The Dutch Italianates

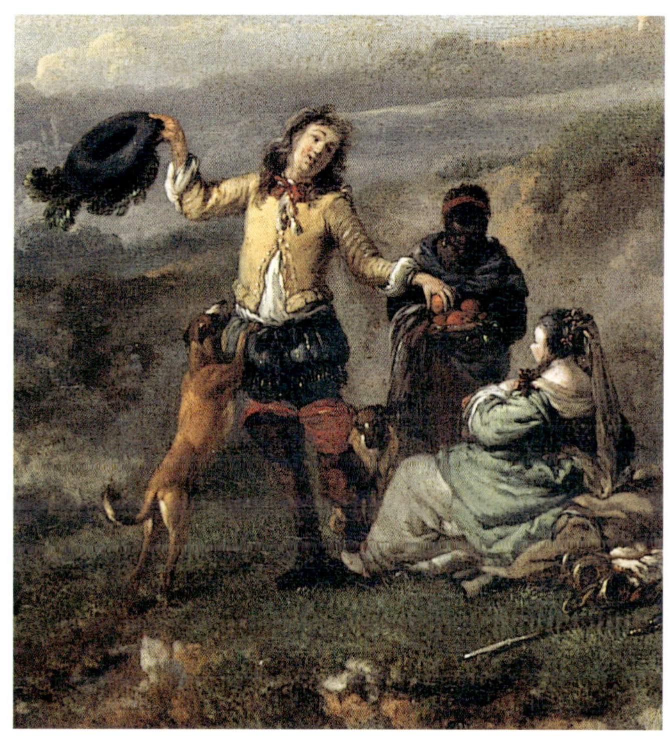

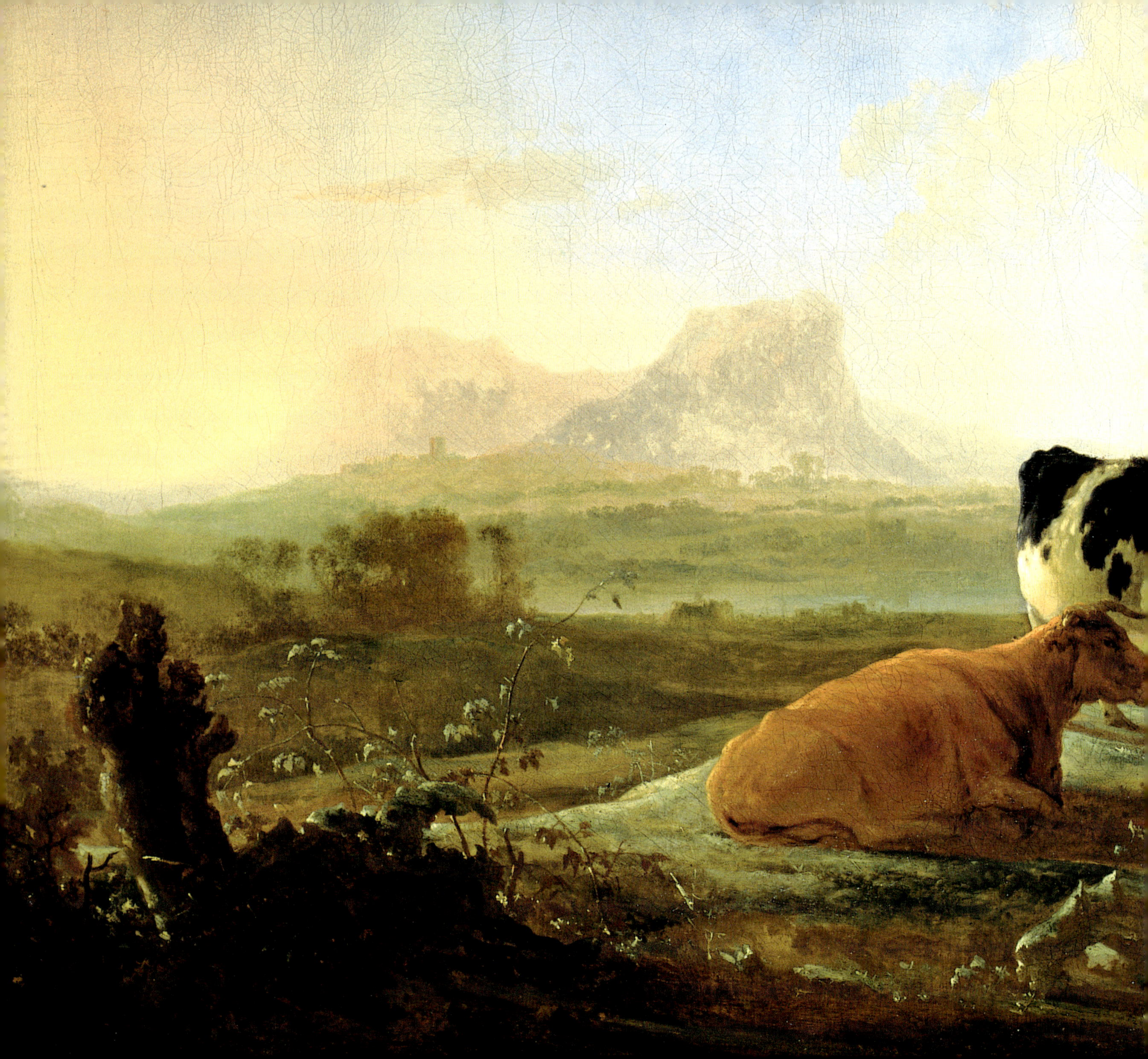

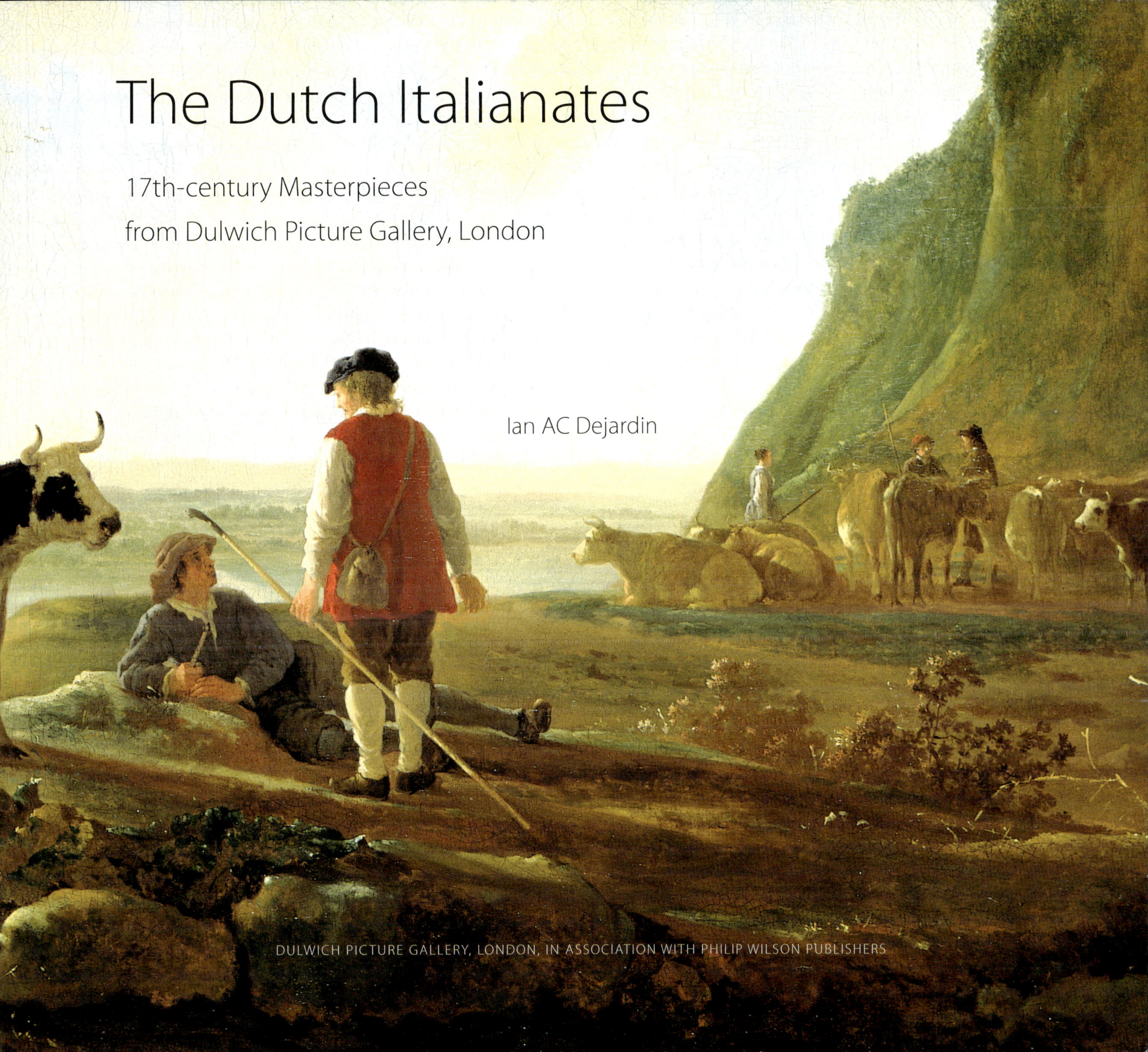

The Dutch Italianates

17th-century Masterpieces
from Dulwich Picture Gallery, London

Ian AC Dejardin

DULWICH PICTURE GALLERY, LONDON, IN ASSOCIATION WITH PHILIP WILSON PUBLISHERS

Published to accompany the touring exhibition 'The Dutch Italianates: 17th-century Masterpieces from Dulwich Picture Gallery, London' organised in collaboration with International Arts & Artists, Washington.
Participating venues include:
Muscarelle Museum of Art, The College of William and Mary, Williamsburg, VA
Fresno Metropolitan Museum of Art and Science, Fresno, CA
The Frick Art Museum, The Frick Art & Historical Center, Pittsburgh, PA
Oklahoma City Museum of Art, Oklahoma, OK

Dulwich Picture Gallery
Gallery Road
London SE21 7AD
www.dulwichpicturegallery.org.uk

First published in 2008 by
Philip Wilson Publishers Ltd
109 Drysdale Street
The Timber Yard
London N1 6ND
www.philip-wilson.co.uk

Distributed throughout the world (excluding North America) by:
I.B. Tauris & Co. Ltd
6 Salem Road, London W2 4BU

Distributed in North America by:
Palgrave Macmillan, a division of St. Martin's Press
175 Fifth Avenue, New York NY 10010

ISBN 978-0-85667-657-4

Designed by Caroline and Roger Hillier, The Old Chapel Graphic Design
www.theoldchapelivinghoe.com

Printed in China by Everbest

Photography credits:
Matthew Hollow: Figs. 1–6, 8–9, 12–18, 21–22; cat. nos. 1–39
The Royal Collection © 2008, Her Majesty Queen Elizabeth II: Fig. 7
Benedict Luxmoore: Fig 10
John Hammond: Fig. 11
Herzog Anton Ulrich-Museum: Fig. 19
Rijksmuseum: Fig. 20

half title page:
(detail, cat. no. 35)
Philips Wouwermans *Landscape with Cattle and Figures*

title page:
(detail, cat. no. 16)
Aelbert Cuyp *Herdsmen with Cows*

front cover:
(detail, cat. no. 28)
William Romeyn *Classical Landscape*

back cover:
(detail, cat. no. 2)
Nicolaes Berchem *Travelling Peasants*

Contents

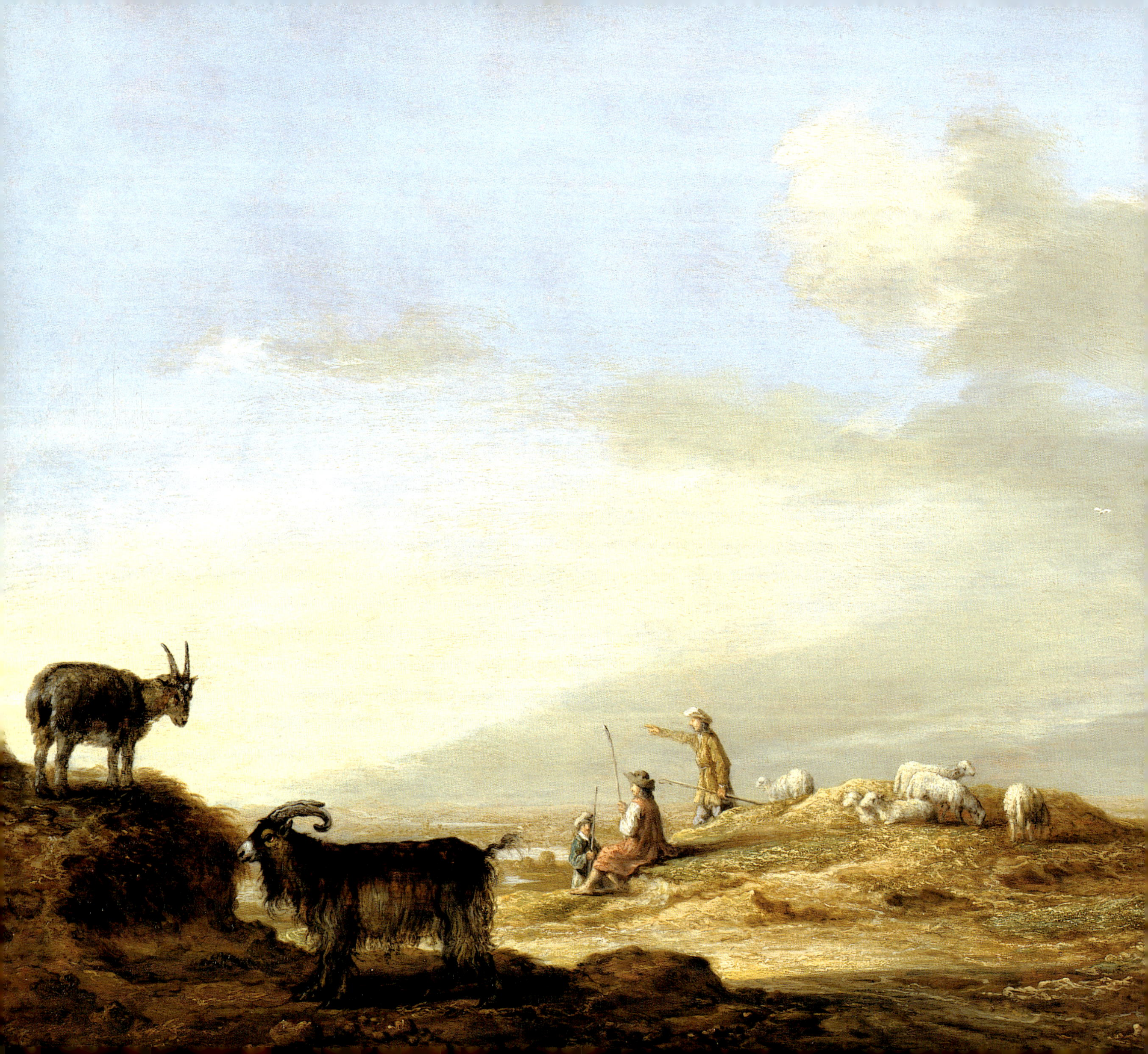

Forewords

This catalogue has been prepared to accompany a touring exhibition of some of Dulwich Picture Gallery's most beautiful Dutch 17th-century paintings. The tour has been organized by International Arts & Artists, Washington, in collaboration with the Gallery. I would like to thank all the team at IA&A, but most specifically Amanda Cane, who responded enthusiastically at extremely short notice to my proposal, and has been a great pleasure to work with.

I would also like to acknowledge the Museums, Libraries and Archives Council in the UK, which has generously supported Dulwich Picture Gallery's ongoing project towards the publication of full scholarly catalogues. The research for our Dutch and Flemish volume, much of it done by Dr Paul Matthews, has provided a great deal of valuable new information for this catalogue. I am deeply grateful to Paul for all his hard work. The same project has been supported by the Embassy of the Kingdom of the Netherlands in London – our thanks go to the Ambassador and his team for this valuable support.

My team here at Dulwich have responded heroically to this additional demand on their time, already stretched by the Gallery's immensely busy temporary exhibition schedule. My heartfelt thanks go to Victoria Norton, Head of Exhibitions, Mella Shaw, Senior Exhibitions Officer, and Sanne Klinge, Exhibitions Officer. Thanks also to Xavier F. Salomon, Curator, and to Jessica Stevens-Campos, Curatorial Intern.

Ian AC Dejardin, Director
Dulwich Picture Gallery

What a pleasure it is to collaborate with Dulwich Picture Gallery, an esteemed British cultural institution with a worldwide reputation, now sharing some of its treasures with America for only the second time in its two-century history. We are deeply indebted to Dulwich Picture Gallery's Board of Trustees and to the Gallery's far-sighted director Ian Dejardin for allowing this wonderful selection from its collection to tour to the United States, and to head of exhibitions Vicky Norton and exhibitions officer Sanne Klinge for their guidance through this process.

Within International Arts & Artists, we acknowledge the director of our Traveling Exhibition Service, Marlene Rothacker and Amanda Cane, the senior exhibitions manager who organized the U.S. part of this collaboration and arranged the tour.

For the Benefit of All,
David Furchgott, President
International Arts & Artists

opposite
(detail, cat. no. 17)
Aelbert CUYP *Landscape with Cattle and Figures*

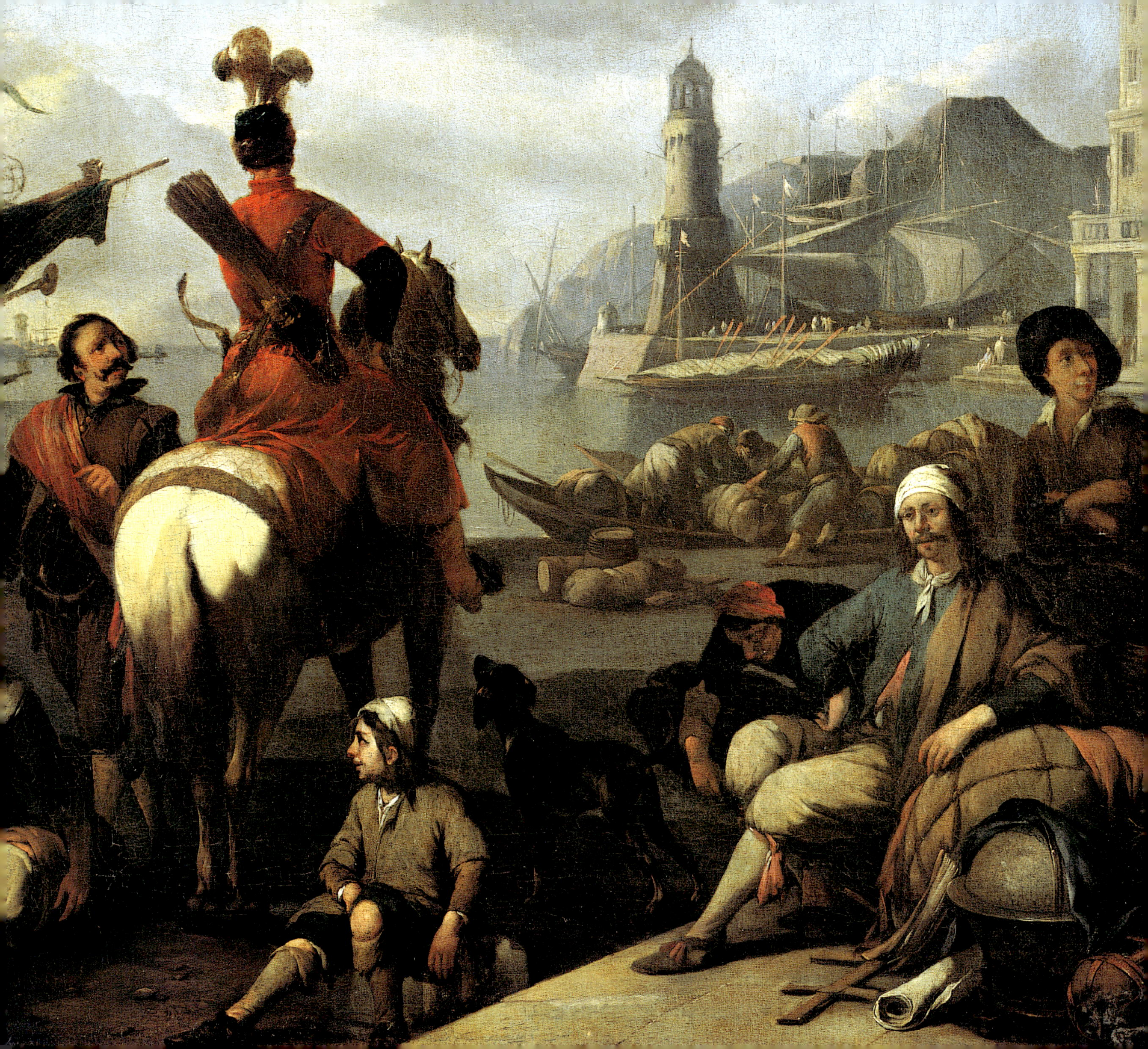

The Story of Dulwich Picture Gallery

Dulwich Picture Gallery was founded in 1811 through the bequest of Sir Peter Francis Bourgeois R.A., painter, art dealer and collector. The collection of 360 paintings that Bourgeois left to Dulwich College was then, and has remained, of international importance. Put together over some thirty years by Bourgeois and his mentor and business partner, Noel Desenfans, the story of its genesis matches larger-than-life characters with stirring times and remarkable opportunities [fig. 1].

Desenfans [fig. 2] was born into a family of shoemakers in 1744 in Avesnes-sure-Helpe, a small market town in Northern France, between Paris and Lille. He studied at the University of

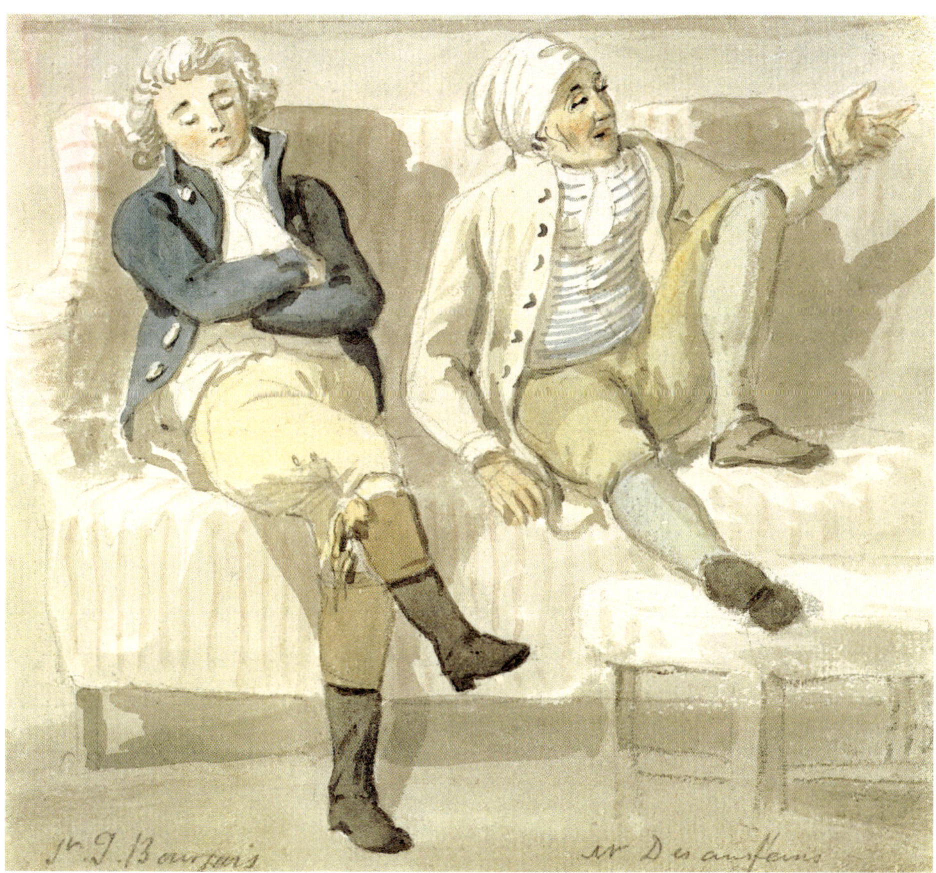

left
Fig. 1
Attrib. to Paul Sandby
Noel Desenfans and Francis Bourgeois
c. 1805
watercolour on card
14.3 x 15.3 cm
DPG No. 645

opposite
(detail, cat. no. 24)
Jan Lingelbach
Italian Seaport

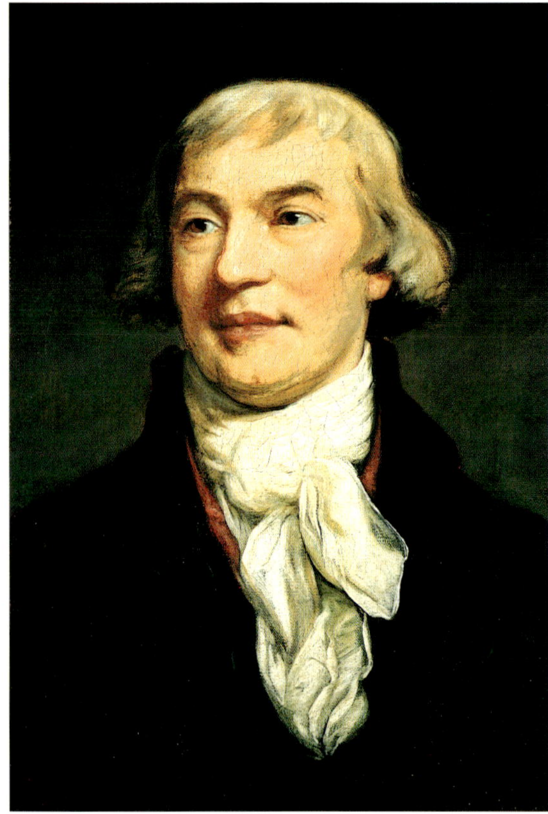

Fig. 2 **James Northcote** *Noel Joseph Desenfans*
c. 1796, oil on canvas, 73.3 x 60.9 cm (oval)
DPG No. 28, Bourgeois Bequest, 1811

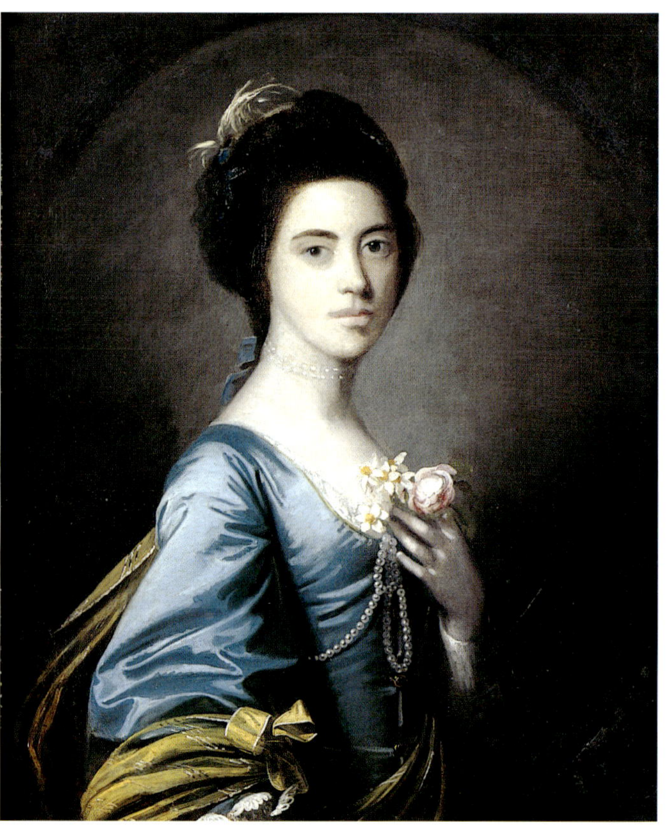

Fig. 3 **Sir Joshua Reynolds** *Margaret Morris (later Desenfans)*
1757, oil on canvas, 74.5 x 61 cm
Private collection, on permanent loan to Dulwich Picture Gallery

Paris, and later Douai, and was intended for the Church. As a young man he had literary aspirations of a Rousseau-like tendency, writing a book entitled *L'Éleve de la Nature* and at least one play.

By 1769 he had given up on literature and the Church and moved to London, where he found work as a French language tutor to young ladies. He lodged with a Swiss watch-maker, Isaac Bourgeois, and his wife Elizabeth. Through his tutoring he met his wife-to-be, Margaret Morris, a minor heiress from a Welsh family distinguished enough to have commissioned Joshua Reynolds to paint the portraits of Margaret [fig. 3] and her sister. She was in fact the aunt and chaperone of one of Desenfans' pupils, and while rather older than her husband-to-be, she was an excellent match for a poor French teacher.

Through Isaac he met Francis Bourgeois, Isaac's son [fig. 4]. Desenfans started dealing in pictures in the 1770s; he was the

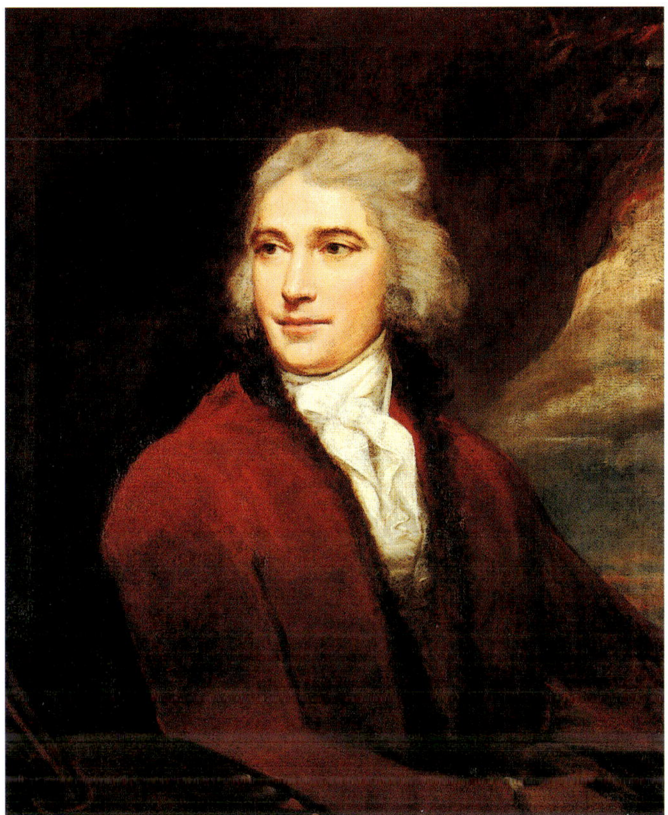

Fig. 4 **James Northcote** *Sir Peter Francis Bourgeois*
c. 1795, oil on canvas, 76.2 x 63.5 cm
DPG No. 172, Bourgeois Bequest, 1811

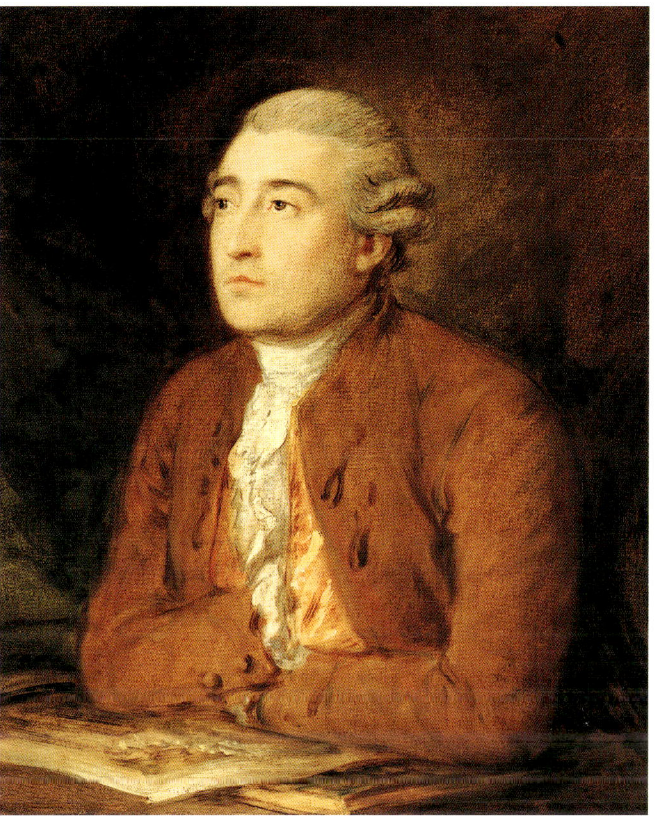

Fig. 5 **Thomas Gainsborough** *Philippe Jacques de Loutherbourg*
c. 1777–8, oil on canvas, 76.5 x 63.2 cm
DPG No. 66, Bourgeois Bequest, 1811

'art historian' of the operation, with useful contacts in Paris, notably J.P. Lebrun, art-dealer husband of the artist Elizabeth Vigée-Lebrun. When Francis's father returned to his native Switzerland after the death of his English wife, Francis decided to stay, and Desenfans effectively adopted the 16-year-old. The young man had some (to our eyes not much) talent for art, and Desenfans undertook to have Bourgeois trained up as a painter – surely not an entirely altruistic decision, since a 'tame' artist was a useful commodity for any art dealer to have on tap in those less ethical days, when pictures were routinely 'prepared' for sale. Francis was briefly apprenticed to the great French landscape-painter, then in England, Philippe Jacques de Loutherbourg [fig. 5]. Desenfans and Bourgeois, aided initially at least by the financial input of Margaret Morris, whom Desenfans married in 1776, gradually became the leading art dealers of the time in London – when the city was rapidly

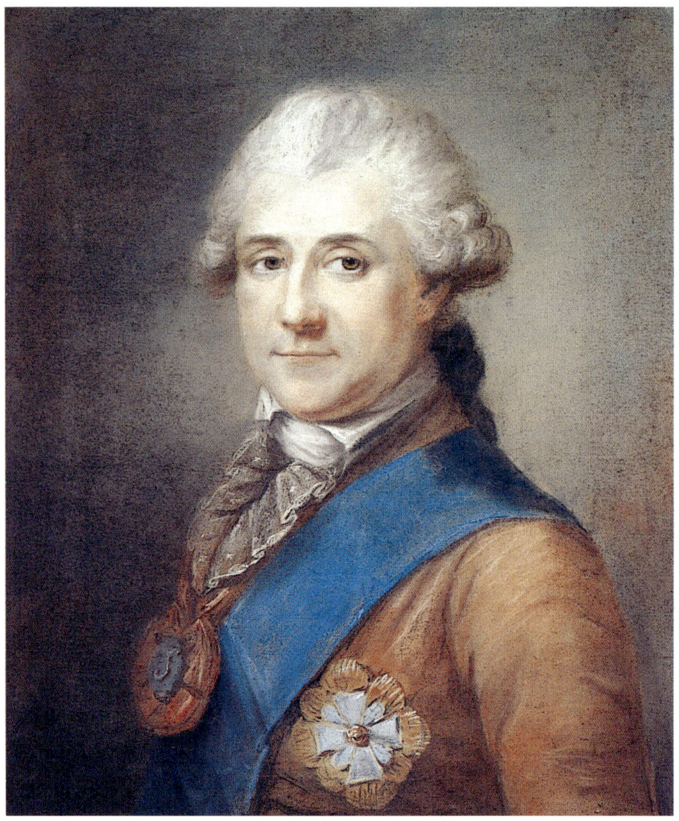

Fig. 6 **After Marcello Bacciarelli** *Stanislaw II Augustus, King of Poland*
c. 1790, pastel on paper, mounted on canvas, 60.9 x 50.8 cm
DPG No. 490, Bourgeois Bequest, 1811

becoming the seat of the most thriving art market in the world. As the French Revolution raged across the Channel, French aristocrats disposed of their pictures in England.

The pair's business took an unexpected turn in 1790, when Michal Poniatowski, Prince Primate of Poland, on behalf of his brother, the King of Poland, Stanislaw II Augustus [fig. 6], commissioned them to put together a Polish national collection, the kind of commission that most art dealers can only dream about. Probably at least as important to Desenfans and Bourgeois as the potential financial rewards was the social cachet that this Royal appointment brought with it. Desenfans became a Consul of Poland (an appointment that came with the right to wear a fine uniform: an overcoat of red, embossed with green, and a white waistcoat beneath), while Bourgeois was knighted and given a court appointment as painter to King Stanislaw. Acceptance as a Royal Academician – something Desenfans had been lobbying for with little success up until then – soon followed for Bourgeois, and George III ratified the knighthood, making Sir Francis Landscape Painter to the King. The importance of these honours was considerable to the pair; doors that had hitherto been closed opened to the newly made royal courtiers. The general attitude of the art establishment and the aristocracy towards Desenfans and Bourgeois seems to have contained considerable elements of snobbery and – possibly – racism. Farington's *Diary*, for instance, contains the following record of a conversation between Benjamin West, President of the Royal Academy, and King George III: *"What is Desenfans?" said the King. "An intriguing Frenchman!" said West. "They are all so, the French," said the King.* Bourgeois, meanwhile, was generally considered to be good-natured, but something of a fool. Dulwich Picture Gallery stands as a 200-year long 'last laugh' against such snobbery.

The Polish royal commission under their belts, business in fact went on much as usual, but with added urgency, maximum social aspiration and a driving concern for quality linked with a certain didactic sense; Stanislaw was insistent that this collection was to present a survey of the best of art as it was then understood. By 1795, they had a magnificent potential royal collection of some 180 paintings on their hands; but Fate and history intervened with the partition of Poland by Russia and Prussia in that year. The King was deposed and went into exile in St Petersburg – he was after all a former lover of Catherine the Great – and died soon after, in 1798. No payment for the collection was forthcoming, either from him or his family. In fact, no money had changed hands at all, apart from for one or two individual paintings that had already been delivered, and for some prints. Nor were the Russian or British governments amenable to taking on the collection – a serious opportunity missed, it has to be said, on the part of the British, who might easily have acquired a dazzling core collection for a new national gallery in one fell swoop. The actual National Gallery was not founded until 1824. However, the rise of Napoleon was diverting both funds and attention at the time.

This should have been a moment of bankruptcy and despair – and Desenfans at least does seem to have suffered from some kind of nervous illness at this time. But in spite of this Desenfans and Bourgeois kept going with their dealership, making maximum use of their former connection with European Royalty for marketing purposes. Indeed, a very modern sense of marketing is one of Desenfans' distinguishing features. Like the great art dealer Lord Duveen for a later generation, he instinctively understood the power of 'branding' long before the term was coined. The secret of their continued success in the face of such a disaster must, I think, lie in the older man's apparent business acumen. For instance, he managed the affairs of a wealthy elderly widow, Elizabeth Glover, until his death. She made at least one loan of £10,000 to him, and he was to have been a major beneficiary of her will, but she outlived all three of the Founders, and drops out of the story. It is clear that Desenfans must have been something of a wheeler-dealer; the source of his apparent wealth and the manner in which he lived were cause for some comment, particularly amongst the Royal Academicians with whom he conducted many skirmishes on various issues. He had also acted as co-mortgagee of the collection of the French ex-Finance Minister, Alexandre de Calonne [fig. 7], whom he knew from University days in Douai, and who was

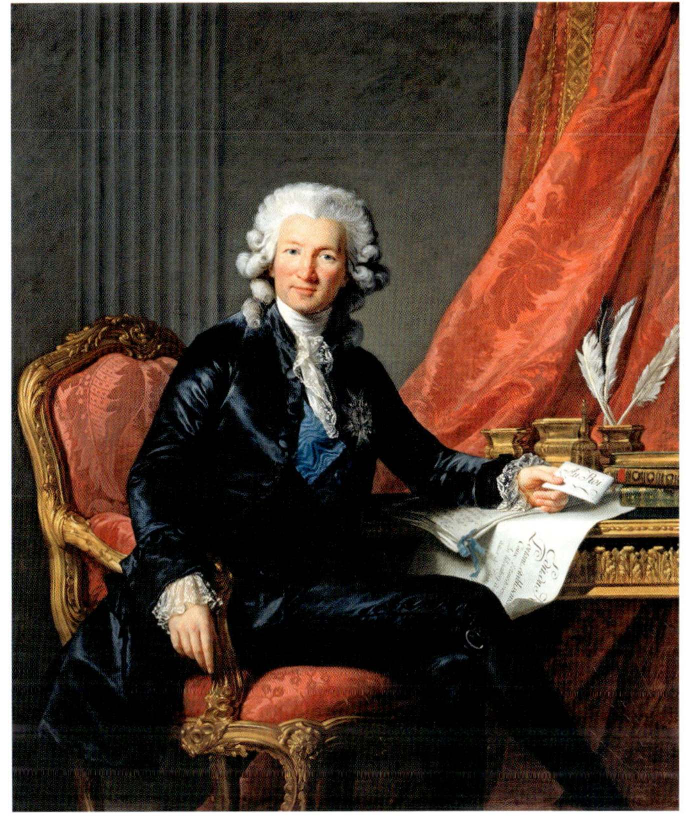

Fig. 7 **Elizabeth Vigée LeBrun** *Alexandre de Calonne*
1784, oil on canvas, 155.5 x 130.3 cm
The Royal Collection © 2008, Her Majesty Queen Elizabeth II

trying to raise money for a counter-Revolution. Calonne's plan failed, and Desenfans arranged for the subsequent sale, purchasing several important pieces himself (and it was not only paintings that he acquired: a few surviving pieces of silverware that Mrs Desenfans left to the Gallery, and which she touchingly believed to be ornamented with her husband's coat of arms, in fact bear those of Calonne). Francis Bourgeois, meanwhile, was always the more rash of the two, and effectively began to spend

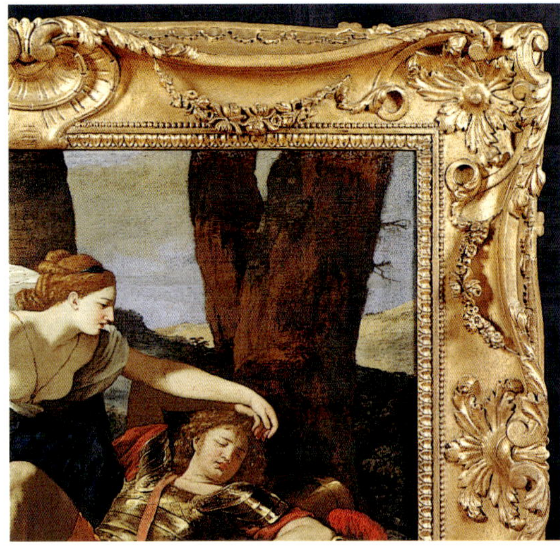

above Fig. 8 Frame of Nicolas Poussin's *Rinaldo and Armida* DPG No. 238 (detail), c. 1805, Carved wood, gilt

below Fig. 9 Frame of Guido Reni's *St. Sebastian* DPG No. 268 (detail), c. 1805, Carved wood, gilt

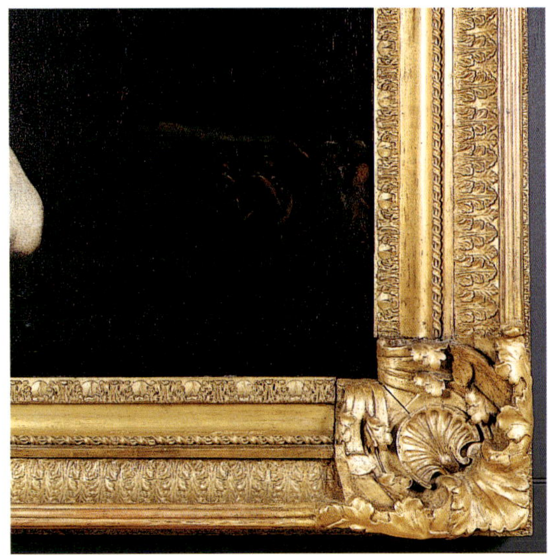

money more like a collector than a dealer. There was at least one occasion when Desenfans threatened to split from his younger partner on account of his extravagance: in a letter to Benjamin West, c. 1803, Desenfans wailed that he was 'at the eve of parting with Sr Francis... if I will not be reduced to Beggary... Such is his passion for pictures, that it will render him miserable, and makes it now impossible for me, to continue with him... he has been... at every sale & every picture Room, where, like a child who wishes for everything in a toy shop, he has been buying whatever he saw; to put where? In my garret...' The threatened split never happened; but by now Sir Francis was clearly marching to a different drummer, and may already have been thinking of posterity.

Meanwhile, the remarkable collection of paintings, rapidly becoming one of the greatest private collections in Europe, was usually reframed in modern, matching frames [figs. 8 & 9], and hung, floor to ceiling, in the Desenfans' by now decidedly imposing house in Charlotte Street (now renamed Hallam Street; the actual site has been demolished). The pair used this extravagant display as a means to entice the high and mighty (along with other artists and art students) to their home, for both financial and social reasons. Their success had brought them pretty high socially – Bourgeois was, after all, a knight, a court painter and a Royal Academician, despite what to a modern eye looks like a dire paucity of talent – but they were never truly integrated into the higher echelons of society that they wished to frequent, and indeed were held in some derision in certain circles. They were not unpopular (Bourgeois certainly not), but they remained outsiders. People laughed at what they saw as Desenfans' pretensions to connoisseurship, and at Bourgeois' dandyism.

The death of Desenfans in 1807 was followed not long after by the premature demise of Bourgeois from injuries sustained in a horse-riding accident in late 1810. By this point the collection had changed radically and numbered some 360 pictures, only a handful of the original 'Polish' stock remaining. Bourgeois lingered for a few weeks, sorting out his affairs, dying on 8th January 1811. The collection was left to Dulwich College, a boys' school in the village of Dulwich, five miles or so south of London (the school is still there, although it moved further up College Road into larger premises in the 1870s; it is now one of England's best-known public schools). Quite how Bourgeois arrived at his decision is a matter of conjecture; the exact nature of the link to the College is now lost, and his will offers no explanation. However, Dulwich College had, from the death of its founder Edward Alleyn in 1626, contained a picture gallery, albeit of more historical than artistic importance – 'a hundred mouldy portraits, among apostles, sibyls, and kings of England' as Horace Walpole with his usual sharp (and disconcertingly accurate) tongue put it later.

Nevertheless, Bourgeois' will did make some priorities clear. The educational remit implied by the bequest going to a school was joined by an early concern for conservation: Bourgeois appreciated Dulwich's distance from the damaging smogs of the city; money was left (not enough, of course; Mrs Desenfans, the oft-neglected heroine of the hour, had to step in with funds) to pay for housing the collection, and Bourgeois stipulated that the new build should be entrusted to his friend, Sir John Soane. In doing so, the jigsaw puzzle of Dulwich Picture Gallery's history was provided with its crowning piece: Soane, who designed the building in honour of his friend without charging a fee, provided an architectural masterpiece to match the quality of Bourgeois' by now astonishing collection. Other stipulations included that of there being a mausoleum incorporated into the building to house the remains of Desenfans, his wife, and Bourgeois himself, as co-founders, which Soane achieved beautifully, flooding it with an amber-tinted *lumiere religieuse*, as he himself put it. He also had to include within the building modest accommodation for six poor almswomen of the village – at the request of the Governors of Dulwich College.

Most importantly, the paintings were specifically bequeathed 'for the inspection of the public'. A charge of sixpence was levied, and tickets had to be bought in town rather than on site. This provided essential income for the running of the Gallery. Education, conservation, and accessibility – these three concepts provide watchwords to this day for Dulwich Picture Gallery, and indeed every major art gallery. Bourgeois' will effectively invented the modern public art gallery in England, and surely earned the Founders the glory of their Mausoleum.

By this sequence of chance events and the conjunction of these diverse characters, a remarkable institution was born. Dulwich Picture Gallery predates the foundation of the National Gallery by thirteen years, and was in fact England's very first purpose-built public art gallery. It would be several decades before the National Gallery caught up in terms of the breadth and value of its collections. Bourgeois' collection is housed in a building that has been the architectural blueprint for countless galleries since – a work of profound brilliance by an architectural genius at the height of his form, and an object of pilgrimage in its own right. Dulwich Village meanwhile has retained its 19th-century village character to a remarkable degree, given that it has long since been encircled by the sprawl of Greater London. The Gallery, surrounded in the first instance by a charming garden with specimen trees, is further embedded in a green area of parkland, playing fields, bluebell woods and cricket pavilions – all within five miles of the city centre. Despite its idyllic immediate surroundings, its catchment area now incorporates some of the most vibrant, culturally and economically diverse districts in this melting-pot of a city. While at the heart of this venerable institution lies a collection of such extraordinary quality and beauty that it is a 'must-see' for anyone with an interest in 17th- and 18th-century

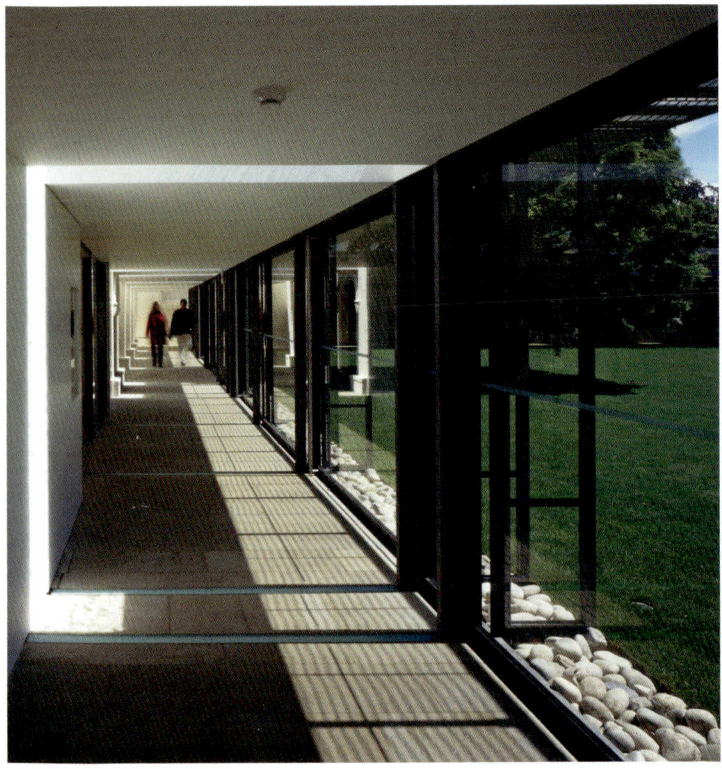

Fig. 10 The Cloister – Rick Mather extension, completed 2000

art - Rembrandt, Cuyp, Pynacker, Rubens, Poussin, Claude, Raphael, Murillo, Gainsborough, Watteau, Canaletto - and more; the list is long and distinguished.

Today the Gallery is vibrant in other ways as well. A Heritage Lottery-funded refurbishment in 1999–2000 not only restored the building to its original splendour, but brought new life to the gardens and added much-needed 21st-century facilities. A stylish café, the Sackler Centre for Art Education, a lecture theatre and extra exhibition space (the Linbury Room), are found in a sensitive and award-winning new building set round a cloister [fig. 10], designed by Rick Mather, one of the foremost architects of the day, and a specialist in museum projects.

Although the famous view down the enfilade, glittering with masterpieces in Bourgeois's favourite gilt frames, may not appear to have changed much since 1817, when the public were first admitted, there is in fact nothing fossilised about Dulwich Picture Gallery. Its Education Department is a world-leader, having received over twenty national awards in as many years. Soane's august galleries welcome learners of all ages and backgrounds; while the Education staff reach out far beyond, into some of the most challenging districts of South London. The exhibitions department delivers upwards of three exhibitions a year on a wide variety of subjects, from Old Masters to 20th-century British. The collection itself has been enhanced and preserved by a sensitive and extensive programme of conservation.

Dulwich Picture Gallery's mission is to encourage enjoyment of the visual arts in as original and accessible a way as possible, while preserving and interpreting its unique heritage as a world-class gallery.

The modern miracle of Dulwich Picture Gallery is that all this is maintained and achieved as an Independent Charitable Trust (set up in 1994, when the gallery finally ceased to be part of Dulwich College). The gallery receives no government funding, and must raise every penny for its activities, be it education programmes, exhibitions or conservation projects. This is a continuous struggle, fought out in an ever-more-competitive arena, against a backdrop of ever-rising costs. In the 19th century the Gallery was opened to the public by a solitary Keeper (and his dog), with the help of an odd-job man. Today more than forty staff, plus dozens of volunteers, guides and teachers are required to deliver the extraordinary service that the Gallery offers to its visitors.

In 2011, Dulwich Picture Gallery celebrates its 200th birthday [fig. 11].

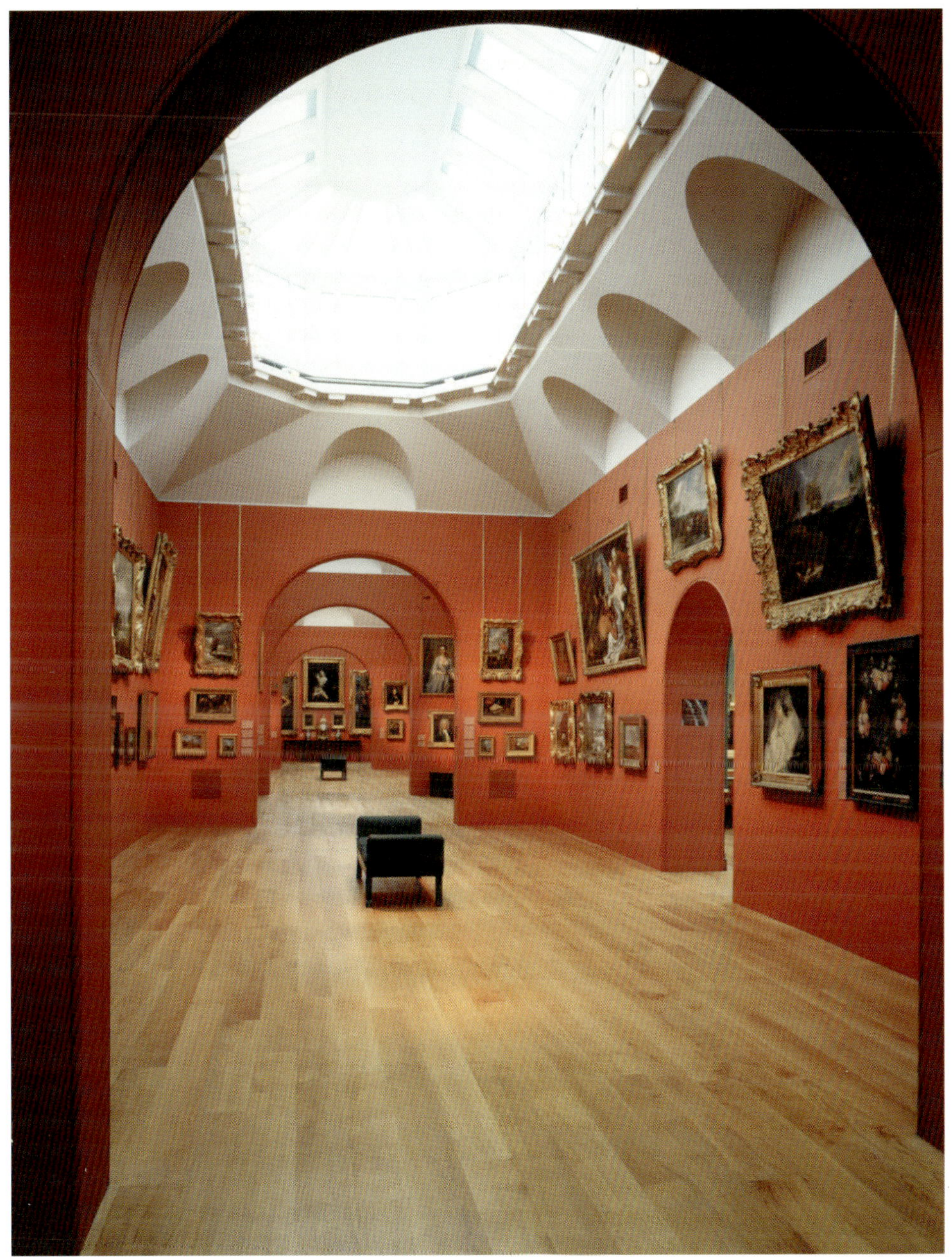

Fig. 11
Dulwich Picture Gallery – the enfilade today

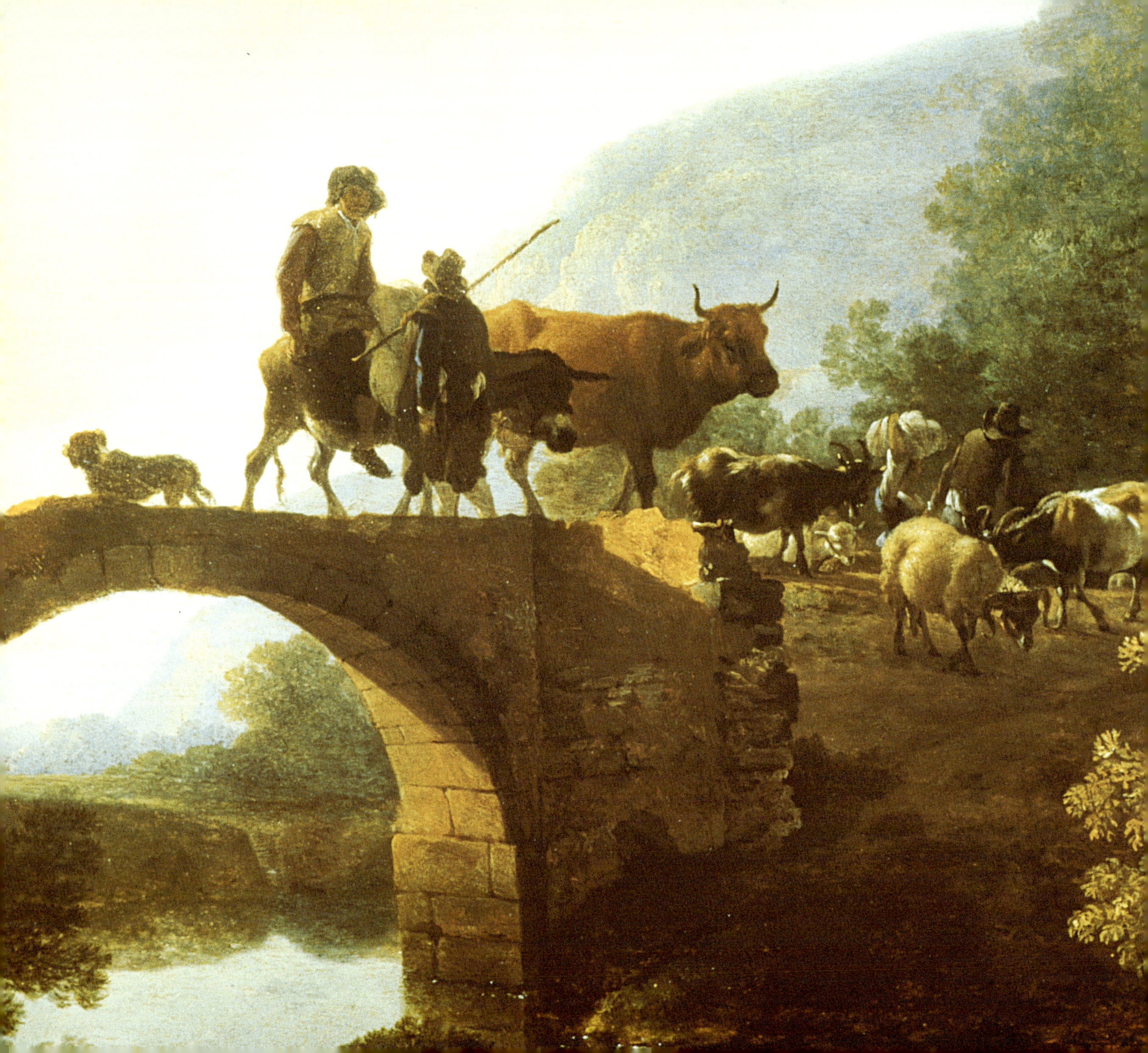

The Dutch Italianates

17th-century Masterpieces from Dulwich Picture Gallery, London

Not the least of Dulwich Picture Gallery's fascination is derived from its status as a document of the history of taste. The Founders probably valued their Guido Renis and their Gerrit Dou more highly than many modern visitors do. In one case, a 'Rembrandt' that was once visited religiously as one of the Gallery's (not to mention the western world's) greatest masterpieces, has turned out to be by one of his best pupils, Arent de Gelder [fig. 12]. The gilt of the magical Rembrandt name left the lily – literally, in one sense, since De Gelder's signature was covered by a much later fake Rembrandt signature, which was removed during conservation. The reattribution inevitably involved some noughts dropping from the end of the picture's value, and the crowds ceased to seek it out. Yet it remains the same masterpiece it always was.

The Gallery's 200 years of history provide many such changes in critical fortune. One painting's story sums this up better than any other – the Gallery's great Guido Reni of *St Sebastian* [fig. 13]. As a masterpiece by the 'Divine Guido', this painting was one of our Founders' most precious possessions, and the glory of the collection. For much of the 19th century it occupied a position of honour at the end of the enfilade, as the Gallery's 'high altarpiece' [fig. 14]. But tastes changed; John Ruskin, one of the Victorian age's most influential opinion-formers, found the work of the great Bolognese distasteful. Reni, and the Bolognese School in general, went catastrophically out of fashion. Meanwhile, in 1880, J.P. Richter declared the picture a production of Reni's school, not an original by the master at all. It crept into store with its tail between its legs. However, as the Bolognese School was rediscovered, largely through the

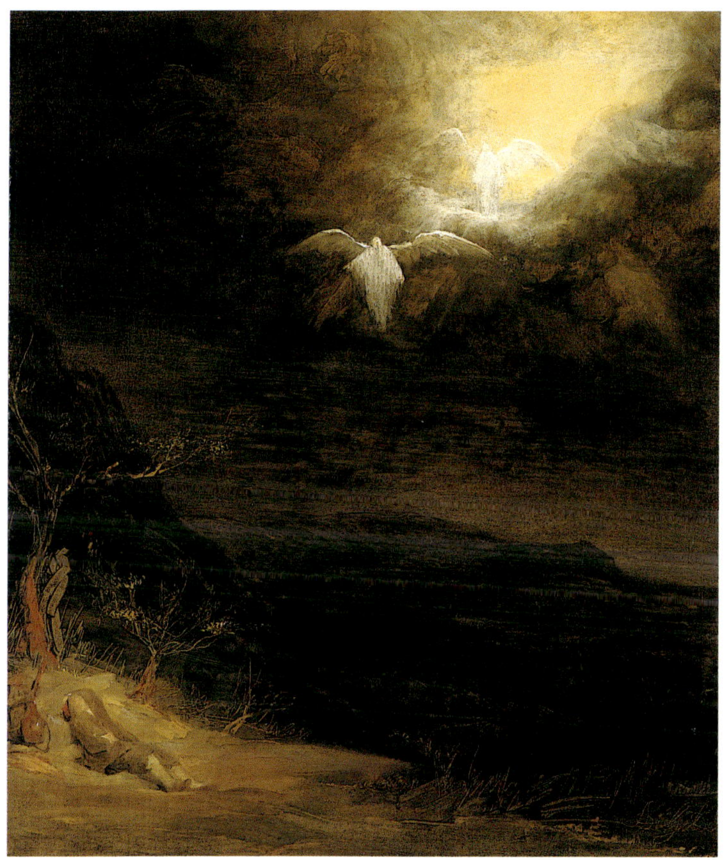

above
Fig. 12 **Arent de Gelder** *Jacob's Dream*
1710–15, oil on canvas, 66.7 x 56.9 cm
DPG No. 126, Bourgeois Bequest, 1811

opposite
(detail, cat. no. 27) **Adam Pynacker** *Bridge in an Italian Landscape*

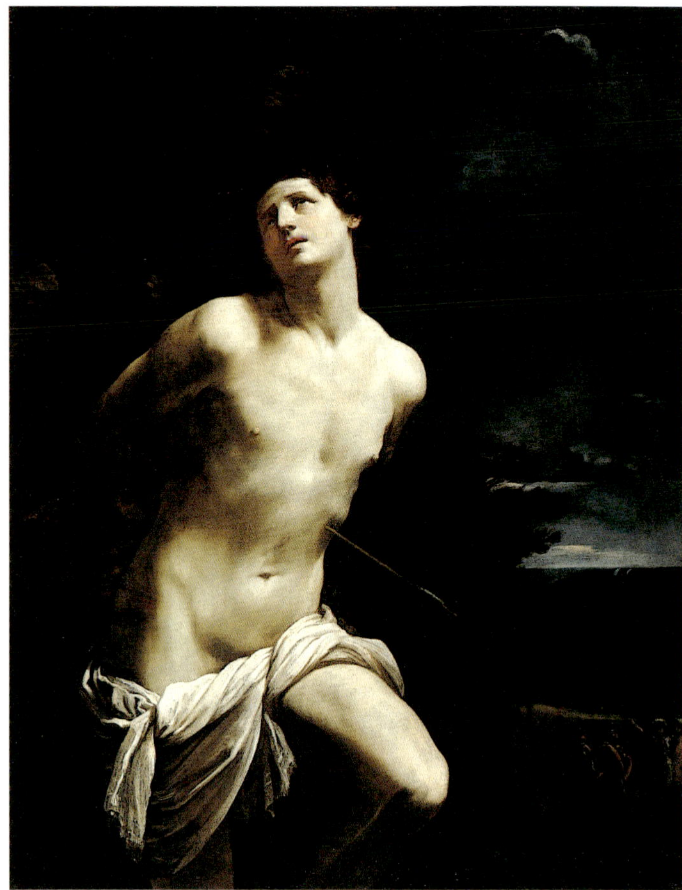

Fig. 13 **Guido Reni** *St. Sebastian*
c. 1625, oil on canvas, 170.1 x 131.1 cm
DPG No. 268, Bourgeois Bequest, 1811

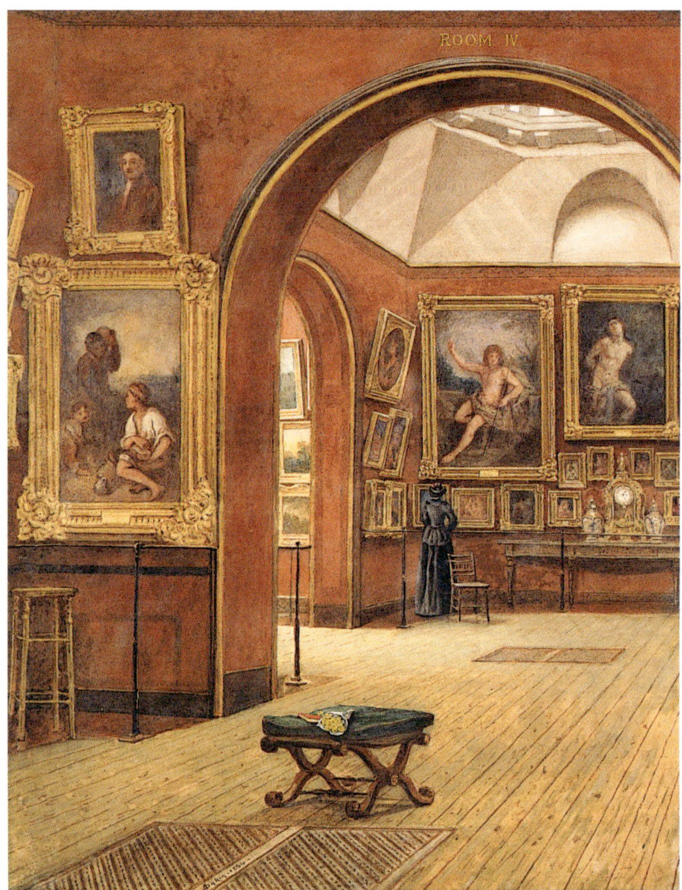

Fig. 14 **Joseph Dakin** *Interior of Dulwich Picture Gallery*
1894, watercolour on paper, 60 x 45 cm
DPG No. G13

work of Sir Denis Mahon in the 20th century, so the Dulwich *St Sebastian*'s fortunes began to improve. Conservation in the 1990s proved that the picture was indeed autograph, and after the Gallery's refurbishment in 2000, Reni's languorous saint once more took its old place at the end of the enfilade. And while we may not yet have learned to rank Reni quite as high as our Founders did, he is not far short, and – arguably – going up in value all the time.

One room demonstrates this aspect of the Gallery's significance more clearly than any other: that which contains the Dutch Italianate paintings. For the founders, collecting in the 1790s, these artists were at the height of their value

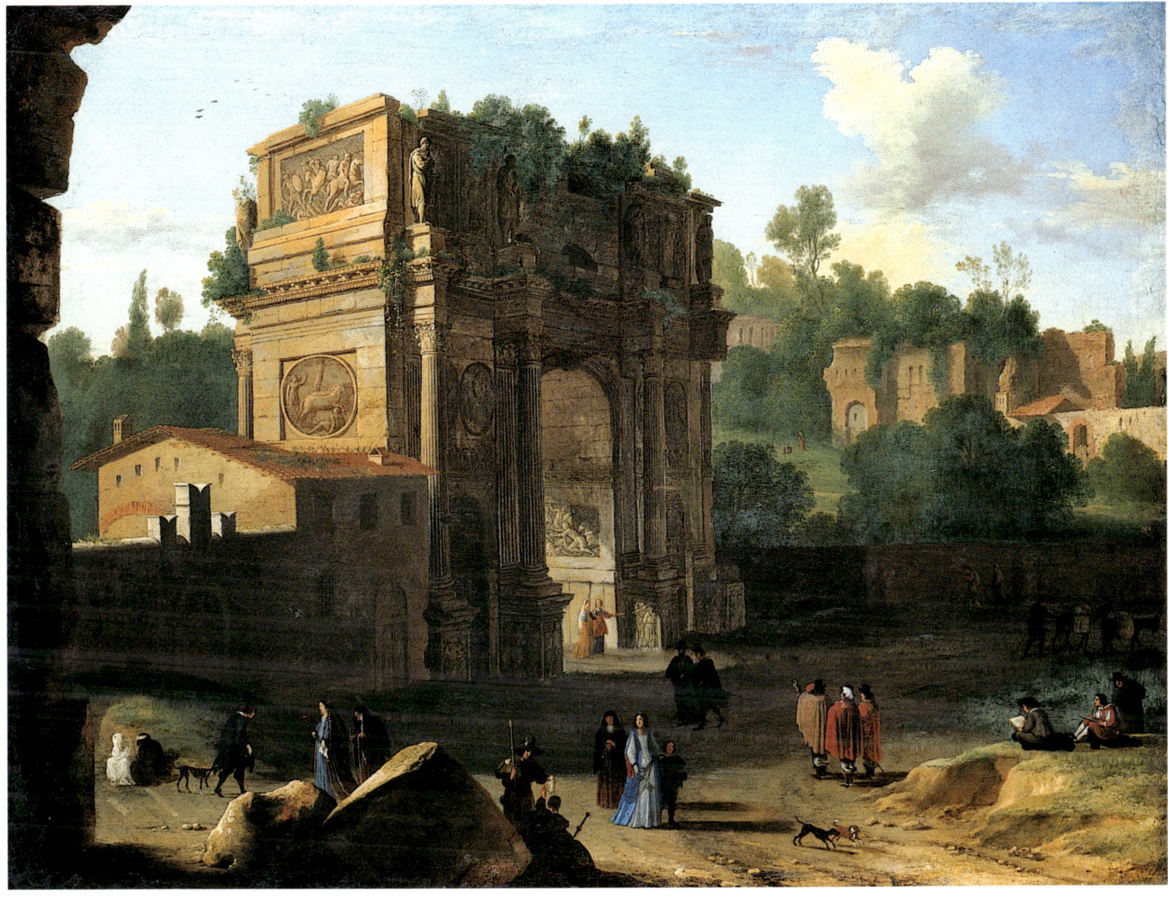

Fig. 15
Herman van Swanevelt
The Arch of Constantine
1645
oil on canvas
89.5 x 116.2 cm
DPG No. 11,
Bourgeois Bequest, 1811

and reputation. Nicolaes Berchem, Karel du Jardin, Philips Wouwerman, Jan Both and Aelbert Cuyp – these were names to mention in the same breath as Rembrandt, and were ranked rather higher than the likes of Jan van Goyen and Salomon van Ruysdael, early masters of the 'domestic' Dutch landscape. Neither of these two undoubted masters is represented in the collection, and the only landscape that does show the tonal style of Van Goyen (Cuyp's early *River Landscape*, cat. no. 13), was 'doctored', probably by Francis Bourgeois, to make it look more 'correct', i.e. more like a Dutch Italianate painting.

Francis Bourgeois' bequest of 1811 contained a magnificent collection of these paintings, by Cornelis van Poelenburch, Herman van Swanevelt [fig. 15], Thomas Wijck, Jan Both, Nicolaes Berchem, Karel du Jardin, Adam Pynacker, Jan Lingelbach, Philips Wouwerman, Aelbert Cuyp, Adriaen van de Velde [fig. 16], Jan Weenix and others. In fact, Noel Desenfans played an important role in the discovery of Aelbert Cuyp, who was utterly revered – and extensively collected – in England in the late 18th century. Dulwich's Cuyps are amongst the best in the world.

By the 1830s, however, the tide was turning against the appreciation of these artists. John Constable, England's great landscapist, delivered a series of lectures in 1836 in which he fulminated against Berchem and Both for their 'bastard style of landscape'. Approached by a gentleman after one lecture who said glumly "I suppose I had better sell my Berghems [sic]," Constable apparently replied "No, sir, that will only continue the mischief, *burn them*." For Constable, it was Ruisdael and Hobbema who represented the only 'true' Dutch landscape; and where landscape was concerned he had the fervour of a fundamentalist. A few years before, in 1830/1, he had demonstrated his commitment to the style of Ruisdael in the clearest manner. That year he was on the committee of Royal Academicians that annually chose half a dozen or so pictures

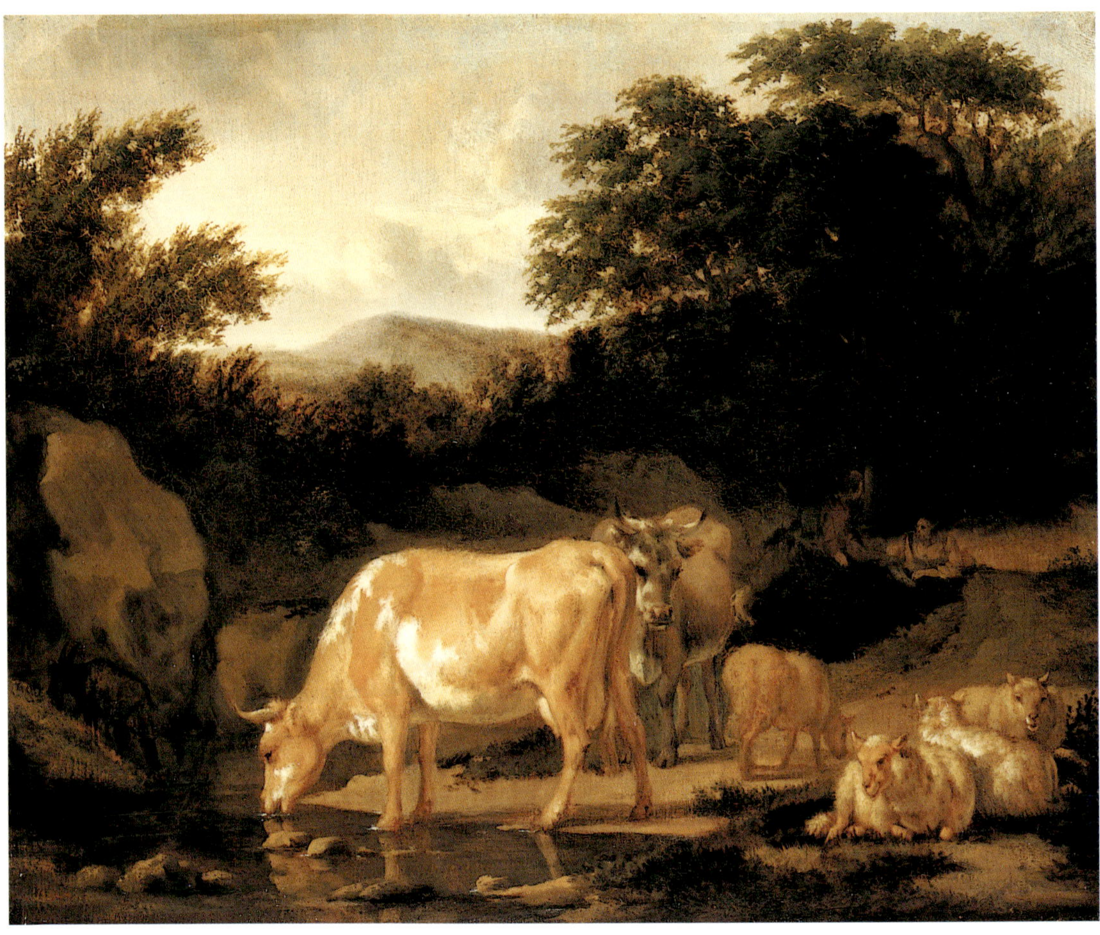

Fig. 16
Adriaen van de Velde
Cows and Sheep in a Wood
c. 1665
oil on canvas
18.4 x 22.5 cm
DPG No. 51,
Bourgeois Bequest, 1811

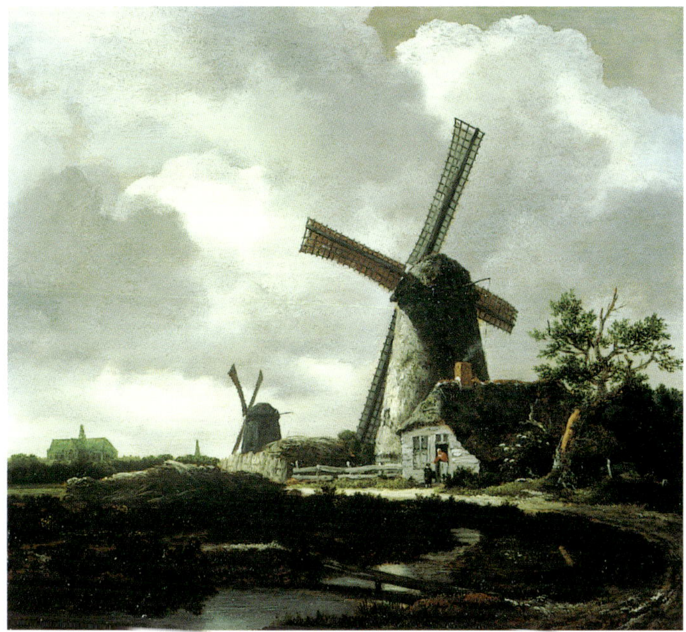

Fig. 17 **Jacob van Ruisdael** *Landscape with Windmills near Haarlem*
c. 1650–2, oil on panel, 31.5 x 33.9 cm
DPG No. 168, Bourgeois Bequest, 1811

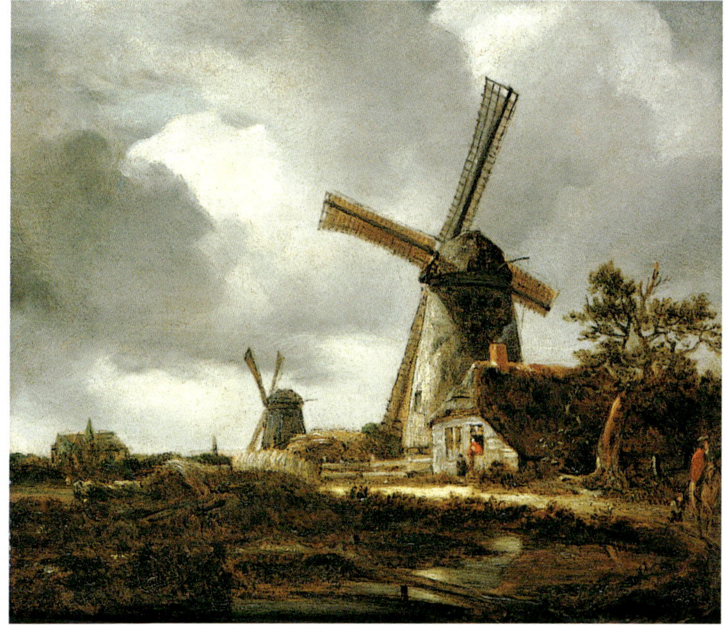

Fig. 18 **John Constable after Jacob van Ruisdael** *Landscape with Windmills near Haarlem*, 1831, oil on panel, 31.5 x 34.5 cm
DPG No. 657

from Dulwich's collection to go to the Royal Academy Schools for the young student artists to copy. For the first time since the foundation, and clearly through Constable's influence, both Ruisdael and Hobbema featured on the list – and, presumably in the course of teaching the students, he executed his own virtuoso copy of Ruisdael's *Landscape with Windmills near Haarlem*. The Gallery was able to acquire Constable's small 'master class' in 2007; this fine copy now hangs next to the original by Ruisdael [figs. 17 & 18]. The additional staffage faithfully reflects the appearance of the original in 1831 – the horseman was found to be a late addition (quite possibly Bourgeois' work again, this time trying to make Ruisdael look more like Wouwermans) and was removed during the work's conservation in 1997.

For more than a century Constable's opinion largely prevailed. The Italianates fell from their pedestal, and it seems to have been more than just an aesthetic depreciation; somehow their unique vision of Italian skies and characters acquired a moral taint, as if there was something actually dishonest about a Dutch artist painting mountains and sunshine, when their own country was (stereotypically) characterised entirely by its flatness and its dour weather (it sometimes seems necessary to remind scholars that the Dutch – like the similarly benighted British – do see sunshine *sometimes*). The Italianates' remarkable qualities – their glorious tonal control, their colour mastery, their magical handling of light, their humour, their sheer technical brilliance – were dismissed as so much meretricious trickery.

Fortunately, the tide began to turn again some forty years ago. A series of exhibitions, including Dulwich Picture Gallery's own 2002 exhibition *Inspired by Italy: Dutch Landscape painting 1600–1700*, curated by Laurie Harwood, has done much to reinstate these great artists to something of their former glory. There have been important monographic exhibitions also: Aelbert Cuyp (National Gallery, London) in 2002, Nicolaes Berchem in 2007 (at the Frans Hals Museum, Haarlem), Karel du Jardin (Rijksmuseum, Amsterdam, 2008) amongst others. We can now enjoy these dazzling paintings without any actual guilt.

So, who were the so-called Dutch Italianates? For some of those artists routinely described in this manner the label is something of a misnomer. Cuyp, for instance, and Philips Wouwerman, certainly never set foot in Italy, and their landscapes – in comparison with the obviously Italian confections of, say, Both and Poelenburch – might more accurately be described as Dutch with some elements of the Italianate about them. But many of their 17th-century compatriots did make the journey, following a by no means easy transalpine trail to the country deemed to be the 'home of art'. Intriguingly, once there, they seem not to have been overly interested in copying from the great masters of the Renaissance (or indeed, of their Baroque contemporaries); they were different to the 18th century's artistic tourists. It was not Raphael or Michelangelo or Reni, but Italy itself that seems to have caught their imagination. Having 'discovered' the *campagna*, and having been electrified by the effect of the flood of warm light on the landscape, they played a crucial role at the birth of a new genre of pure landscape. Some, like Swanevelt, worked directly alongside the Frenchman Claude, who was to prove the most exalted exponent of the new, light-drenched 'classical landscape'. Seminal figures from the 'first generation' of Dutch Italianates, like Poelenburch and Breenbergh, were clearly also influenced by the extraordinary work of the German-born Adam Elsheimer, who had died painfully young in 1610. His work was generally on a miniature scale, but he cast a long shadow. In one or two of Elsheimer's rare, highly-finished works, as well as in the highly influential prints made after them by Hendrick Goudt, the full potential of landscape as a genre in its own right was adumbrated [fig. 19].

A rowdy bunch for the most part, the Dutch in Italy lived in the area around the Spanish Steps in Rome; and they stuck together. They even had a club, the *Schildersbent*, calling themselves the '*bentveughels*' (usually translated as 'birds of a feather'). There were mock initiation rituals, toga parties, much consumption of alcohol, and rude nick-names. During the day they marched out into the *campagna* to sketch together.

Meanwhile, alongside the development of the Italianate landscape, a distinctive figure style evolved, called *Bambocciante* after its progenitor Pieter van Laer (known by his typically rumbustious, not to mention insensitive, '*bentveughel*' nickname *Il Bamboccio* – 'rag-doll' – he was a hunch-back.). We know some other nick-names: Poelenburch was 'Satyr'; Du Jardin, who seems not to have formally joined, still did not escape the nick-name 'Goat's Beard'; Breenbergh was 'the Ferret'; Jan Baptist Weenix was 'Rattle' after his distinctive speaking voice. Van Laer painted so-called 'low-life' characters – the people of the streets, shepherds, drinkers, beggars, travelling musicians – in a style of exaggerated comic theatricality that nevertheless stopped short of caricature. This figurative style influenced many, if not most, of the Dutch Italianates, and variants of *Il Bamboccio*'s characters saunter, beg, and interact through paintings by, amongst others, Berchem, Lingelbach, Du Jardin and Wouwermans. Furthermore, given that the principle of collaboration between artists was common at the time, some of the masters of the *Bambocciante* figure type went on to provide the figures for other non-Italianate colleagues' work. These figures were frequently painted in a loose, flickering decorative style that prefigures the 18th-century Rococo. The Italian art

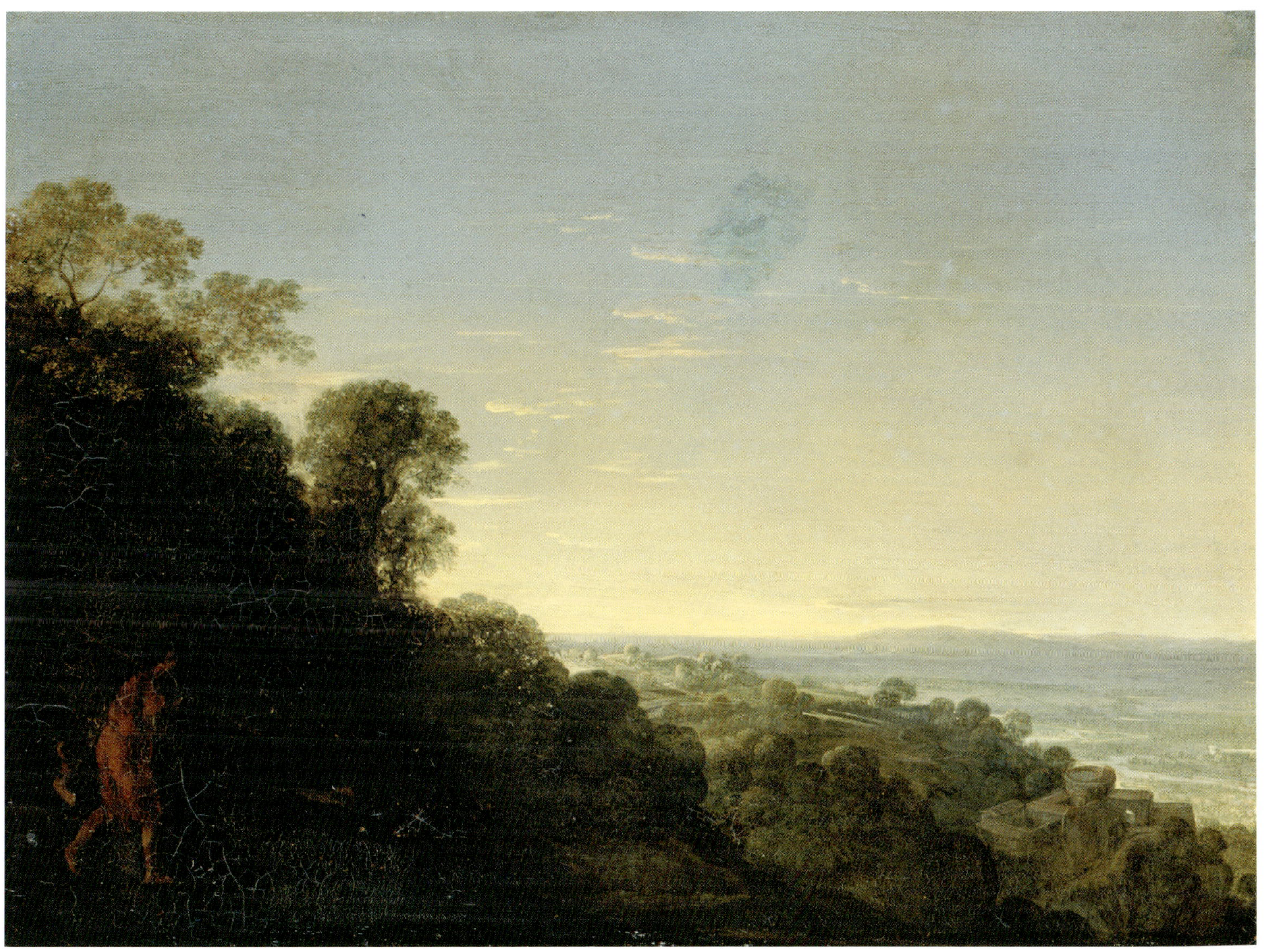

Fig. 19 **Adam Elsheimer** *Aurora*
c. 1606, Oil on copper, 17 x 22.5 cm
Herzog Anton Ulrich-Museums Braunschweig, Kunstmuseum des Landes Niedersachsen

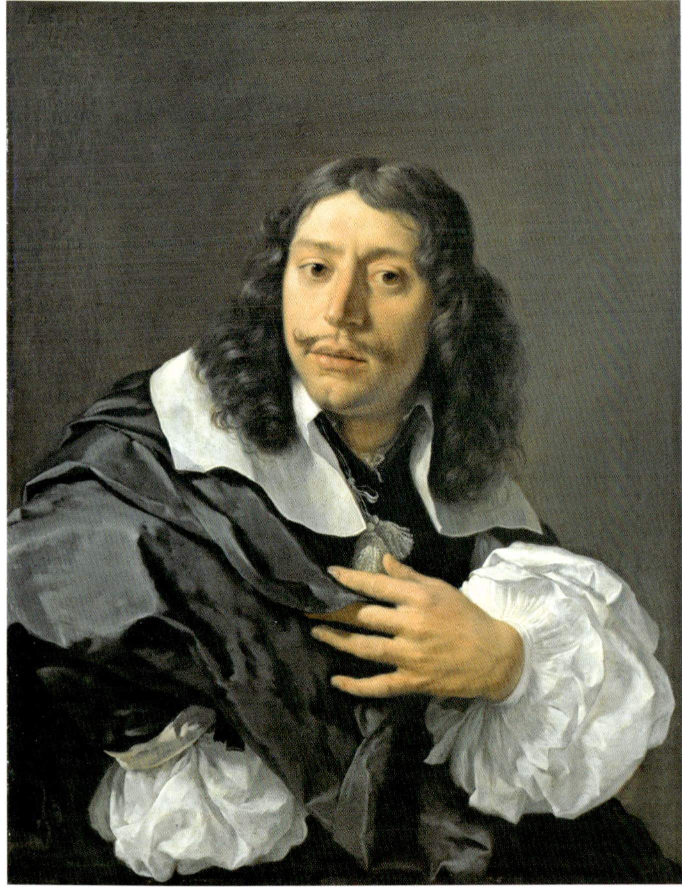

Fig. 20 **Karel du Jardin** *Self-Portrait*
1662, oil on copper, 28.5 x 22 cm
Rijksmuseum, Amsterdam

establishment was predictably scandalised by the Dutch taste for low-life staffage (not to mention their apparent obsession with defecating dogs – a recurring detail that can mystify even the dog-loving British to this day); consequently patronage of this new style was thin on the ground. The Italians preferred Claude, who peopled his limitless distances and luminous classical landscapes with mythological or religious figures.

A third Italianate genre was to emerge, through the work of artists like Jan Baptist Weenix and Jan Lingelbach. These two developed an elaborately decorative type of harbour scene, densely populated with exotic merchants and assorted colourful characters. Their carefully husbanded sketchbooks provided them with *capriccios* of picturesque buildings, Roman ruins, Baroque churches and classical statues that they could arrange decoratively to form theatrical backdrops, suggestive of the Italy of the imagination. Amsterdam was the marketplace of the world at this time – these harbour scenes functioned as a kind of collective Dutch fantasy of a colourful world increasingly within their grasp. After all, what location was so exotic that Dutch merchants could not reach it?

There was no denying, however, that the market for the Italianates' work was back home in Holland, so very few stayed in Italy for good. Some managed a decade, most less, some just a year or two. Occasionally an artist sojourned more than once, like Du Jardin, but for most a single visit was enough. The style certainly did not depend upon residence in Italy for inspiration. Memory, and sketchbooks full of motifs, served just as well. Most of their careers were spent in their various native towns in Holland, where the so-called Italianate style was just another specialist genre – like marine painting, or architectural painting – calculated to appeal to a section of that buoyant art-buying market, a 'performance indicator' of Dutch society's growing cosmopolitanism. The Italianates were not viewed as exotic, or separate, in any way once back home. Indeed, many of these artists could, and did, paint in very different styles if the market was there for them – both Berchem and Du Jardin painted large-scale history pieces; Du Jardin [fig. 20] and Cuyp painted fine portraits.

Analysis of the style has tended to conclude that it lasted almost exactly a century (c. 1600–c. 1700), and fell into three

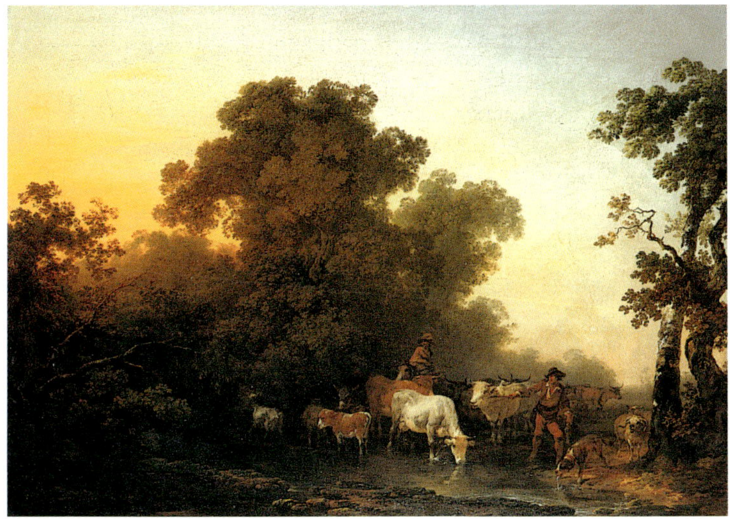

left
Fig. 21 **Philippe Jacques de Loutherbourg** *Landscape with Cattle and Figures*
c. 1765, oil on canvas, 70.8 x 97.2 cm
DPG No. 339, Bourgeois Bequest, 1811

phases or 'generations', of which the second was probably the most characteristic and successful. (It is from this period – roughly the 1640s–1670s – that most of Dulwich's great collection comes.) But the neatness of this analysis slightly ignores the influence that these artists had on the 18th-century aesthetic, particularly in France, but in England also – and even in 19th-century America. The Italianate style did not end around 1700; or if it did, it managed a vigorous afterlife by moving out into Europe. Berchem's milkmaids are the grandmothers of Francois Boucher's; his cattle continue their plod into the landscapes of Philippe de Loutherbourg [fig. 21] and from him, incidentally, into the rather inferior paintings of Francis Bourgeois; and the more romantic fantasy found in Weenix and Lingelbach's exotic harbour scenes feeds into those of Claude-Joseph Vernet [fig. 22].

The Dutch Italianates were an international phenomenon. *Pace* Constable, it is more than possible to admire Ruisdael *and* Both, Hobbema *and* Du Jardin. The Italianates conquered the world once – it is surely time for them to do it again.

below
Fig. 22 **Claude-Joseph Vernet** *An Italianate Harbour Scene*
1749, oil on canvas, 104.4 x 117.8 cm
DPG No. 319, Bourgeois Bequest, 1811

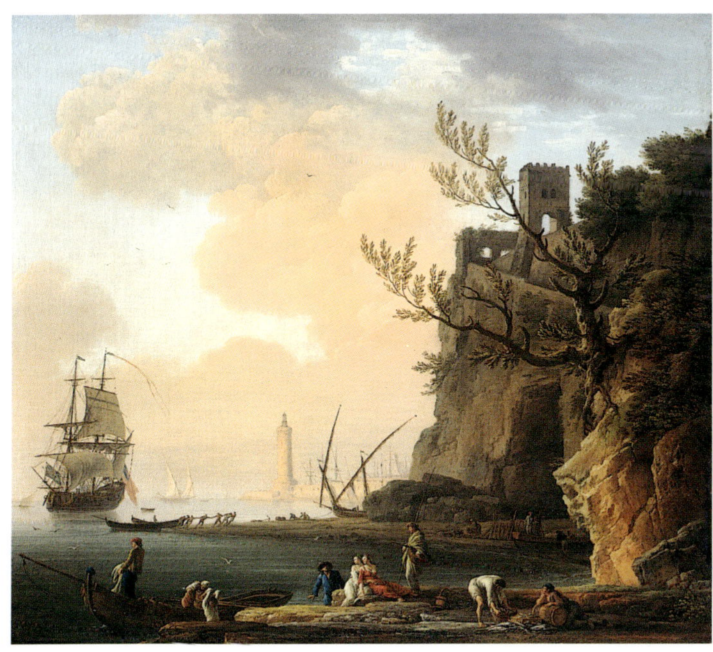

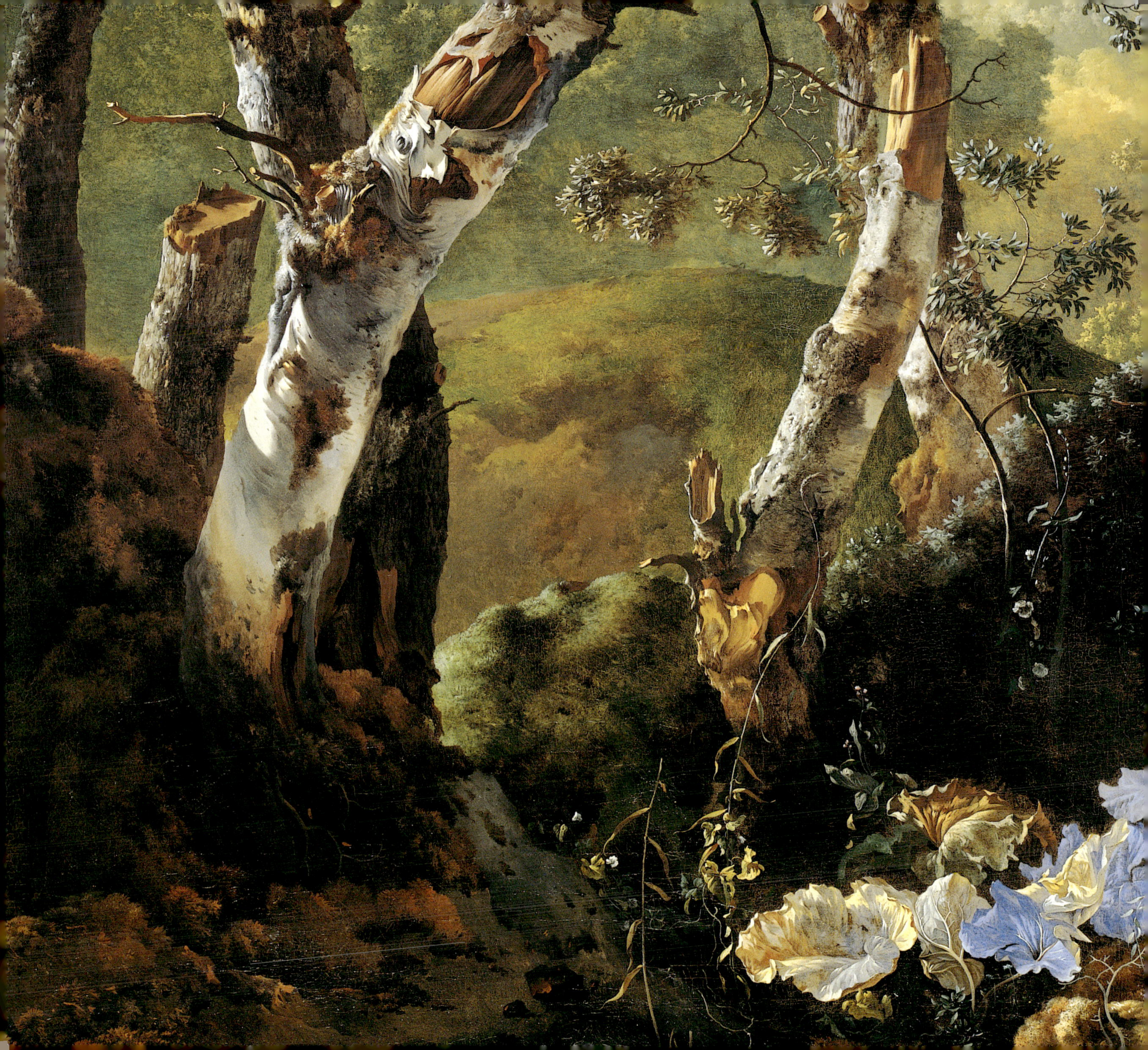

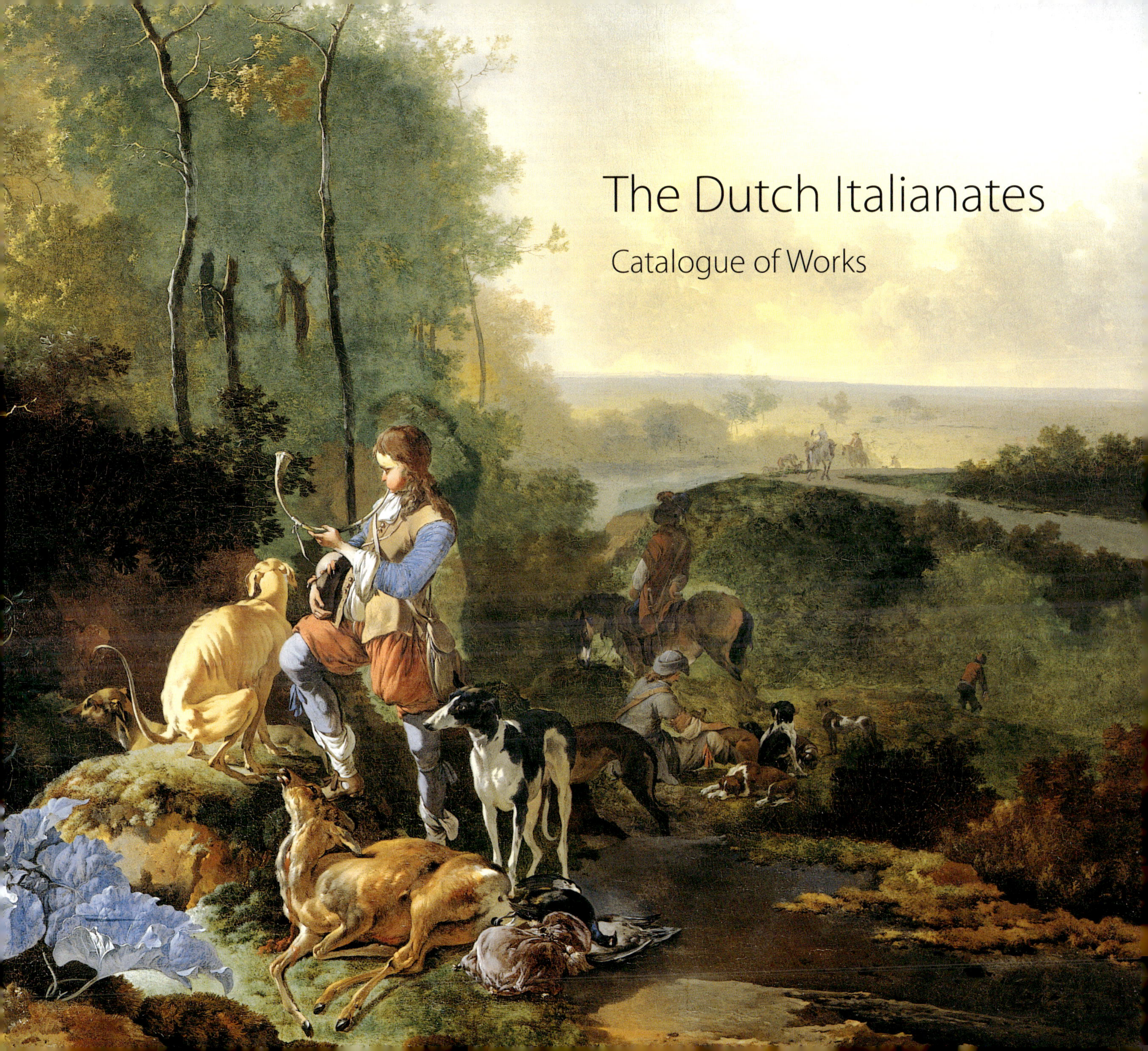
The Dutch Italianates
Catalogue of Works

1

Nicolaes BERCHEM

(Haarlem 1620–1683 Amsterdam)

A Farrier and Peasants

DPG No. 88, Bourgeois Bequest, 1811

Signed, bottom right: Berchem.F.
Canvas, 67.3 x 81.3 cm, including a made-up strip of 1.2 cm at the left edge.

Prov.: London, Noel Desenfans, 1794–1807: London, ?Desenfans sale, 16 June 1794 lot 99 ('Landscape, cattle and figures, with a farrier shoeing an ass, companion to 97 3 ft. 9 by 3 ft. 3, on canvas'); London, Sir Francis Bourgeois, 1807–1811; Bourgeois Bequest, 1811.

Ref.: Patmore, 1824b, p. 188; Jameson, 1842, p. 464, no. 132; Hazlitt, 1843, p. 29; Richter and Sparkes, 1880, p. 10, no. 132; Ruskin, 1843, I, p. 37; 1905 cat., pp. 22–3, no. 88; HdG, 1907–26, IX, p. 101; no. 174; Cook, 1914, p. 51–3, no. 88; Schaar, 1958, p. 85; Murray, 1980a, p. 28; Murray, 1980b, p. 7; London, 1995, pp. 54–5, no. 10; Beresford, 1998, p. 38.

This is a more romantic and dynamic variant of the theme that Du Jardin handles in his *Smith Shoeing an Ox* (cat. no. 19). Here the simple Italian smithy is replaced by a great Roman ruin that at first glance looks like a natural cliff. Animals and people mill round the smith, at work in the foreground.

With the decline of appreciation for the Dutch Italianates during the 19th century, *A Farrier and Peasants* was singled out for particular criticism. In 1843 Hazlitt wrote that 'There is a truth of character and delicate finishing; but the fault of all Berghem's [sic] pictures is that he continues to finish after he has done looking at nature, and his last touches are different from hers. Hence comes that resemblance to tea-board painting, which even his best works are chargeable with.' In 1873 Ruskin, in his *Modern Painters*, having listed six 'legitimate sources of pleasure in execution', added another: 'strangeness' (that is an unusual technique or effect), comparing the bull's head in Rubens' *Adoration of the Magi* with the cow in this painting. Ruskin, who loved the Rubens, strongly criticized Berchem's technique, writing that in *A Farrier and Peasants* 'a dark back-ground is first laid in with exquisite delicacy and transparency, and on this the cow's head is actually modelled in luminous white, the separate locks of hair projecting from the canvas. No surprise, nor much pleasure of any kind, would be attendant on this execution, even were the result equally successful; and what little pleasure we have in it vanishes, when on retiring from the picture, we find the head shining like a distant lantern, instead of seeming substantial or near.'

Schaar proposed that this belonged to a group of grotto pictures that Berchem produced in the late 1650s or early 1660s, in particular noting a similar type of composition in *Gypsy camp* in the Munich Alte Pinakothek (inv. no. 6313).

previous pages
(detail, cat. no. 26)
Adam PYNACKER
Landscape with Sportsmen and Game

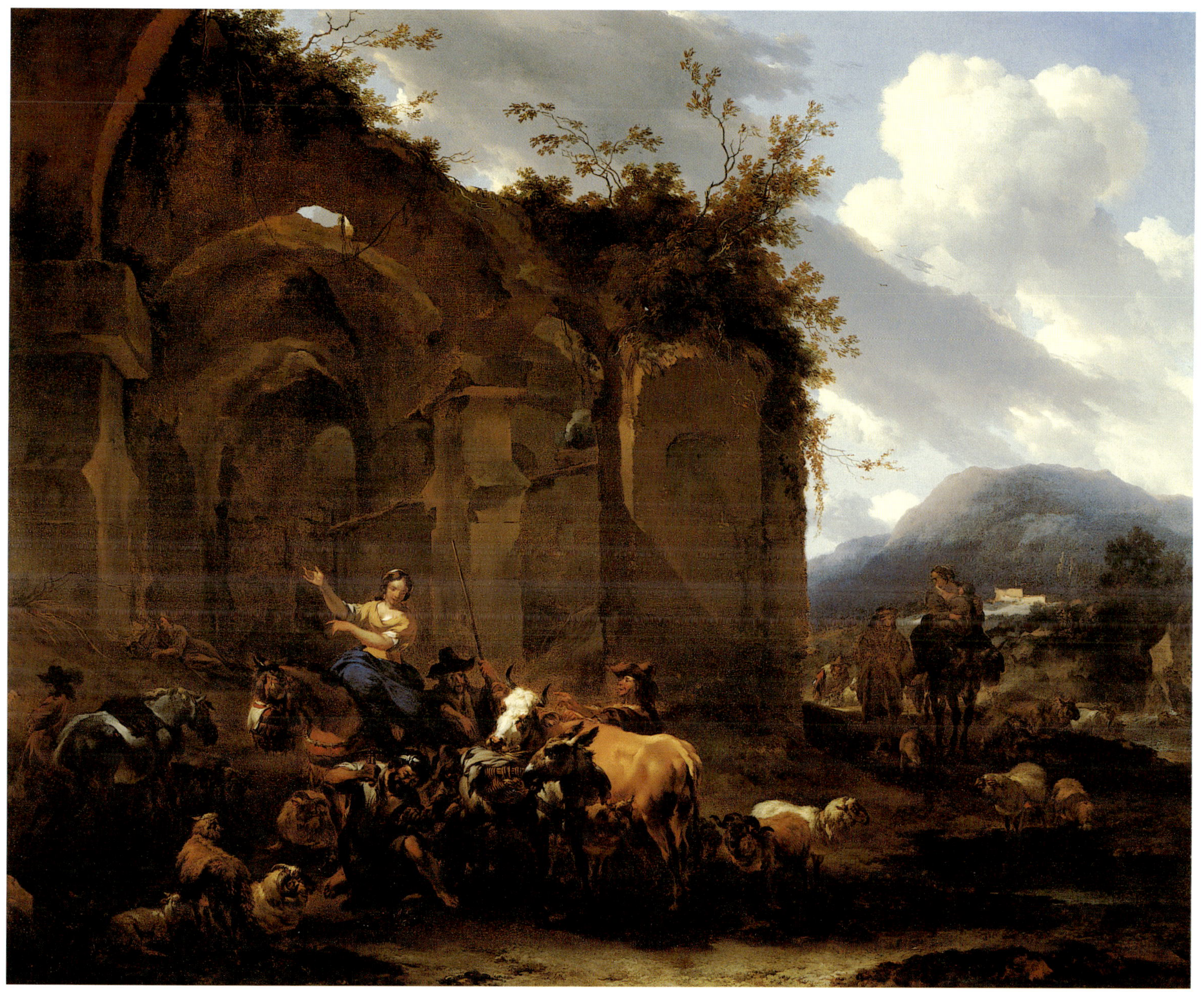

2

Nicolaes BERCHEM

(Haarlem 1620–1683 Amsterdam)

Travelling Peasants

[previously called *Le Soir*]

DPG No. 157, Bourgeois Bequest, 1811

Signed, bottom left: Berchem f
Oak panel, 34.4 x 45.6 cm

Prov.: ?London, ?Desenfans' sale, 16 Jun. 1794, lot 56 ('Berchem – Landscape, with cattle and figures, fording a brook 2 ft. 2 by 1 ft. 10, on pannel'); Bourgeois Bequest, 1811.

Ref.: Smith, 1829–42, V, p. 12, no. 18; Jameson, 1842, p. 475, no. 200; Waagen, 1854, II, p. 344; Richter and Sparkes, 1880, p. 10, no. 200; 1905 cat., p. 41, no. 157; HdG, 1907–26, IX, p. 161, no. 380; Cook, 1914, p. 97, no. 157; Murray, 1980a, p. 28; Murray, 1980b, p. 8; Beresford, 1998, p. 40; Houston and Louisville, 1999–2000, p. 180, no. 61.

The story of this painting is an object lesson in how an art historical mistake can take on a life of its own, becoming 'accepted fact'. Around 1750, a different painting – another of Dulwich's Berchems in fact, *Roman Fountain with Cattle and Figures* (cat. no. 3) – was recorded in the collection of the Marquis de Voyer d'Argenson[1]. It was described as being one of a pair. The two pictures next appear in the posthumous sale of the collection of Louis-Jean Gaignat in 1769. They were bought by an engraver, Jean-Georges Wille. He had the two pictures engraved by Nicholas-Barthélemy-Francois Dequevauviller (1745–1807); the prints name them as *Le Midi* (Dulwich's picture) and *Le Soir*. Wille owned them until 1784, at which point they disappear from view. *Roman Fountain*, however, certainly turns up – without its partner – in the 1813 posthumous inventory of Sir Francis Bourgeois' collection, and consequently remains at Dulwich Picture Gallery. However, Desenfans and Bourgeois liked to hang pictures as pairs (they were not, in fact, above adapting non-matching canvasses to fit matching frames[2]). So they framed another of their Berchems, *Travelling Peasants*, to 'match' *Roman Fountain*. John Smith, writing twenty years later, knew of the Gaignat provenance of the latter painting, and the existence of the Dequevauviller engravings, but he must not have known the prints personally. He jumped to the not unreasonable conclusion that the Bourgeois 'pair' must be identical to the Gaignat pair. Later art historians failed to question this, and as a result *Travelling Peasants* has spent nearly 200 years wrongly identified with an entirely different painting, wrongly (if not inappropriately) labelled 'Le Soir', and hanging in association with a painting that is not only slightly different in size, but clearly painted at a different time and in a different style.

Travelling Peasants is in fact the later of the two by some years, probably painted in the mid to late-1650s, possibly in Italy, where the artist is thought to have been for a few years from 1653. Its handling is soft and impressionistic, the hazy distances of the background mountain intimated by broken brushstrokes with the ground left to show through – a bold and confident effect that allows the grain of the wood to play an important visual role.

1 As was first pointed out by Mme Anne Leclair (DPG archive, letter on file, 27 April 2004).
2 This is what seems to have happened, for instance, in the case of Van Dyck's *Madonna and Child* (DPG90), to which 30cm of canvas was added to make it fit the magnificent matching frame to the Van Dyck studio production, *Charity* (DPG81).

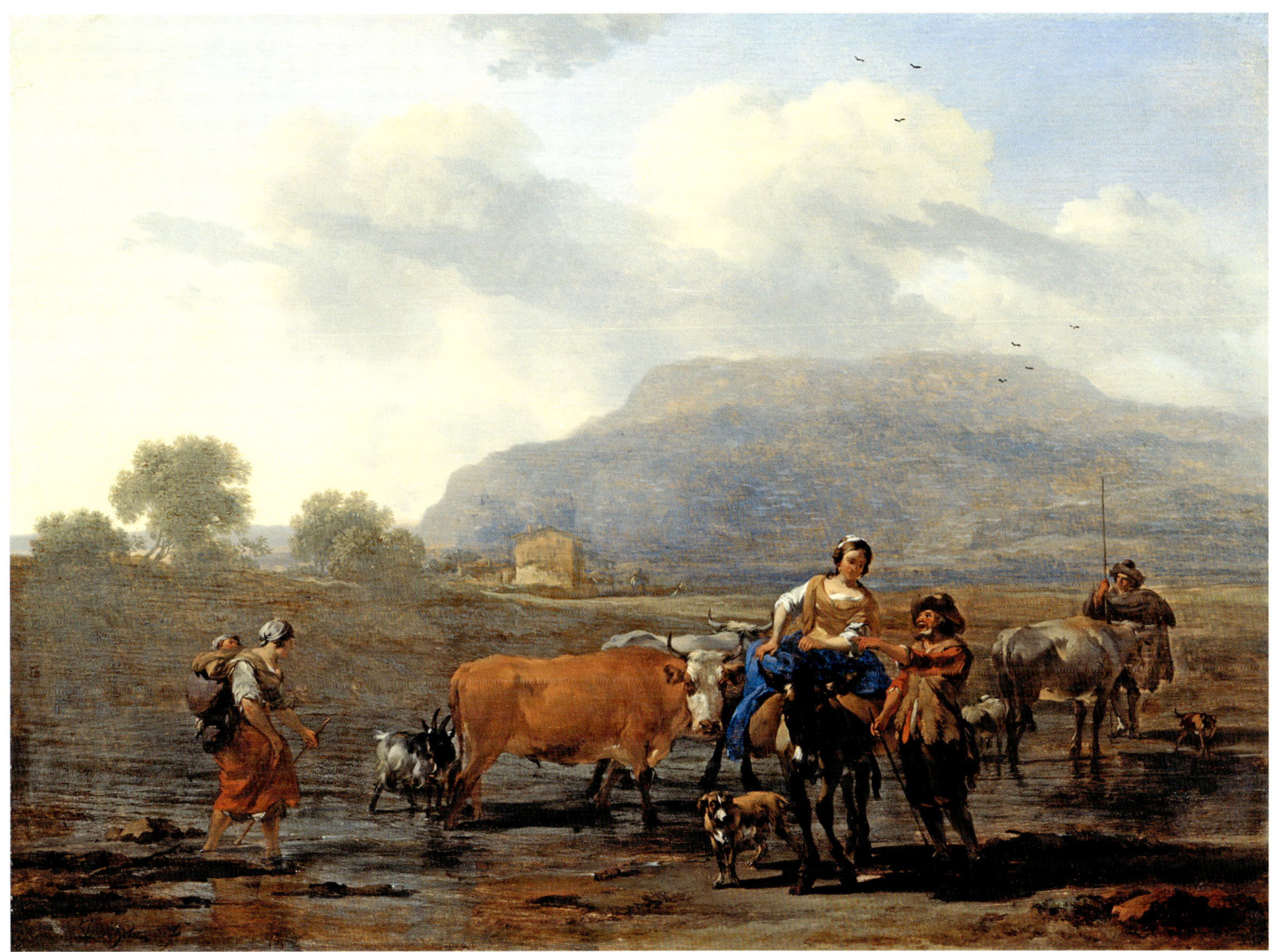

3 Nicolaes BERCHEM

(Haarlem 1620–1683 Amsterdam)
Roman Fountain with Cattle and Figures (Le Midi)
DPG No. 166, Bourgeois Bequest, 1811

Signed, bottom left: Berchem
Oak panel, 36.8 x 48.4 cm

Prov.: Asnières castle, Marquis Marc-Antoine René Marquis de Voyer d'Argenson (1722–1782), his inventory [Poitiers, Bibliothèque Universitaire, section IV, pièce 1, f° 13], c. 1750; Paris, Louis-Jean Gaignat (d. 1768): his posthumous sale, Paris, Rémy,Poirier, 14 Feb. 1769, lot 42; Bt Wille ['Wille le graveur', according to RKDH copy of sale catalogue], 4001 livres; Paris, Jean-Georges Wille (1715–1808): his sale, Paris, Basan, 6–10 December 1784, lot 3; London, Sir Francis Bourgeois, 1811; Bourgeois Bequest, 1811.

Ref.: Smith, 1829–42, I, p. 12, no. 17; Jameson, 1842, p. 476, no. 209; Waagen, 1854, II, p. 344; Richter and Sparkes, 1880, p. 9, no. 209; 1905 cat., pp. 43–4, no. 166; HdG, 1907–26, IX, p. 106, no. 192; Cook, 1914, p. 103, no. 166; Schaar, 1958, p. 19; Murray, 1980b, p. 28; Murray, 1980, p. 8; Beresford, 1998, p. 40; Houston and Louisville, 1999–2000, p. 182, no. 62.

Versions and copies: 1. Nicolas-Barthélemy-François Dequevauviller. Engraving, 39 x 46 cm. 2. Engraving, R. Cockburn.

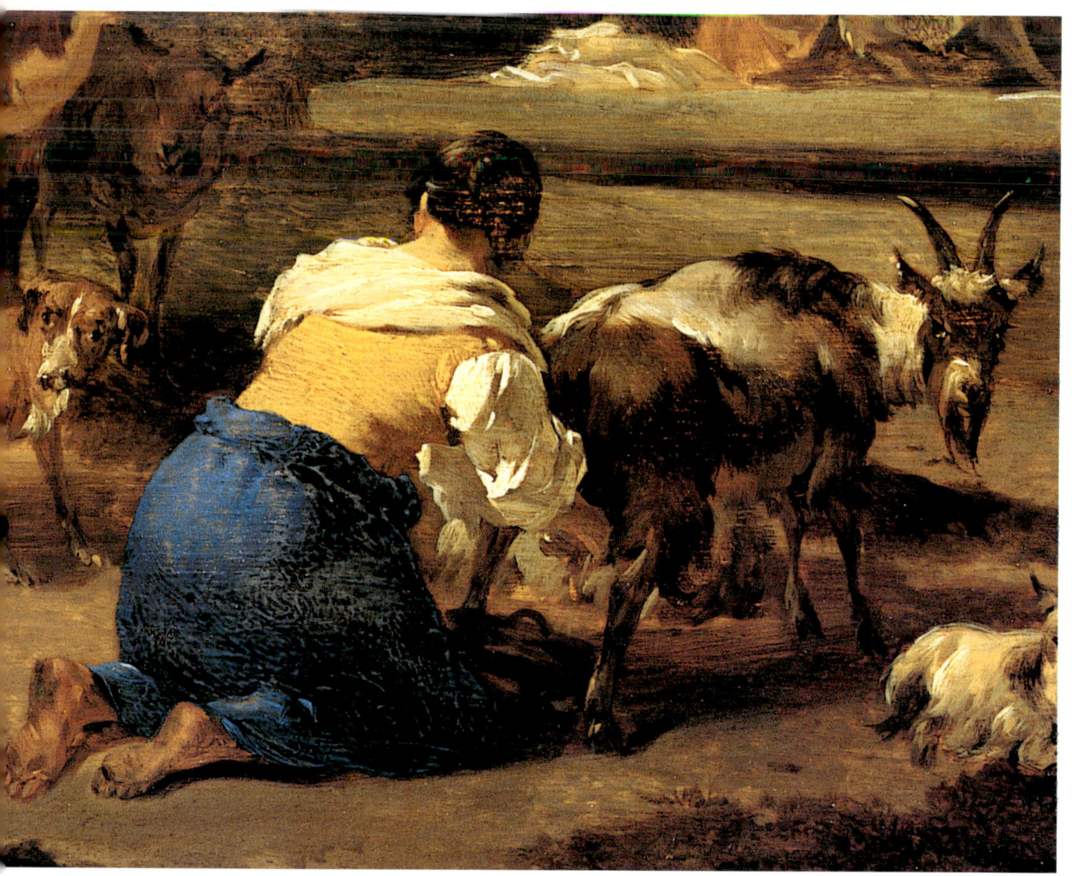

detail

Schaar associated this painting with works datable to c. 1645/6, but a drawing of an identical fountain at the Teylers Museum is dated 1653[3], so it may be later. See entry for *Travelling Peasants* (cat. no. 2).

3 See M.C. Plomp, *The Dutch Drawings in the Teylers Museum. Volume II. Artists Born Between 1575 and 1630*, Haarlem/Ghent/Doornspijk 1997, p. 65 no. 35.

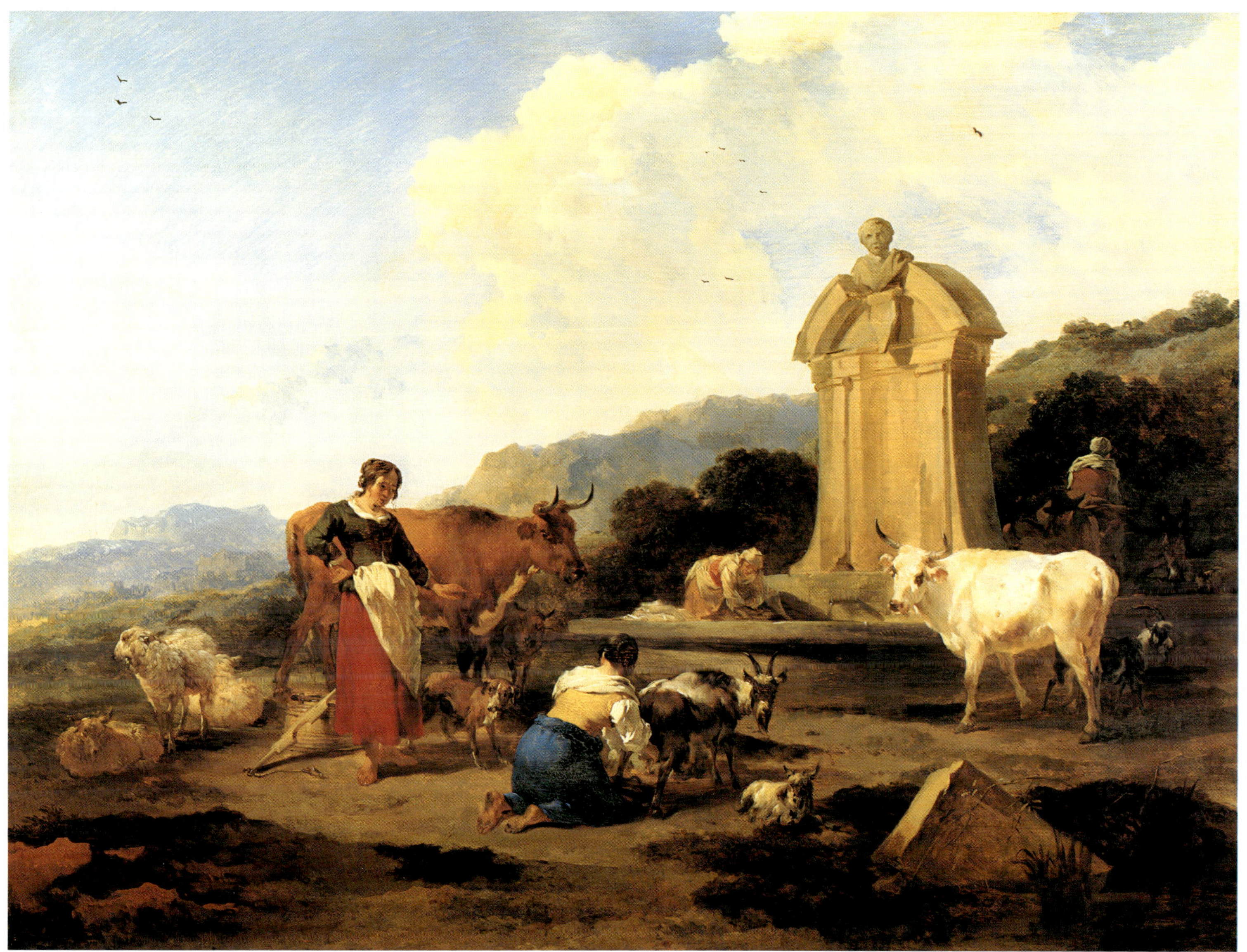

4 Nicolaes BERCHEM

(Haarlem 1620–1683 Amsterdam)
A Road through a Wood
DPG No. 122, Bourgeois Bequest, 1811

Signed, bottom right: CBerrighem (CB in monogram)
Canvas, 119.5 x 89.6 cm

Prov.: London, Noel Desenfans and/or Sir Francis Bourgeois: 1804 Insurance List, no. 87; London, Sir Francis Bourgeois, 1807–1811; Bourgeois Bequest, 1811.

Ref.: Richter and Sparkes, 1880, p. 9, no. 160; 1905 cat., p. 31, no. 122; HdG, 1907–26, IX, p. 106; Cook, 1914, p. 72, no. 122; Murray, 1980, p. 28; Murray, 1980b, p. 7; Beresford, 1998, p. 39.

The form of the signature indicates an early date: Schaar implies that it should be dated in the late 1640s. This picture reminds us that Berchem was a friend of Ruisdael – it was soon after this that the pair of them went to Westphalia together on a sketching trip. Were it not for the signature, this painting might conceivably have been allocated to one of the most populous 'black holes' of attribution in Dutch art history: 'Follower of Jacob van Ruisdael'. However, no-one could ever have doubted the attribution of the figures to Berchem; and the blue hills shining through the tree trunks, allied to the light, almost rococo brushwork would have given pause for thought. The cattle, and the mounted milkmaid, are classic Berchem types. Most fascinating is the sheer scale of the piece – very large by Berchem's standards – but the young artist has controlled the space with a series of brilliant diagonals upwards to the sky, and brought light and air into play through the aforementioned pure blue stripe of distant hills just below the centre line. Another wonderfully spontaneous detail plays itself out on the far right of the foreground, where two mounted huntsmen are about to gallop out of the frame; the further away of the two has just fired his rifle, and so a sleepy, timeless scene is transformed into an instantaneous moment by means of a burst of flame and a speeding bullet.

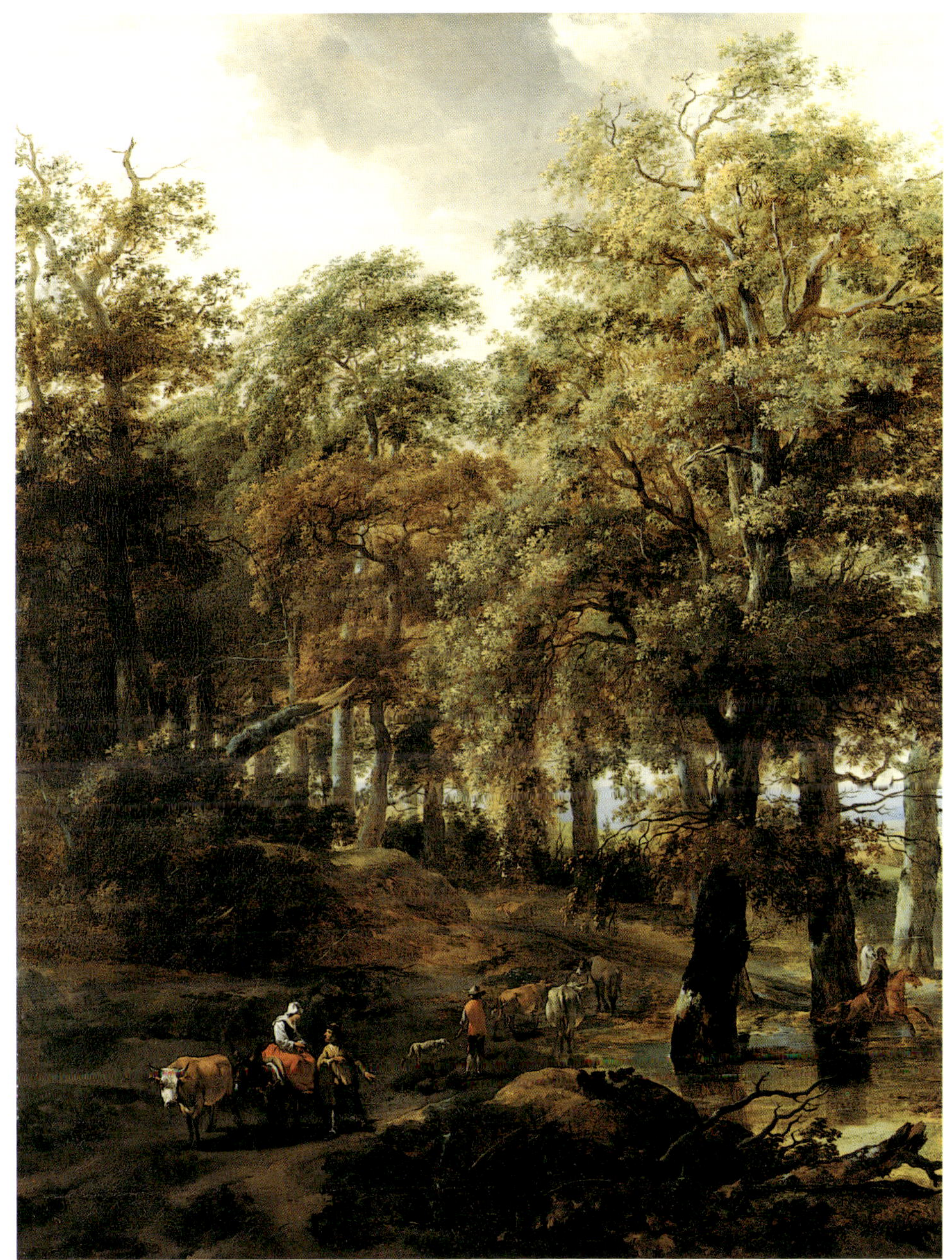

5 Attributed to Jan BOTH

(Utrecht? c. 1615–1652 Utrecht)
Banks of a Brook
DPG No. 12, Bourgeois Bequest, 1811

The status of this picture is problematic, thanks to its condition. Burke proposed that it might be a replica, by Both himself, of the original in the Koninklijk Museum voor Schone Kunsten in Antwerp (inv. no. 26, 56 x 70cm) – and certain elements (the trees and distant mountain) certainly appear fine enough to be from Both's own hand.

Canvas, 55.2 x 68.9 cm

Prov.: London, Sir Francis Bourgeois, 1811; Bourgeois Bequest, 1811.

Ref.: Patmore, 1824, pp. 58–9, no. 184; Smith, 1829–42, VI, p. 213, no. 113; Jameson, 1842, p. 447, no. 30, or p. 449, no. 41; Richter and Sparkes, 1880, p. 17, no. 41 (as follower of Both); 1905 cat., p. 4, no. 12 (as J. Both); Cook, 1914, p. 10, no. 12; HdG, 1926, IX, p. 487, no. 234; Burke, 1976, pp. 219–20, no. 62 (as a copy, c. 1641–5, possibly by Both, of the painting at Antwerp); Murray, 1980a, p. 30; Murray, 1980b, p. 9; Beresford, 1998, p. 46.

Versions and Copies: 1. Original, Antwerp, Koninklijk Museum voor Schone Kunsten, canvas, 56 x 70 cm, inv. no. 26.

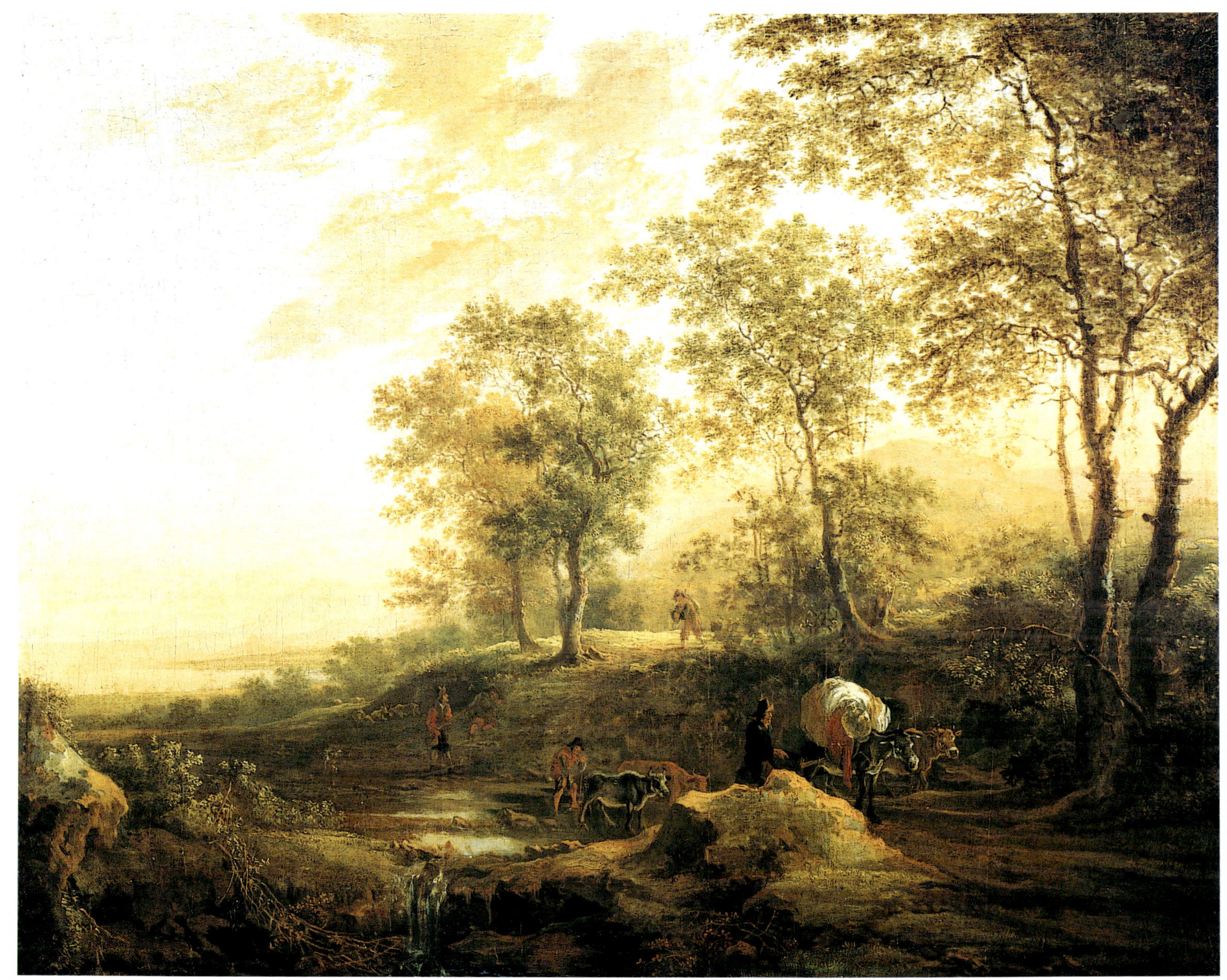

6 Jan BOTH

(Utrecht? c. 1615–1652 Utrecht)

Road by the Edge of a Lake

DPG No. 15, Bourgeois Bequest, 1811

John Smith was of the opinion that this was a 'very indifferent' example of the master's work – probably more an indicator of the taste of the time (he was writing in the 1830s) for the more grandiose works such as Dulwich's *A Mountain Path* (cat. no. 7) than a valid criticism. The painting has its own poetic qualities, particularly in the way the light catches the leaves of the trees, and the individual blades of grass to the side of the path – a detail reminiscent of (the younger) Paulus Potter.

Burke suggests that this painting dated from Both's period in Rome between about 1638 and 1641. It is first recorded in Paris in 1781 as part of the Poullain collection. There it was stated to be a collaboration between Moucheron and Both, and in the 1905 Dulwich catalogue it was suggested that Andries Both, Jan's elder brother, may have had a hand in it too. Certainly Jan collaborated with other artists regularly, particularly figure painters, and in this he was not unusual. The peasants in this painting are reminiscent of the Roman 'low-life' figures of Pieter van Laer – *Il Bamboccio* as he was known – hence the suggestion that Andries, who was a follower of Van Laer, may have been involved. The broad characterisation and handling of the figures certainly contrasts with the delicacy of the landscape detail, but the evidence is not conclusive.

Oak panel, 57 x 51 cm

Prov.: Paris, Antoine Poullain (Moitte Cat. 1781, no. 62, as by Both and Moucheron); ?London, Noel Desenfans, 1791–1807: ?Evening Mail inventory, 1791 (Little Parlour: 'Both – A Landscape, with figures'); ?undated list of 'Pictures to be sold', no. 306 (Small Parlour: 'Both – a Landscape & figures'). 36 gn; London, Sir Francis Bourgeois, 1811; Bourgeois Bequest, 1811).

Ref.: Smith, 1829–42, VI, p. 214, no. 115; Richter and Sparkes, 1880, p. 17, no. 205 (as follower of Both); 1905 cat., p. 4, no. 15 (as 'J. & A. Both'); HdG, 1926, IX, no. 142; Cook, 1914, p. 11, no. 15; Burke, 1976, p. 220, no. 63 (as painted in Jan's Roman period, c. 1638–41); Murray, 1980a, p. 30; Murray, 1980b, p. 9; Beresford, 1998, p. 44; Houston and Louisville, 1999–2000, p. 144, no. 44.

Versions and Copies: 1. Engraving in Francois Basan Collection de Cent vingt estampes, gravees d'apres les tableaux & dessins qui composoient le cabinet de M. Poullain, Receveur General des Domaines du Roi, decede en 1780; Precedee d'un Abrege historique de la Vie des Auteurs qui la composen; Dediee a M. Paris, 1781 (as in Poullain collection), p. 12, plate 62. 2. Engraving, R. Cockburn (as 'Morning').

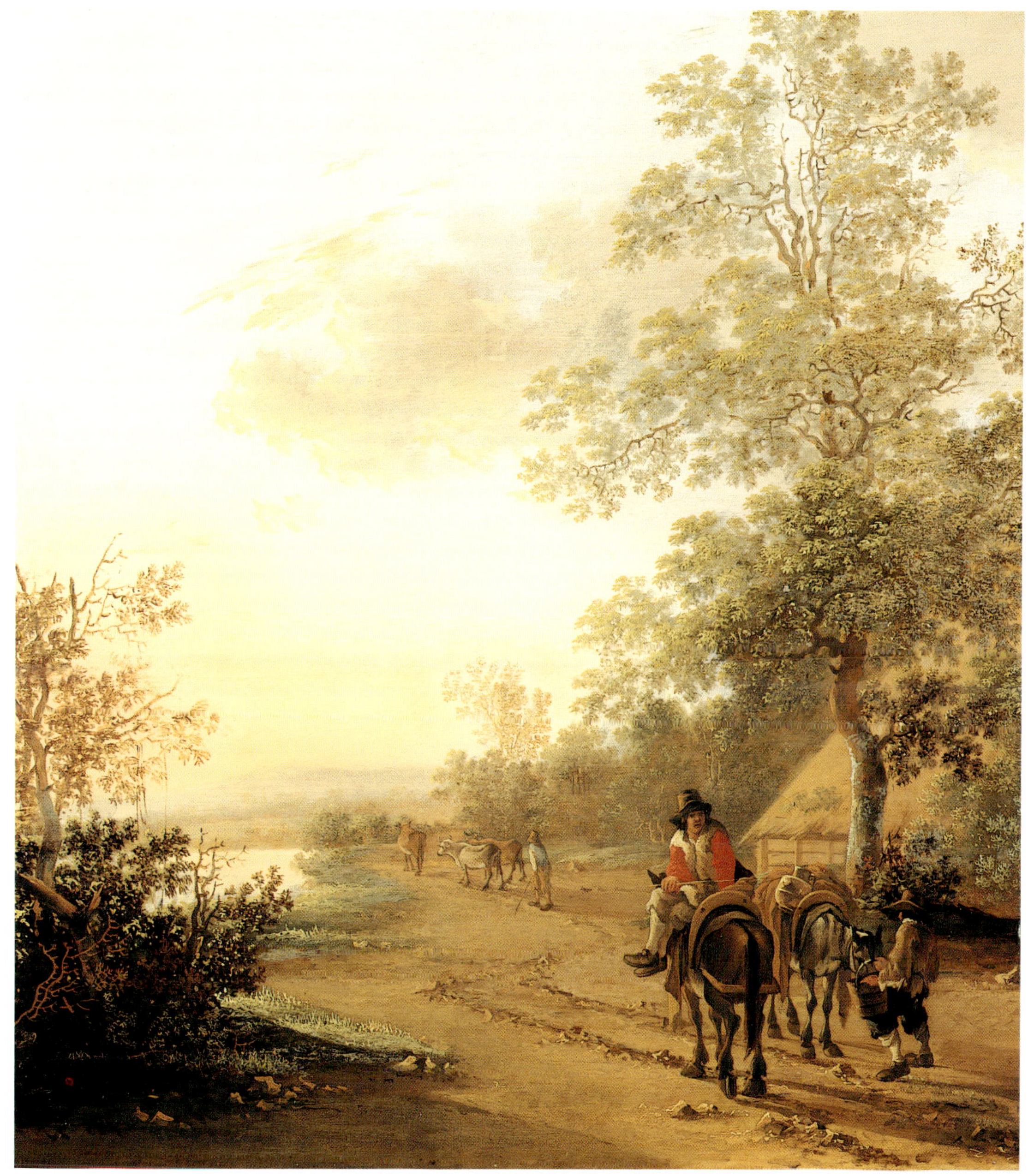

7 Jan BOTH

(Utrecht? c. 1615–1652 Utrecht)
A Mountain Path
DPG No. 208, Bourgeois Bequest, 1811

Signed, lower centre left: JBoth . f (JB in monogram)
Canvas, 70.8 x 111.4 cm

Prov.: London, Sir Francis Bourgeois, 1811, Bourgeois Bequest, 1811.

Ref.: Patmore, 1824a, p. 36, no. 125; Smith, 1829–42, VI, p. 214, no. 116; Jameson, 1842, p. 448, no. 36; Waagen, 1854, II, p. 344; Richter and Sparkes, 1880, p. 16, no. 36; 1905 cat., p. 56, no. 208; HdG, 1907–26, ix, p. 487, no. 235; Burke, 1976, n. p., no. 64; Murray, 1980a, pp. 30–1; Murray, 1980b, p. 9; Warsaw, 1992, p. 56, no. 2; Beresford, 1998, p. 45.

Versions and Copies: 1. Miniature replica by an anonymous copyist, Leiden, Welcker Coll.[1]

Burke dated this grand composition to the second half of the 1640s, linking its blues and greens (albeit now rather difficult to make out due to chemical change) to a painting in the Staatens Museum voor Kunst, Copenhagen. At any rate, it follows Both's return to his native Utrecht in 1642, and compares nicely with the earlier *Road by the Edge of a Lake* (cat. no. 6) which has been dated to his Roman period. The picture produced in Holland is less ethereal in its colouring and more dense in its landscape detail; silver has given way to gold. Images like these proved powerfully influential; surely Aelbert Cuyp's *A Road near a River* (cat. no. 15) might almost be a conscious variation on this very painting. Comparison of the two is interesting, at any rate, since Both is revealed as less Classical and measured in his composition. His painting has two focal points – the busy path to the left, bathed in sunshine, and the stupendous crag in the distance, which Both has consciously framed with trees, leaving an inner frame of sky. A comparison of busy humanity with eternal nature seems intended.

The painting has suffered from a condition known as 'blanching', a clouding of pigment and/or varnish that has rather impaired appreciation of the landscape elements of the painting. This interferes with what must once have been a masterclass in the handling of the progression of light and shade across rocky, wooded terrain.

1 See Amsterdam, Rijksmuseum, Rijksprentenkabinet, *De verzameling van Dr. A. Welcker. I: Nederlandse tekeningen de zestiende en zeventiende eeuw*, exh. cat. 1956.

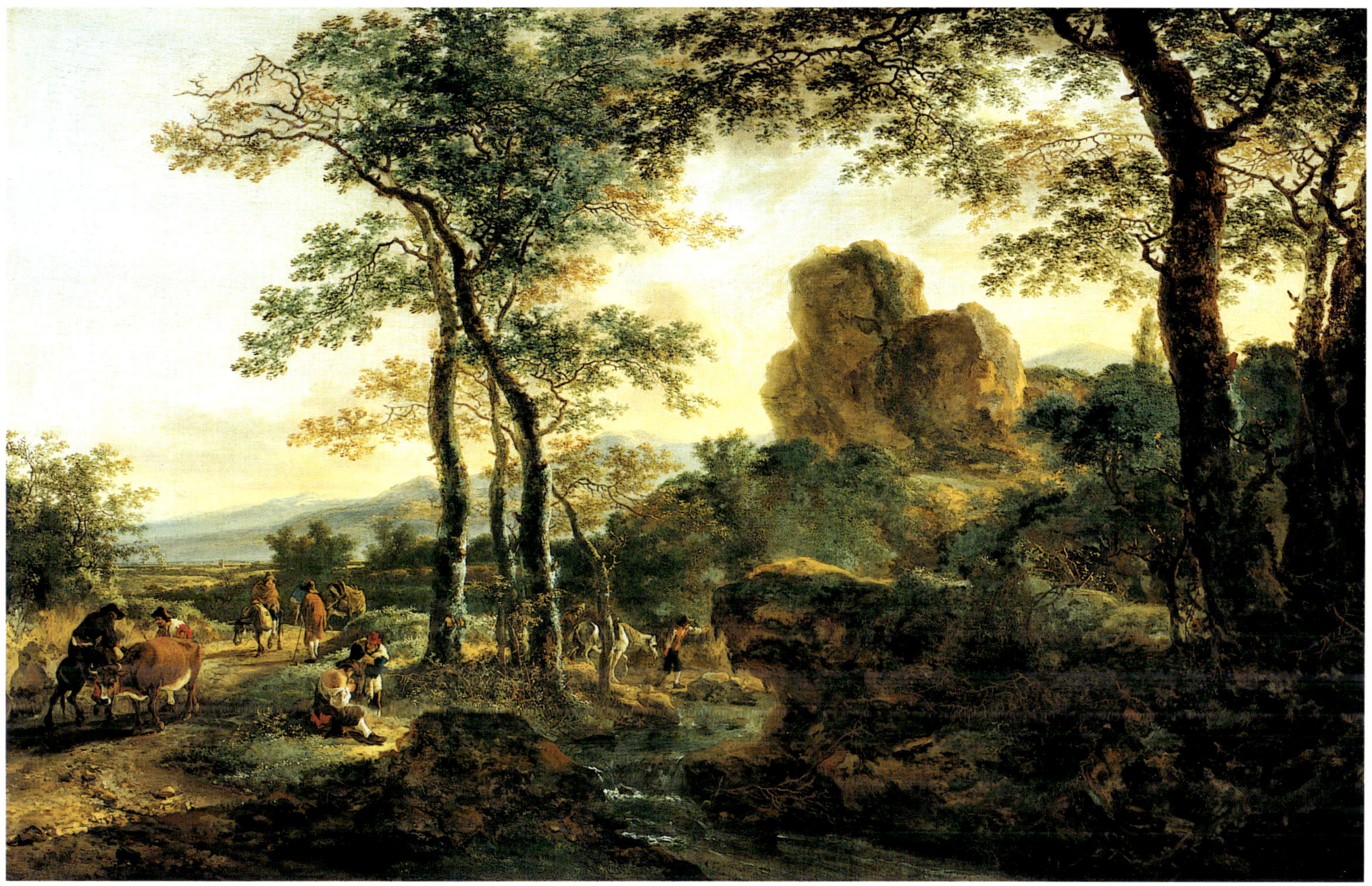

8

Abraham van CALRAET

(Dordrecht 1642–1722 Dordrecht)

White Horse in a Riding School

DPG No. 65, Bourgeois Bequest, 1811

The theme of the riding school found its genesis in the work of both Cuyp and Wouwermans. Here, Calraet makes good use of one of Wouwermans' trademarks – the white horse – while some near-identical prototypes of Calraet's chestnut horse being put through its paces in the middle ground can be found prancing down the road to the right of Cuyp's *An Evening Ride near a River* (cat. no. 14). In terms of atmosphere, however, Calraet's interior is curiously monochrome, and the relative proportions of the figures a little dubious. Nonetheless, the existence of at least two autograph copies of the picture suggests it was one of Calraet's most popular works.

Signed on plank, bottom right: AC
Oak panel, 34.9 x 52 cm

Prov.: London, Noel Desenfans, ?1804–1807: 1804 Insurance List, either no. 102 ('Cuyp – Horses and Figures'), £100, or 103 ('Ditto [Cuyp]–Ditto [Horses and Figures]'), £80; London, Sir Francis Bourgeois, 1807–1811; Bourgeois Bequest, 1811.

Ref.: Patmore, 1824, p. 14, no. 73 (as Cuyp); Jameson, 1842, p. 56, no. 114 (as Cuyp); Richter and Sparkes, 1880, p. 44, no. 114 (as by Cuyp); 1905 cat., p. 16, no. 65; HdG, 1908, II, p. 179, no. 604 (as Cuyp); Cook, 1914, p. 37, no. 65; Bredius, 1919, p. 120 (first tentative attribution to Calraet); London and Leeds, 1947, no. 9 (attributed to Cuyp, but suggesting Calraet); 1953 cat., p. 13; Murray, 1980a, p. 38; Murray, 1980b, pp. 9–10; Waterfield, 1988, p. 10; Chong, 1992, no. 239; Beresford, 1998, p. 57.

Versions and Copies: 1. Autograph copy, Woburn Abbey, Duke of Bedford 2. Autograph copy, Location unknown, panel, 33 x 49.5 cm, signed (?) with initials (formerly London, Christie's, 12 Jul 1985, lot 62; London, Christie's, 19 Jun 1987, lot 139; London, Phillip's, 14 Feb. 1989, lot 9). 3. Engraving, R. Cockburn.

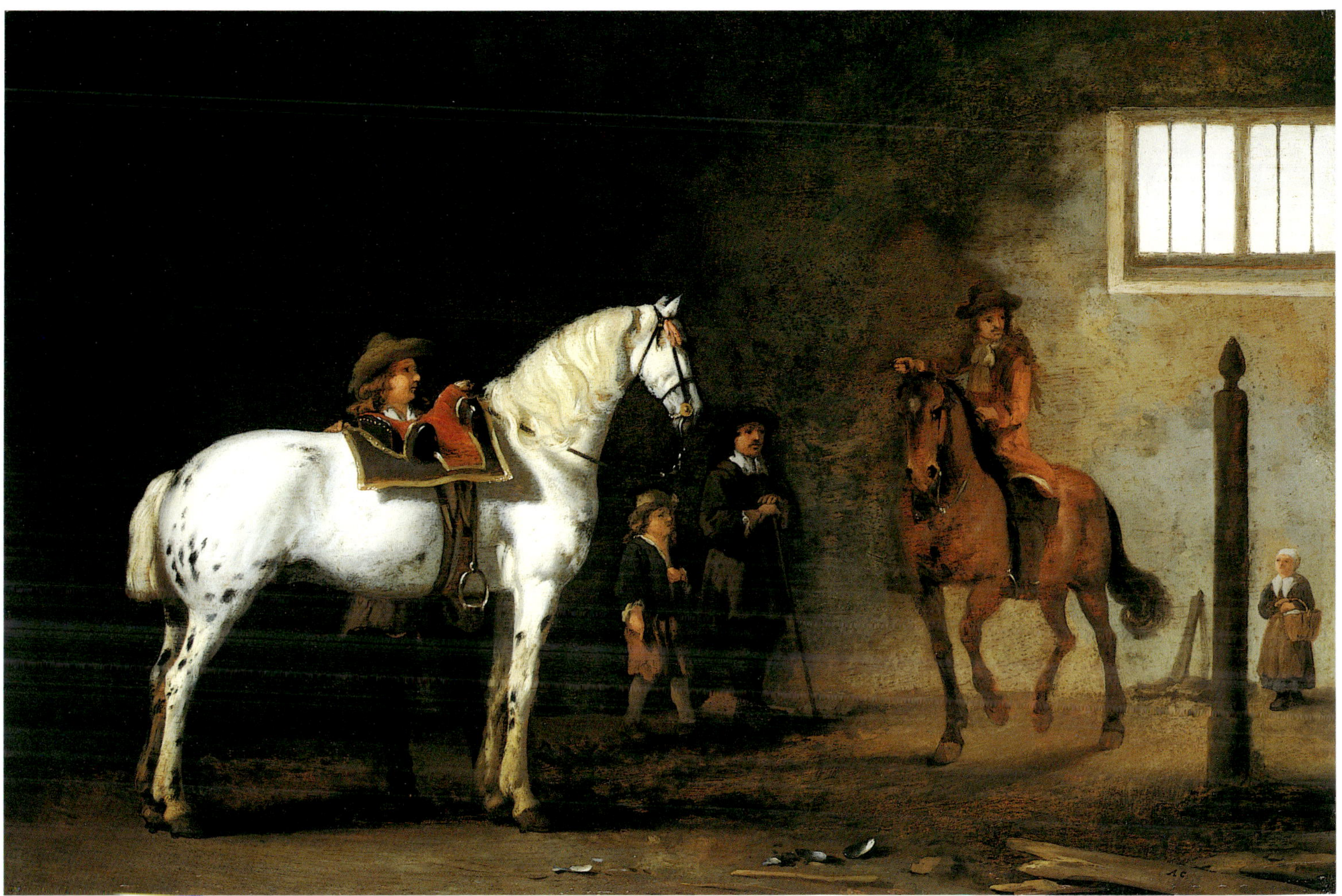

9 Abraham van CALRAET

(Dordrecht 1642–1722 Dordrecht)

Two Horses

DPG No. 71, Bourgeois Bequest, 1811

Signed, bottom left: AC
Oak panel, 29 x 40.4 cm

Prov.: London, Noel Desenfans, 1804–1811: 1804 Insurance List, either no. 102 or 103 (as Cuyp); London, Sir Francis Bourgeois, 1807–1811; Bourgeois Bequest, 1811.

Ref.: Patmore, 1824, p. 14, no. 74 (as Cuyp); Hazlitt, 1843, p. 29; Richter and Sparkes, 1880, p. 44, no. 156 (as by Cuyp); 1905 cat., p. 18, no. 71 (as Cuyp); HdG, 1908, II, p. 158, no. 551 (publ. 1926: as Calraet); Thieme-Becker, 1907–50, XIX, p. 483; Cook, 1914, p. 41, no. 71; Bredius, 1919, p. 120 (first attribution to Calraet); London and Leeds, 1947, no. 10 ('hitherto called Cuyp, but perhaps by Calraet'); 1953 cat., p. 13 (as Calraet); Murray, 1980a, p. 38; Murray, 1980b, p. 10; Chong, 1992, no. 240; Beresford, 1998, p. 59.

Versions and Copies: 1. Copy or version, Location unknown, panel, 32 x 44 cm (formerly Brussels, R. Zomer sale, 11 Dec. 1923, lot 50). 2. Copy or version, Location unknown (formerly Brussels, De Fursac sale, 1 Dec. 1923, lot 50). 3. Engraving, R. Cockburn.

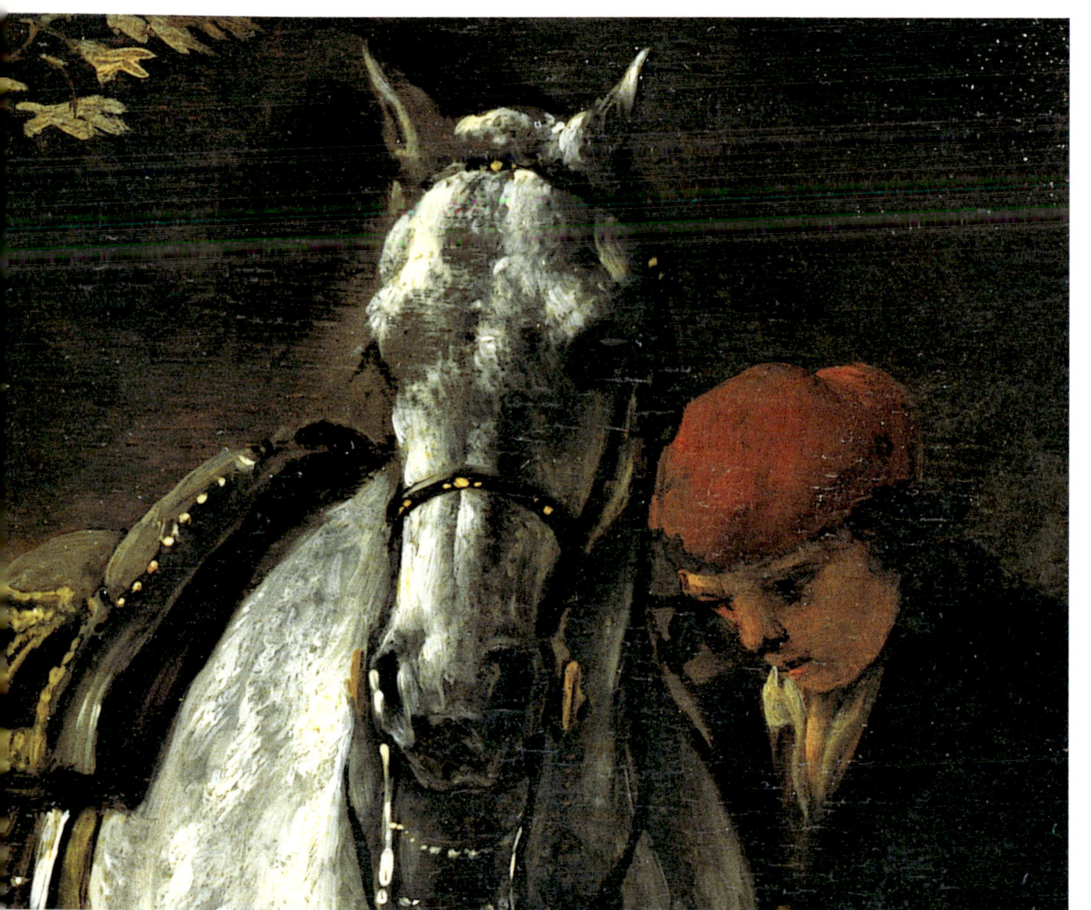

detail

Writing in 1843, when the picture was attributed to Cuyp, William Hazlitt commented of *Two Horses* that 'Nature is scarcely more faithful to itself than this delightfully unmannered, unaffected picture is to it'. Bredius first attributed the painting to Calraet in 1919, but it was not until 1953 that this gained widespread acceptance.

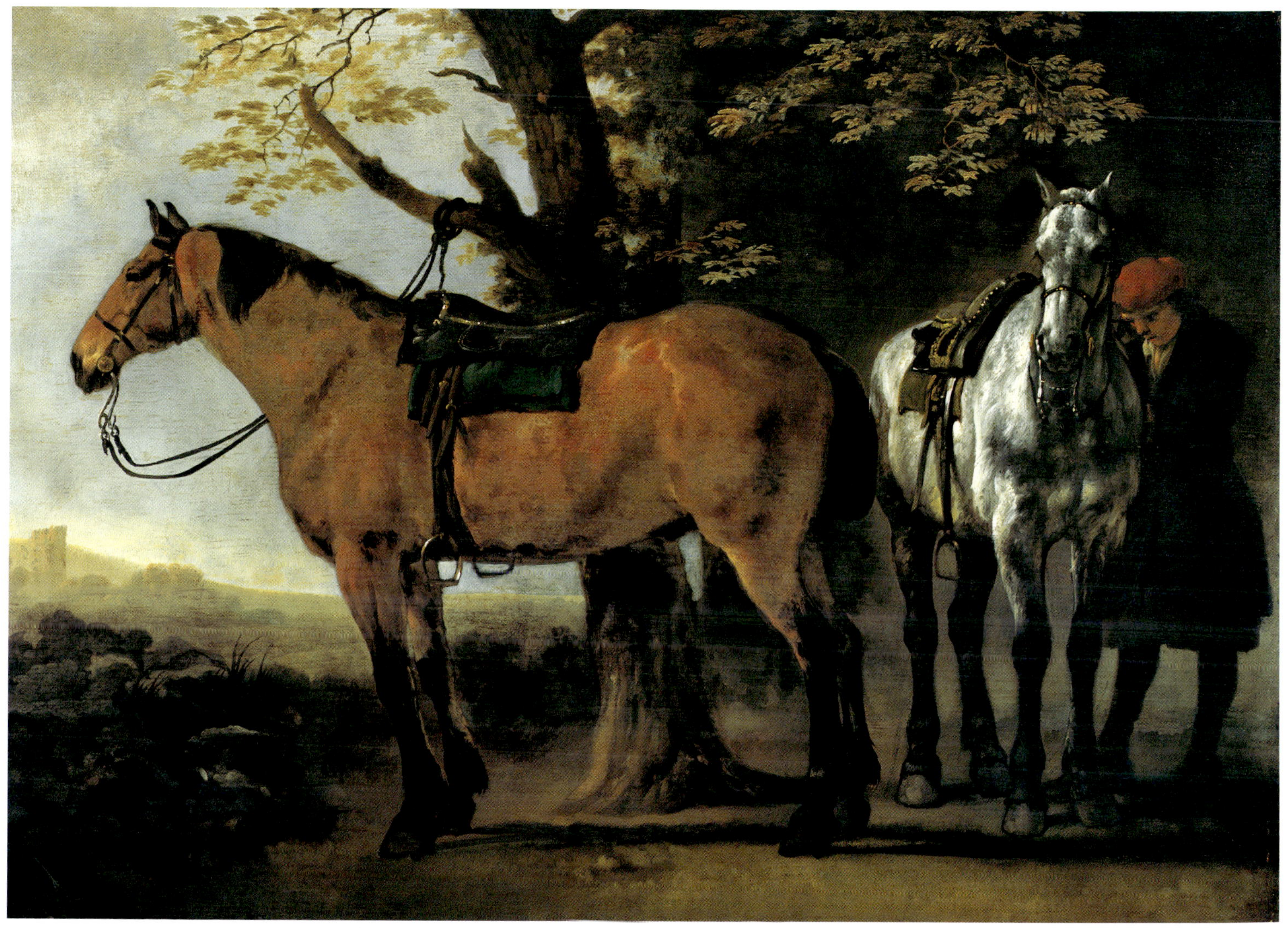

10 Abraham van CALRAET

(Dordrecht 1642–1722 Dordrecht)
A Riding School in the Open Air
DPG No. 296, Bourgeois Bequest, 1811

Signed, bottom left: AC.
Oak panel, 32 x 51.6 cm

Prov.: ?J. van der Linden van Slingelandt, 1785, his sale, Dordrecht, sale, 22 Aug. 1785, lot 88. Bt Roos for 470 fl.; Amsterdam, Sale, 11 Jul. 1798, lot 24. Bt Gruyter (along with lot 23 [HdG594b]); London, Noel Desenfans, ?1804–1807: ?1804 Insurance List, either no. 102 ('Cuyp – Horses and Figures'), £100, or 103 ('Ditto [Cuyp] – Ditto [Horses and Figures]'), £80; London, Sir Francis Bourgeois, 1811; Bourgeois Bequest, 1811.

Ref.: Smith, 1829–42, V, p. 295, no. 28 (as the Cuyp formerly in the Slingelandt collection); Jameson, 1842, p. 445, no. 13 (as Cuyp); Richter and Sparkes, 1880, p. 48, no. 13 (as by School of Cuyp); 1905 cat., p. 81, no. 296 (as Cuyp); HdG, 1907–26, II, p. 180, no. 605 (as Cuyp); Bredius, 1919, p. 120 (tentative identification as Calraet); Murray, 1980a, pp. 38–9 (first attribution as Calraet); Murray, 1980b, p. 10; Chong, 1992, no. Calr 242 (as Calraet); Beresford, 1998, p. 59.

Calraet returns to his favourite theme of the riding school, this time out of doors. The riders and their horses look as if they are auditioning for a role in a late painting by Wouwermans; while the instructor with his riding crop is a variant of the riders in Cuyp's *An Evening Ride near a River* (cat. no. 14). Otherwise, the influence of Cuyp is fairly minor, the landscape background with its castle having none of the subtlety of lighting that that master might have brought to the scene. However, as with all works by Calraet, this composition has considerable unpretentious charm.

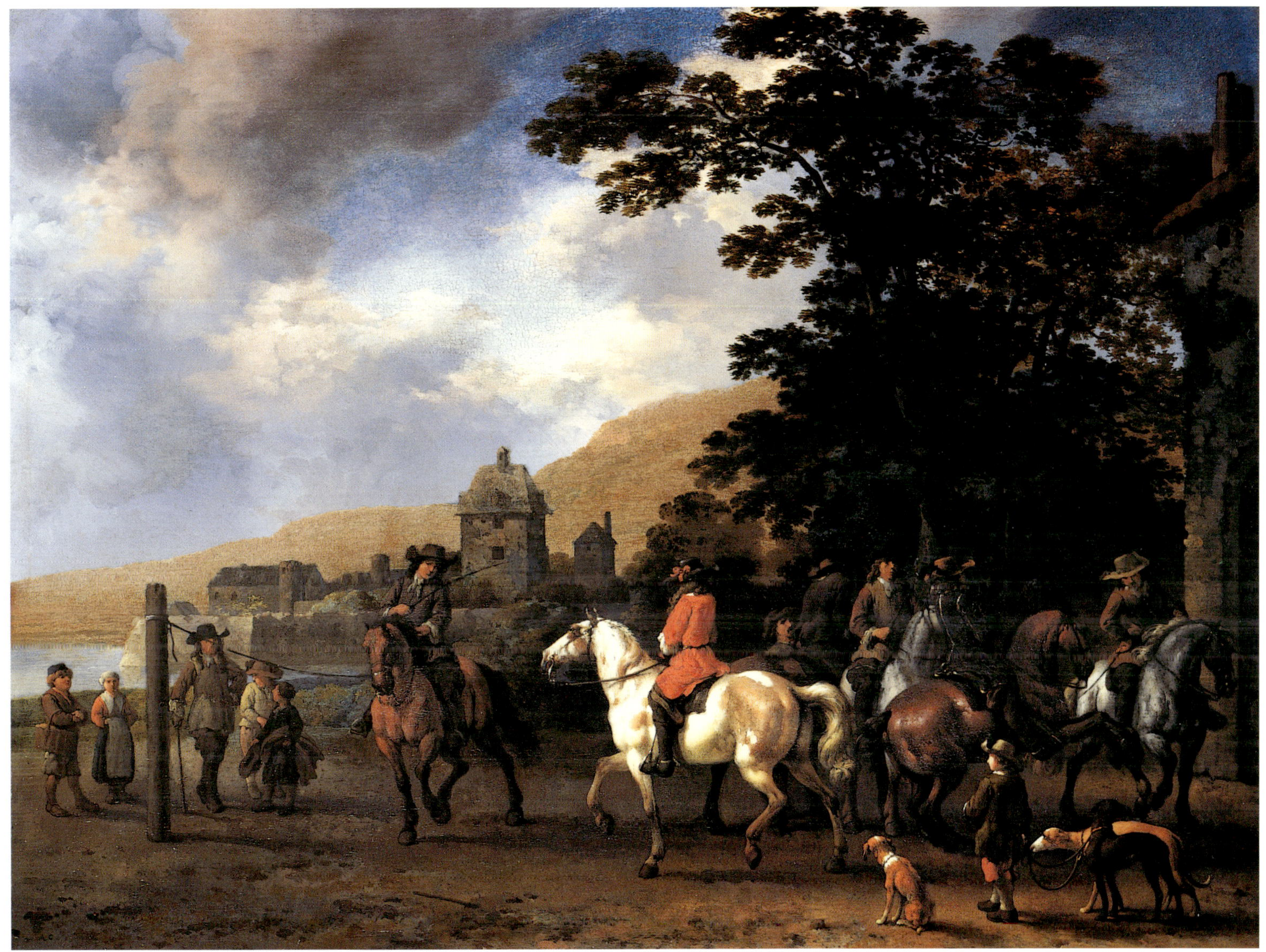

11 Govaert CAMPHUYSEN

(Gorinchem? 1623/4–1672 Amsterdam?)

Two Peasants with Cows

DPG No. 64, Bourgeois Bequest, 1811

Due to a forged signature (presumably removed by Dr Johannes Hell in his conservation campaign of 1952–3), for much of the 19th century this was attributed to Paulus Potter – and it is likely to be the picture bought by Sir Francis Bourgeois as by that artist, in 1798. In 1880 Richter first attributed the picture to Camphuyzen, a suggestion confirmed by comparison with other signed works by the artist, most notably examples in the National Gallery of Canada in Montreal and in the Wallace Collection, London. Like Potter, Camphuyzen excelled in rustic naturalism, concentrating on realistic detail such as the farmer on the right's bare feet and the shoes tied round his waist. *Two Peasants with Cows* is a typical work from around 1650.

Signed, bottom right: G.C.
Oak panel, 47.3 x 62.8 cm

Prov.: ?London, Michael Bryan; ?his sale, London, Christie's, 27 Apr. 1798, lot 82 ('Potter – A small landscape with cattle, and figures, a beautiful cabinet picture of this scarce and admired master'). Bt 'Sr F Bourgeois' £15.15; London, Sir Francis Bourgeois, ?1798–1811; Bourgeois Bequest, 1811.

Ref.: 1816 cat., no. 120 (as Potter); Richter and Sparkes, 1880, pp. 28–9, no. 120 (first attribution to Camphuysen); Bredius and Moes, 1903, p. 213; 1905 cat., p. 15, no. 64; Thieme-Becker, 1907–50, V, p. 465; Cook, 1914, pp. 36–7, no. 64; Murray, 1980a, p. 39; Murray, 1980b, p. 10; Beresford, 1998, p. 59.

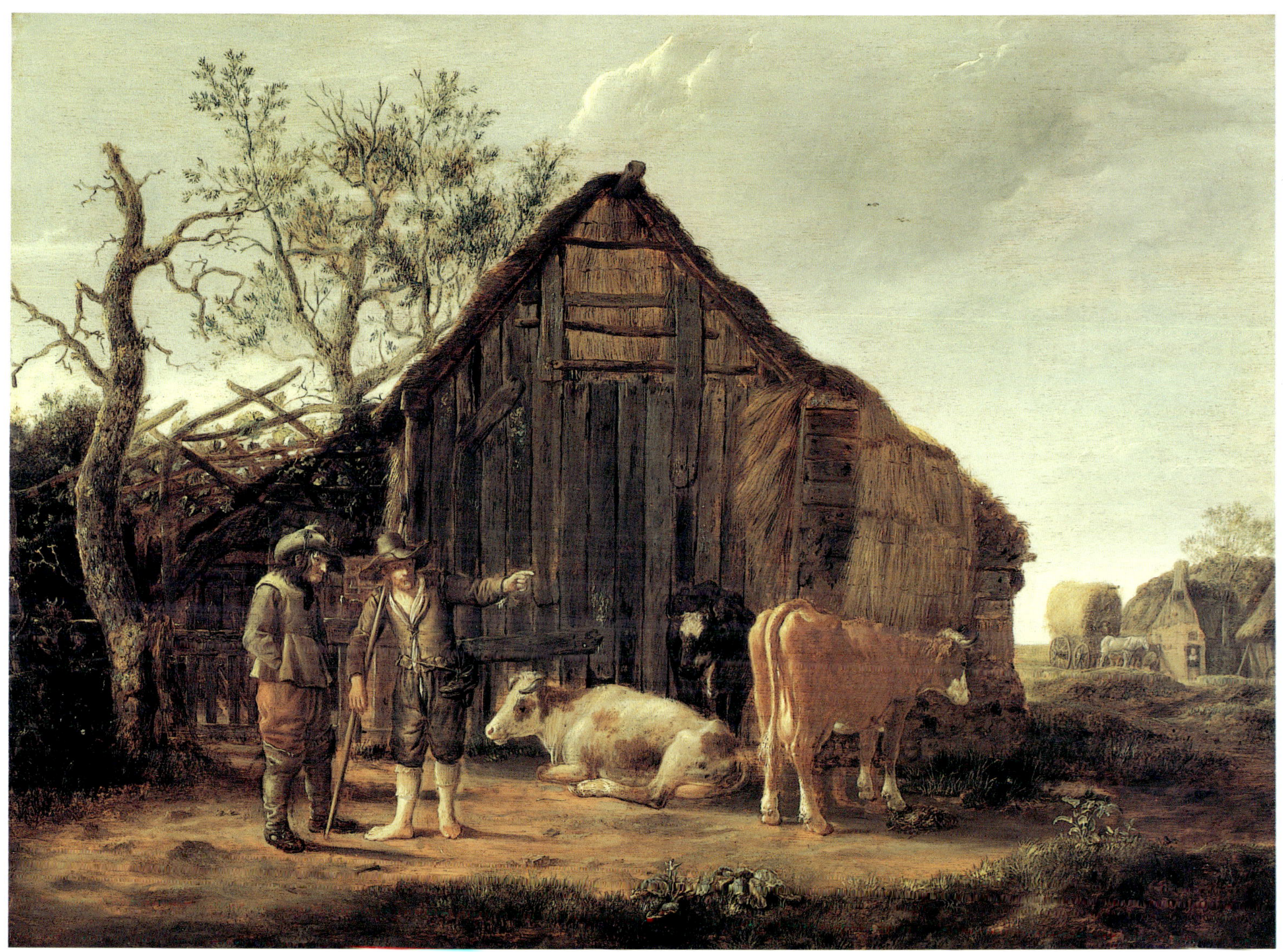

12 Aelbert CUYP

(Dordrecht 1620–1691 Dordrecht)

View on a Plain

DPG No. 4, Bourgeois Bequest, 1811

Nothing is known of Cuyp's training, although presumably he learned the trade from his father Jacob, also an artist. The influence of Jan van Goyen's tonal landscape style is clear in his early work, including this example, painted about 1644. But even here there is something both romantic and heroic about the position of the shepherd against the horizon, and in the general atmosphere. The view is thought to be near Rhenen. The horizon is dominated by the tower, built between 1492 and 1531, of the church of St Cunera there.

Cuyp visited and sketched a view of Rhenen from a distance in 1641, most likely from the Grebbeberg, a 50 m high hill to the east of the city.[4] This sketch provides the detail for *View on a Plain*, but was first used for the background of *A Portrait of a Family* (Switzerland, private collection, dated 1641).

4 H.J. Scholten, *Musée Teyler à Haarlem. Catalogue raisonné des dessins des écoles française et hollandaise*, Haarlem, 1904, p. 172; M.C. Plomp, *The Dutch Drawings in the Teyler Museum. Volume II. Artists Born Between 1575 and 1630*, Haarlem/Gent/Doornspijk 1997, p. 116, no. 98. There is also another view of Rhenen by Cuyp from a different viewpoint (Cambridge, MA, Fogg Art Museum, paper, 175 x 488 mm, inv. 1943.33).

Signed, bottom centre: A. cúÿp
Oak panel, 48 x 72.2 cm

Prov.: London, Sir Francis Bourgeois, 1811, Bourgeois Bequest, 1811.

Ref.: Patmore, 1824, p. 15, no. 68; Jameson, 1842, p. 444, no. 9; Hazlitt, 1843, p. 23; Illustrated London News, 12 Apr. 1856, p. 386; Richter and Sparkes, 1880, p. 44, no. 9; 1892, no. 4; H. Wallis, Magazine of Art, 1881; 1905 cat., p. 2, no. 4; HdG, 1908, II, p. 197, no. 694; Cook, 1914, pp. 4–7, no. 4; London and Leeds, 1947, no. 4; Reiss, 1953, p. 45 (as Jacob Cuyp, bef. 1650); Gerson, 1953 (as Aelbert Cuyp); 1953 cat. no. 4; Burnett, 1969, p. 375; Reiss, 1975, p. 75, no. 42 (rejecting his earlier attribution to Jacob Cuyp); Murray, 1980a, p. 47; Murray, 1980b, p. 12; Yapou, 1981, p. 161; Chong, 1992, no. 69; London, 1995, pp. 48–9, no. 7; Beresford, 1998, p. 81; Houston and Louisville, 1999–2000, p. 174, no. 58.

Versions and Copies: Related drawings: 1. View of Rhenen, Haarlem, Teyler Museum, paper, 190 x 305 mm, inv. no. P42, dated 1641. 2. Netherlands, private collection (see DM 1977, no. 59), Standing shepherd. 3. Netherlands, private collection (see DM 1977, no. 63), Sheep. 4. London, BM, Hind 36, Seated cow. Engravings: 1. R. Cockburn. 2. J. Cousen.

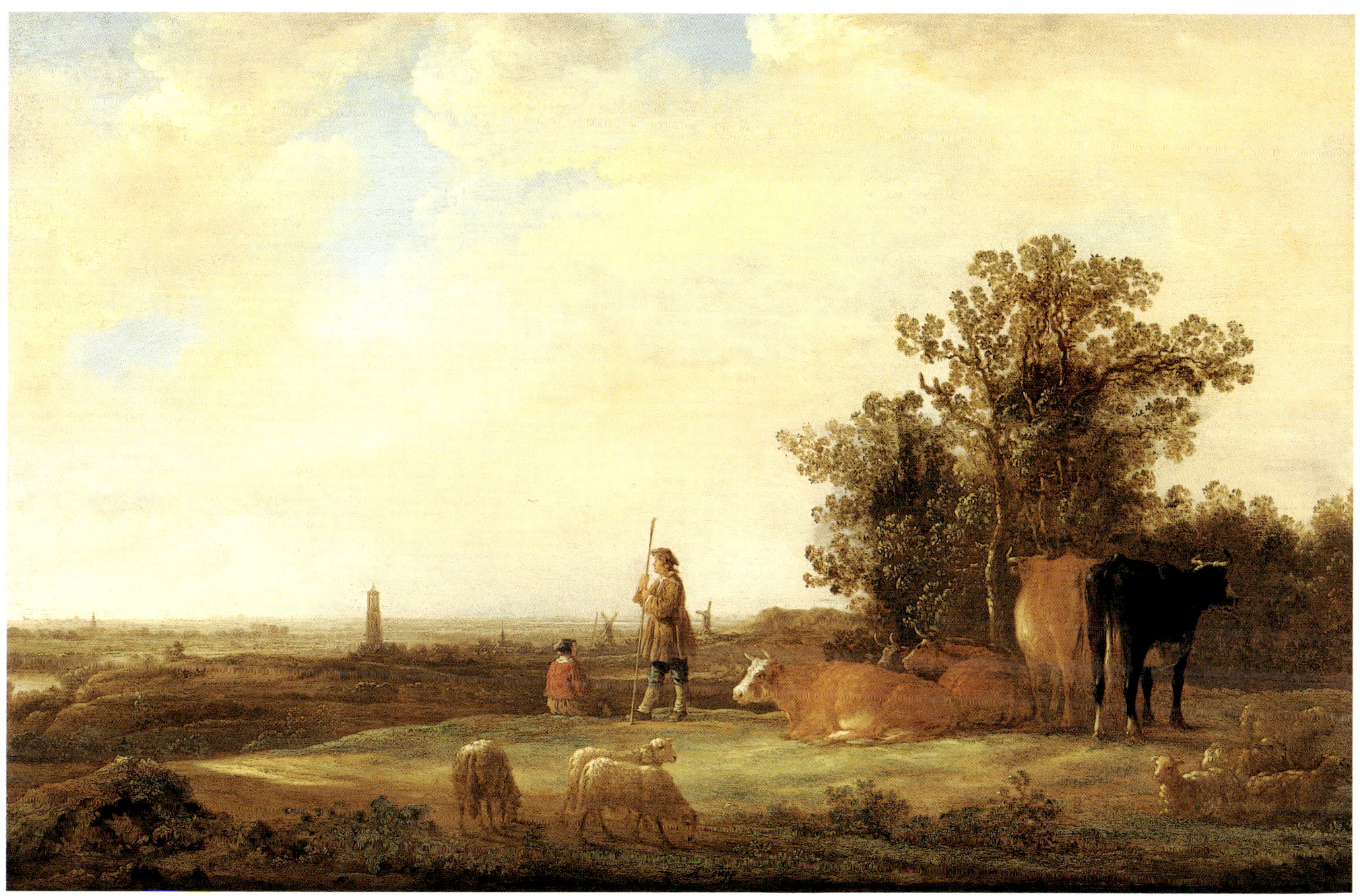

13 Aelbert CUYP

(Dordrecht 1620–1691 Dordrecht)

River Landscape (formerly *Landscape with Cattle*)

DPG No. 60, Bourgeois Bequest, 1811

Signed, lower right: A cuÿp
Oak panel, 16 x 36.8 cm, excluding additions of 8.9 x 36.8 cm

Prov.: London, Noel Desenfans, ?1804–1807; ?1804 Insurance List, no. 33 ('Cuyp–A small Landscape'). £250; London, Sir Francis Bourgeois, ?1807–1811; Bourgeois Bequest, 1811).

Ref.: Patmore, 1824, p. 16, no. 58; Richter and Sparkes, 1880, p. 43, no. 76; 1905 cat., p. 14, no. 60; HdG, 1908, II, p.197, no. 695; Cook, 1914, p. 35, no. 60; Murray, 1980a, p. 299; Waterfield, 1989, pp. 45–6; Chong, 1992, no. 29; Beresford, 1998, p. 81.

Versions and Copies: 1. Preparatory drawing, Amsterdam, A. Schwarz collection (in 1968), black crayon on paper, 14.1 x 19.4 cm. 2. Engraving, R. Cockburn.

Painted early in the artist's career, c. 1640, when still under the influence of his presumed master Jan van Goyen, this little signed work was until recently not in an exhibitable state. Its 18th-century fate is revealing of the period's attitude to Cuyp's emerging reputation for collectors as a more available Dutch answer to Claude. The signature was 'right' – but to 18th-century eyes a Van Goyen-style Cuyp just looked 'wrong' in every other respect. Where was the luminous sky? Where were the poetic cows? Therefore someone (and other examples of such activity within the collection indicate that it was probably Sir Francis Bourgeois himself) set out to 'improve' this tiny, limpid masterpiece – i.e. to make it more obviously 'Cuyp-like' – with some lumpen foreground cows and an extra 8.9cm of sky at the top and 1.8cm at the bottom. Dr Johannes Hell, the estimable conservator who worked on the collection after the Second World War, recognised the anomaly. Indeed, Stephen Poyntz Denning, Dulwich Picture Gallery's second Keeper from 1821, had already pointed the finger of suspicion at Bourgeois for the additions to the panel. Hell started to remove the cows but did not complete the job – probably for fear of causing irremediable damage – leaving them ghost-like and see-through. Analysis of the area at the National Gallery in 1996 provided the proof of late 18th-century pigment, and further conservation proceeded. This has not only removed the additional pieces of panel, but finally disposed of the phantom remains of the cows, revealing in the process a tiny fisherman in a boat. A preparatory drawing – minus cows – survives in a private collection.[5]

5 See Amsterdam, Rijksprentenkabinet, *De Verzameling van A. Schwarz*, exh. cat., 1968, pp. 14–15, no. 31.

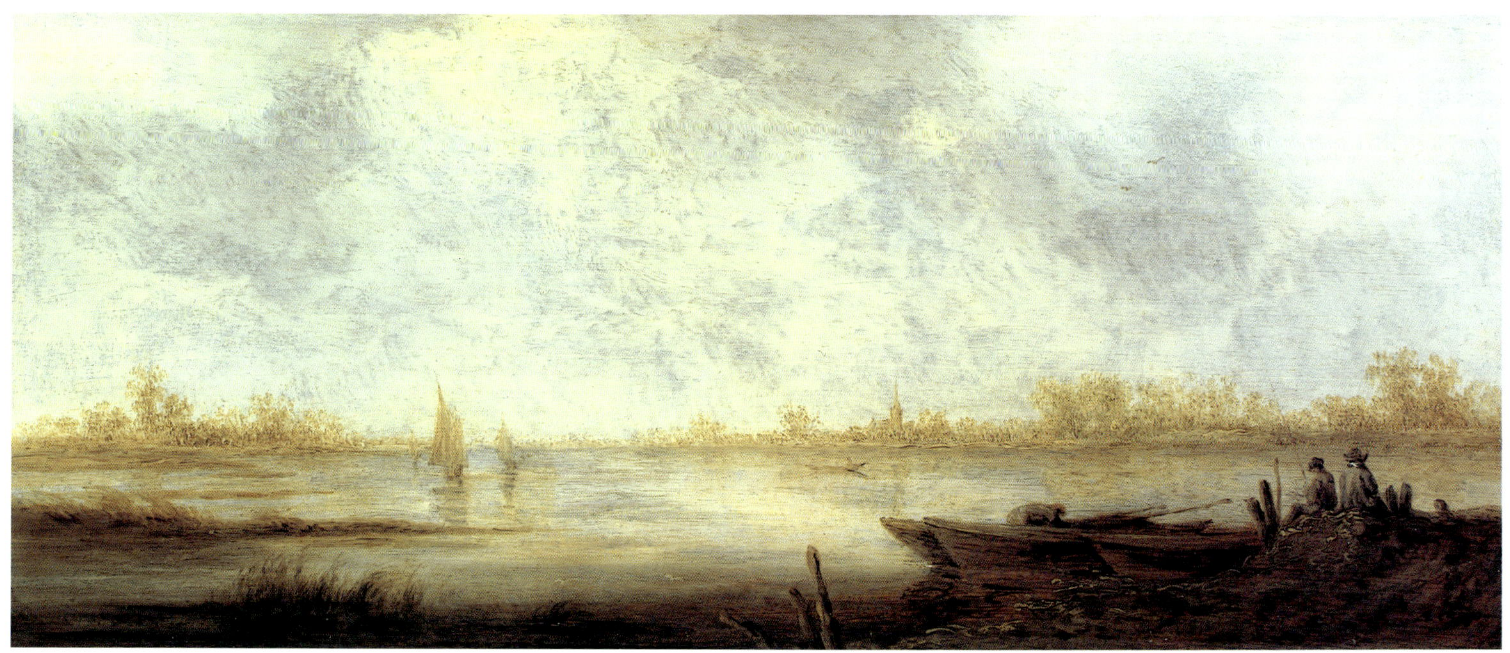

14

Aelbert CUYP

(Dordrecht 1620–1691 Dordrecht)

An Evening Ride near a River

DPG No. 96, Bourgeois Bequest, 1811

The painting is in poor condition which is probably what led Reiss to reject it, although Alan Chong reinstated it suggesting it was the 'work of a pupil under Cuyp's supervision or tutelage'. Certainly the muddy handling and sketchy sheep are atypical of Cuyp's usual precision but the overall composition is strong, the *contre-jour* is perfectly acceptable for Cuyp, and the signature seems genuine and contemporary with the picture itself.

In 1769 *An Evening Ride near a River* was in the collection of John Barnard (1709–1784), one of the foremost collectors of his day, where it was engraved by John Major as 'The contented peasants'. Chong has related the picture to a Cuyp in John Barnard's collection in 1761 that was described as 'Landskip with cattle and figures by Cuyp...'[6] It seems likely to have passed on Barnard's death to his nephew Thomas Hankey who put it up for auction in 1799, whereupon it was bought by Sir Francis Bourgeois. It is difficult to locate this piece in Desenfans and Bourgeois' subsequent records due to the generic descriptions given to landscapes of this kind.

6 R. and J. Dodsley, eds., *London and its environs described*, London, 1761, I, p. 280. Nor can the picture be that described in *The English Connoisseur*, London, 1766, I, p. 8, which replicates the description in Dodsley.

Signed, bottom left: A. cúÿp
Oak panel, 48.9 x 64.1 cm

Prov.: London, Berkeley Square, John Barnard (1709–1784), 1769 (acc. to print by John Major, 'The contented peasants'); Thomas Hankey (as collected by John Barnard) his sale, London, Christie's, 7 Jun. 1799, lot 31; Bt Bourgeois, £47.5, London, Noel Desenfans and/or Sir Francis Bourgeois, 1799–1807; London, Sir Francis Bourgeois, 1807–1811; Bourgeois Bequest, 1811).

Ref.: Patmore, 1824a, p. 16, no. 83; Smith, 1829–42, V, p. 307, no. 261 (as still in collection of John Barnard) [but not p. 360, no. 83: see text]; Jameson, 1842, p. 465, no. 141; Waagen, 1854, II, p. 344; Richter and Sparkes, 1880, p. 45, no. 141; 1905 cat. p. 24, no. 96; HdG, 1908, II, p.126, no. 434 and probably p. 136, no. 467; Cook, 1914, p. 57, no. 96 Reiss, 1975, p. 208 (identifying DPG96 with Smith no. 261 and HDG no. 434, but rejecting Cuyp's authorship); Murray, 1980a, p. 47; Murray, 1980b, p. 12; Chong, 1992, no. C14 ('work of a pupil under Cuyp's supervision or tutelage'), Beresford, 1998, p. 81.

Versions and Copies: 1. Engraving, R. Cockburn. 2. Engraving, T. Major, 1769. 3. Copy, Location unknown, (Photograph in the archive at Gainsborough's House, Sudbury). 4. Watercolour copy (prob. 19th century), Maldon (Essex), Owen collection, 1986 (DPG archive, letter on file).

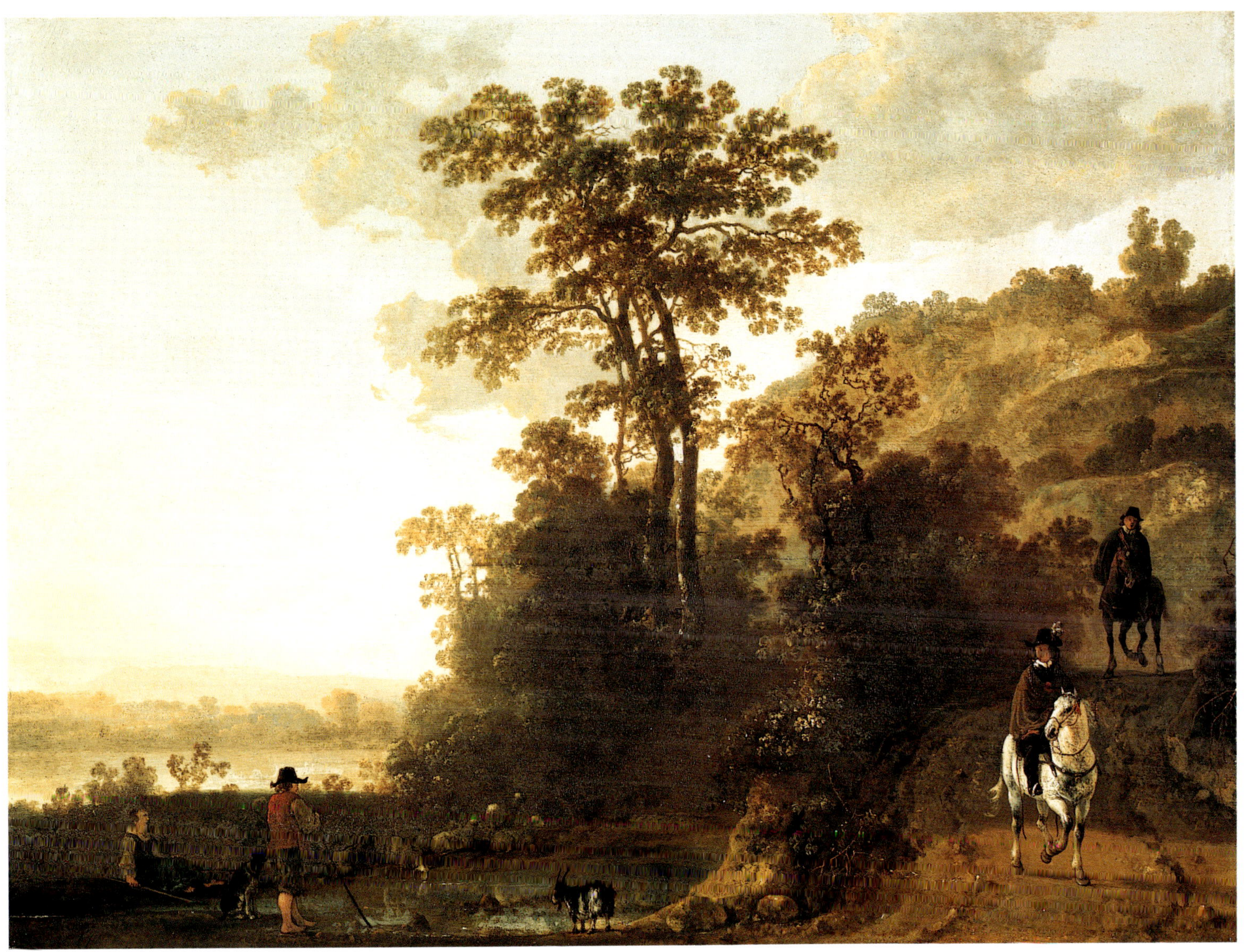

15

Aelbert CUYP

(Dordrecht 1620–1691 Dordrecht)

A Road near a River

DPG No. 124, Bourgeois Bequest, 1811

Cuyp's personal story took a dramatic turn when he married in 1658. His wife, Cornelia Boschman was a wealthy widow, with extensive property in the countryside around Dordrecht. Cuyp's later career is therefore played out away from painting, as an ever more respectable civic worthy. At his wife's death, he was worth 42,000 guilders.

This means that, although he was to live another thirty years, this painting is probably one of his last, from c. 1660. The raking evening light and silhouetted trees, and the division of the landscape into two compartments, reveal a deep appreciation of Jan Both.

Canvas, 115.6 x 170.6 cm

Prov.: London, Noel Desenfans, 1802–1807: London, Skinner and Dyke, Desenfans sale, 18 Mar. 1802, lot 162 ('A large Landscape with Cattle and Figures'. Descriptive Catalogue, no. 142; Bt Elliot for £189.0 (Bt in). Handwritten note in copy of catalogue at The Hague, RKD: '65. [i.e. 6 x 5] – 2 High trees & 2 shepds sitting und.r it & sheep & a dog – a Man ridg on Ass w.h Panniers &c'; 1804 Insurance List, no. 60 ('Cuyp–A large landscape with shepherds, £600'); London, Sir Francis Bourgeois, 1807–1811; Bourgeois Bequest, 1811).

Ref.: Patmore, 1824, pp. 13, no. 18; Smith, 1829–42, V, pp. 304–5, no. 72; Jameson, 1842, p. 468, no. 163; Waagen, 1854, II, p. 344; Ruskin, 1873, p. 38; Richter and Sparkes, 1880, pp. 45–6, no. 163; London, 1903, p. 25, no. 93; 1905 cat., p. 32, no. 124; HdG, 1908, II, pp. 126–7 no. 435; Cook, 1914, pp. 72–3, no. 124; Whitley, 1928b, p. 32; London and Leeds, 1947, no. 5; Reiss, 1953, p. 42; Burnett, 1969, pp. 372–80; Reiss, 1975, p. 181; Murray, 1980a, pp. 47–8; Murray, 1980b, p. 12; Amsterdam, Boston, and Philadelphia, 1987, p. 303; Norwich, 1988, p. 52, fig. 38 (as the 'Landscape with figures' lent to the RA in 1816 and 1817); Chong, 1992, no. 170; Madrid, 1994, p. 104, no. 19; London, 1995, p. 52, no. 9; Beresford, 1998, p. 83; Houston and Louisville, 1999–2000, p. 178, no. 60; Washington, London, and Amsterdam, 2001–2, p. 22; London, 2002, p. 189, no. 51.

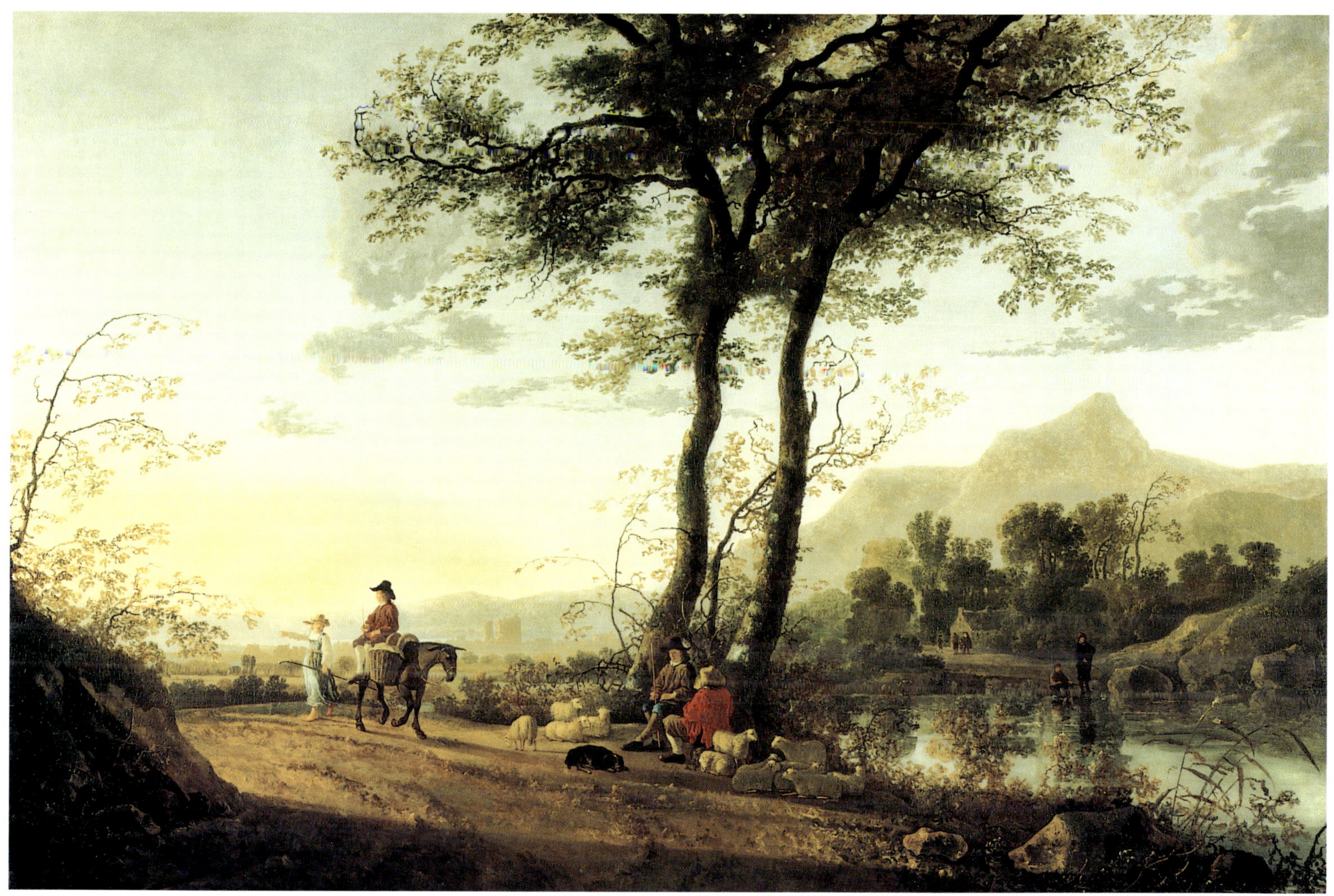

16 Aelbert CUYP

(Dordrecht 1620–1691 Dordrecht)

Herdsmen with Cows

DPG No. 128, Bourgeois Bequest, 1811

Signed, lower right: A. cúÿp
Canvas, 101.4 x 145.9 cm

Prov.: Paris, Delaroche, 23 Apr.1803, lot 53. Bt Paullet, for 13,500 frs; Alexandre Joseph Paillet (1743–1814); London, Sir Francis Bourgeois, 1811; Bourgeois Bequest, 1811.

Ref.: Patmore, 1824a, pp.11–13; Patmore, 1824b, pp. 171–2, no. 3; Hazlitt, 1824, p. 30; Smith, 1829–42, V, p. 306, no. 80 (wrongly identified with a picture in Desenfans' 1802 catalogue); Jameson, p. 469, no. 169; Ruskin, 1843, I, p. 206; Waagen, 1854, II, p. 344; Richter and Sparkes, 1880, p. 46, no. 169; 1905 cat., pp. 32–3, no. 128; HdG, 1907–26, II, pp. 78 & 101, no. 237e and no. 330 (repeating Smith); Cook, 1914, pp. 75–6, no. 128; Reiss, 1953, p. 42ff; Reiss, 1975, p. 77; Murray, 1980a, p. 48; Murray, 1980b, p. 12; Chong, 1992, pp. 257, 323–5, no. 80; London, 1995, pp. 50–1, no. 8; Beresford, 1998, p. 83; Houston and Louisville, 1999–2000, p. 176, no. 59; Washington, London, and Amsterdam, 2001–2, pp. 120, 192–3, no. 14.

Burton Fredericksen (DPG archive, letter on file, 2000) recently recognised this picture in the extended description in Delaroche's sale catalogue of 1803, making it clear that the painting has a French provenance. Previously it had been thought to have passed through a Michael Bryan sale of 1798 – but this is a more generic description, presumably of a different painting[7]. How it passed from its buyer at the sale, the dealer Alexandre-Joseph Paillet, to England is unclear, but it had the distinction of being the most expensive work of art sold in France in that year. Its popularity was such that this painting was the third most copied in the collection during the 19th century; in 1824 William Hazlitt called it 'the finest Cuyp perhaps in the world', and Peter George Patmore waxed poetic: 'indescribable... It seems... made out of woven air and sunshine'. Ruskin, typically, was harder to please, likening the sky to an unripe nectarine, and criticising the artist's lack of naturalism.

Herdsmen with Cows was probably painted in the mid-1640s and is a vivid demonstration of how the influence of the returning Dutch Italianates – Jan Both was back in Utrecht in 1642 – impacted on Cuyp's original style. Ruskin's accusations of not being true to nature were surely right, although we may disagree with him in our appreciation of the final result. The steep cliff to the right and the mountainous outcrop on the horizon look rather like theatrical scenery, dropped into position behind Cuyp's usual flat stage. It is as if he has heard of mountains, but no-one has ever mentioned foothills. The light, however, with its astonishing diffuse vaporised quality, is expertly managed, even if, again, there is a hint of stage management about it. A comparison with another, much smaller, painting in Dulwich's collection, is instructive. The little *Landscape with Cattle and Figures* (cat. no. 17) is an earlier essay in exactly the same subject-matter, but in the Van Goyen manner. Even the arrangement of the clouds, and the implied position of the sun, are the same. Both's fantastic visions of Italy have effectively provided the vocabulary to achieve the effects for which Cuyp was always striving.

7 London, Michael Bryan; his sale, London, Coxe, Burrell & Co., 19 May 1798, lot 39 ('A view in Holland, a clear and brilliant picture representing the morning of a fine summer's day, with cattle and figures on the fore ground. The Works of this admirable painter exhibit an acquaintance with aerial perspective which perhaps is peculiar to himself. – This is in his fine manner').

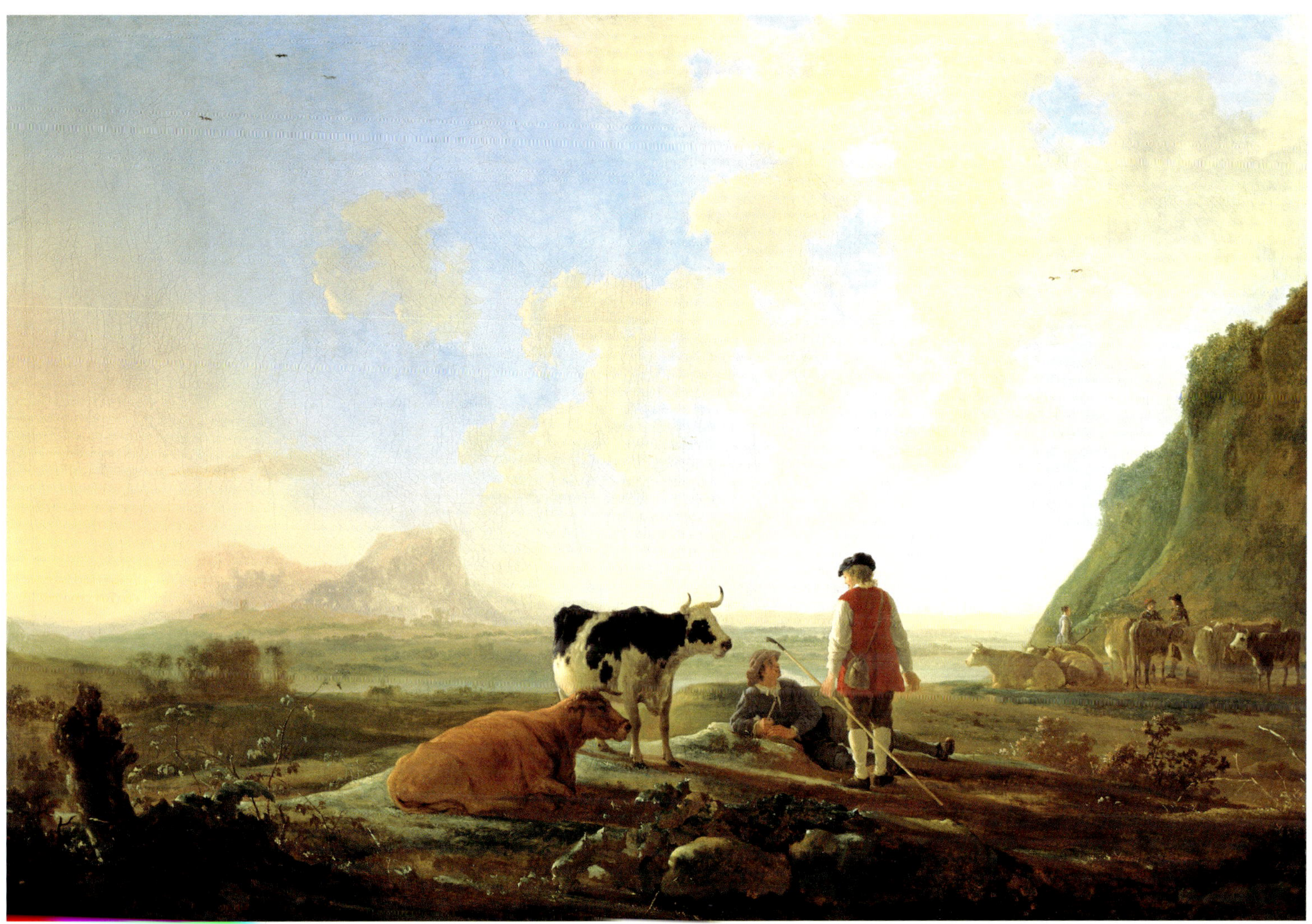

17

Aelbert CUYP

(Dordrecht 1620–1691 Dordrecht)
Landscape with Cattle and Figures
DPG No. 348, Bourgeois Bequest, 1811

Some themes are there from the beginning with Cuyp – and this picture is very early indeed, probably dating from 1640–1. The group of cows, the shepherd pointing to something far outside the picture frame on the left, the sense of a diagonal thrust to the sky created by a low sun (also out of the picture off to the left), the build up of clouds to the right, a darker foreground *repoussoir* to the left, the low horizon, the big sky, the primary interest in light – every single one of these elements can be found in Cuyp's much larger, later, masterpieces in Dulwich's collection – the *Herdsmen with Cows* (cat. no. 16) from c. 1645 and *A Road near a River* (cat. no. 15) of the late 1650s. What differs is the more monochrome tonality derived at this early stage from Jan van Goyen, and the colder quality of the light. The goats – which seem to have wandered in from another picture entirely – play an uncharacteristically dominant part in the composition. They act almost more as a visual barrier than a *repoussoir*, in startling contrast with the shepherds behind them, as a result creating an emphatic sense of distance. Comparison with *A Road near a River* is interesting, where Cuyp goes for the same effect, but with a more subtle hand, using a patch of shadow and foliage in the foreground in the same relation to a pointing figure in the sunny middle distance. As it happens, the two goats are, in a sense, foreigners here – they were copied from drawings executed by Cuyp's father Jacob, used for engravings in *Diversa Animalia Quadrupedia* of 1641.

Signed, lower right: A cúÿp.
Oak panel, 37.5 x 57.5 cm

PROV.: ?London, Noel Desenfans, 1802–1807: ?London, Skinner and Dyke, Desenfans sale, 18 Mar. 1802, lot 158 (Descriptive Catalogue no. 143) £110.5. Bt Elliott (bt in); ?1804 Insurance List no. 31, £100; London, Sir Francis Bourgeois, 1811; Bourgeois Bequest, 1811.

REF.: Patmore, 1824a, p. 18, no. 26; Smith, 1829–42, V, p. 306, no. 77 (as in Desenfans' collection in 1802); Denning, 1858, no. 192 (as after Cuyp); Richter and Sparkes, 1880, p. 43, no. 192 (first identification of the painting as an early work by Cuyp in the style of Jan van Goyen); 1905 cat., p. 96, no. 348; HdG, 1908, II, p. 75, no. 239 and p.198, no. 697; Whitley, 1928a, p. 253 (as lent with other DPG paintings to RA 1816, but this now appears incorrect); London and Leeds, 1947, no. 8; London, RA, Dutch, 1952/3, no. 358; Reiss, 1953, p. 42ff; London, 1973, p. 36, no. 1; Reiss, 1975, p. 43, no. 15; Murray, 1980a, pp. 48–9; Murray, 1980b, p. 12; Chong, 1992, pp. 273–4, no. 12; Beresford, 1998, p. 83; Washington, London, and Amsterdam, 2001–2, p. 92 and pp. 186–7, no. 2.

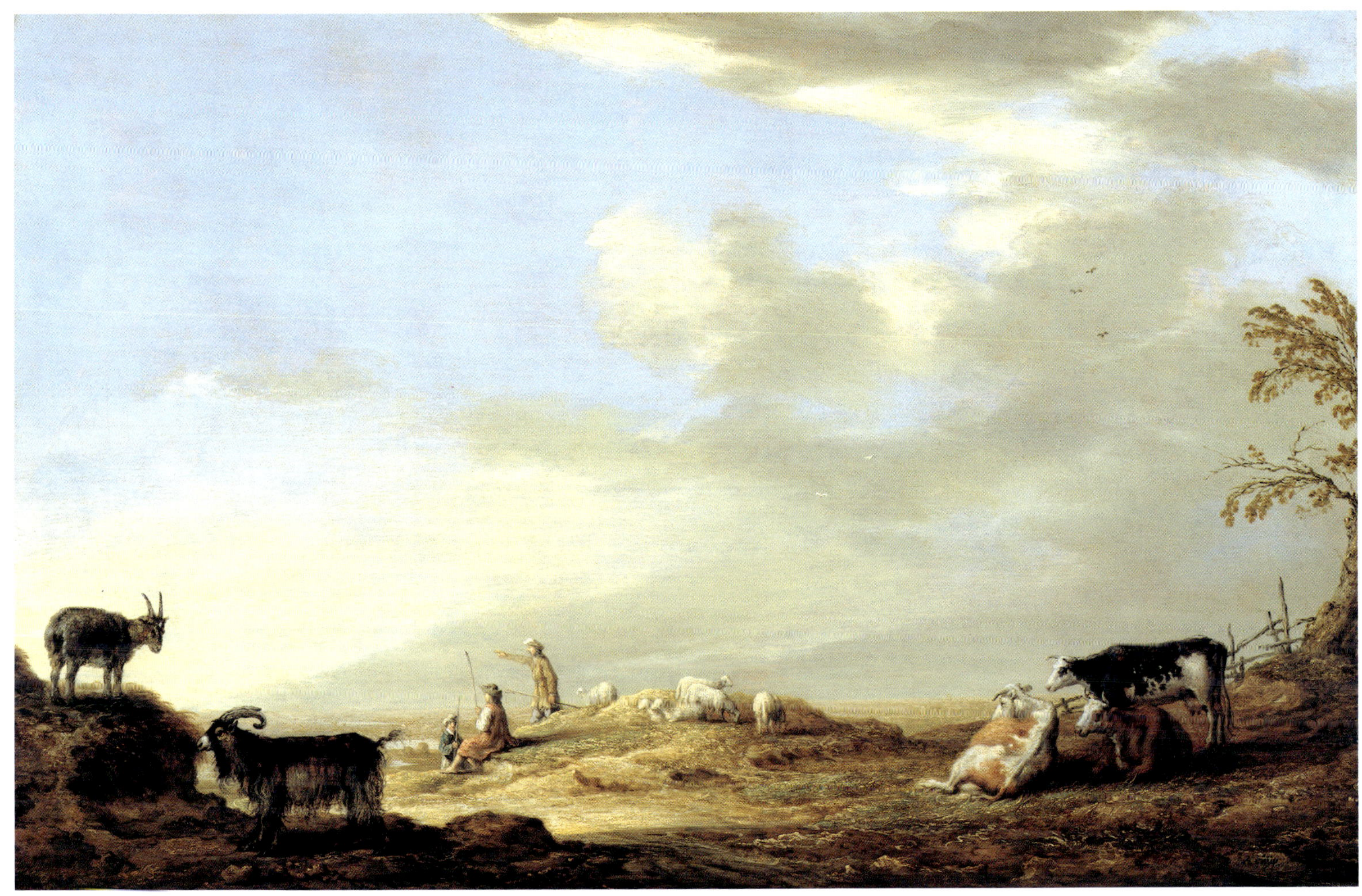

18

Karel DU JARDIN

(Probably Amsterdam 1621/2–1678 Venice)

Peasants and a White Horse

DPG No. 72, Bourgeois Bequest, 1811

Canvas, 44.1 x 39.7 cm

Prov.: London, Noel Desenfans, 1802–1807: London, Skinner and Dyke, Desenfans sale, 18 Mar. 1802, lot 148 (Descriptive Catalogue no. 133); 1804 Insurance List, no. 89, £150; London, Sir Francis Bourgeois, 1807–1811; Bourgeois Bequest, 1811.

Ref.: Smith, 1829–42, V, p. 236, no. 15; Jameson, 1842, p. 453, no. 62; Richter and Sparkes, 1880, p. 60, no. 62; 1905 cat., pp. 18–19, no. 72; HdG, 1926, IX, p. 313, no. 70; Cook, 1914, pp. 41–2, no. 72; Brochhagen, 1957, pp. 241, 244, 255; Brochhagen, 1958, p. 128, no. 420; Murray, 1980a, p. 52; Murray, 1980b, p. 12; Warsaw, 1992, p. 70, no. 8; Trnek, 1992, pp. 124, 126, fig. 44a; Beresford, 1998, p. 94.

Versions and Copies: Engraving, R. Cockburn.

An intensely beautiful and typically individual work by the artist, probably made during his last visit to Italy, when a new, darker tonality took over his painting. A crocus-yellow sky blooms over lavender hills, the extraordinary beauty of the colours powerfully suggesting twilight, and a chill in the air. The buildings in the middle ground are already sunk in semi-darkness, and the trees behind cast long shadows. These poetic atmospheric touches are nicely undercut by the foreground group, in particular the grinning white horse who is illuminated so exquisitely by the last of the sun. This rackety-looking but loveable nag could almost be a joke at the expense of Wouwermans' famous white horses, which prance a courtly minuet through countless examples of that master's aristocratic hunting scenes.

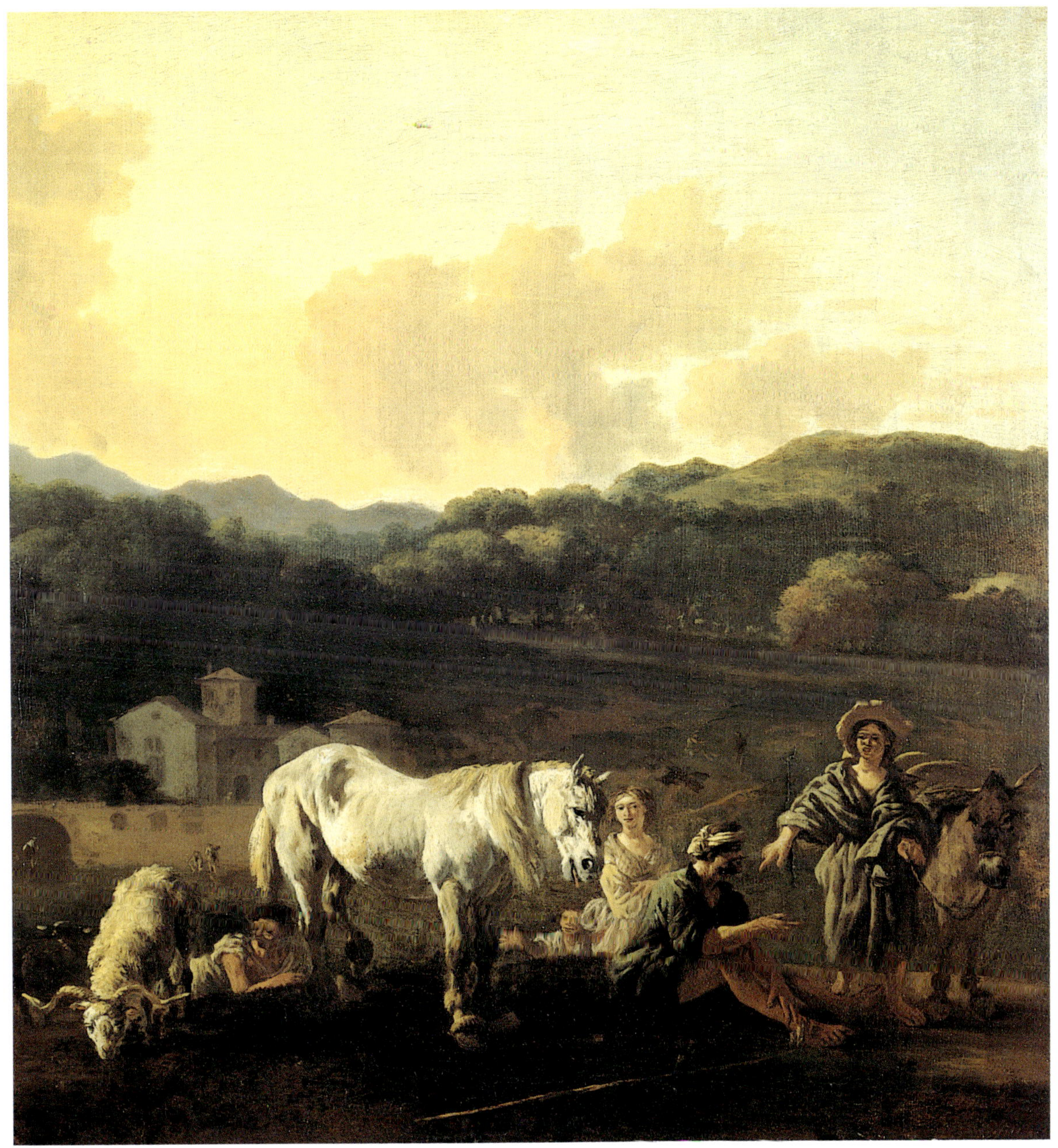

19 Karel DU JARDIN

(Probably Amsterdam 1621/2–1678 Venice)
A Smith shoeing an Ox
DPG No. 82, Bourgeois Bequest, 1811

Signed, bottom right: . K .. DV IARDIN . fe
Canvas, 38 x 42.8 cm

Prov.: Cornelis van Dijck, 1713, his sale, The Hague, Wegewert, 10 May 1713, lot 6; The Hague, J.H. van Heemskerk sale, 29 Mar. 1770, lot 64. Bt J. van der Marck, 305 g.; his sale, Amsterdam, 25 Aug. 1773, lot 142. Bt Van der Schley, 330 g.; Amsterdam, Catherina Bullens (widow of Justus Oosterdijk) sale, 23 July 1777, lot 15. Bt Gilden, 510 g.; Leiden, P. van Spijk; his sale, Leiden, Reyers, Coclers, 23 Apr. 1781, lot 44 (sold for 370 g.); Amsterdam, Jan Gildemeester; his sale, Amsterdam, Schley, Bosch, Yver, Roos, Pruysenaar, 11 Jun. 1800, lot 103). Bt [?Jan]Yver for 814 g. [MS. note in the copy of the catalogue in the National Gallery Library gives the price as 840 g.]; Rotterdam and London, George Craufurd, to 1806; his sale, London, Christie's, 26 Apr. 1806, lot 1. Bt North for £126; London, Sir Francis Bourgeois, 1811; Bourgeois Bequest, 1811.

Ref.: Smith, 1829–42, V, p. 236, no. 15; Buchanan, 1824, II, p. 181; Jameson, 1842, p. 480, no. 229; Richter and Sparkes, 1880, pp. 59–60, no. 229; 1905 cat., p. 21, no. 82; HdG, 1926, IX, pp. 386–7, under no. 336; Cook, 1914, p. 47, no. 82; Brochhagen, 1958, p. 57 and no. 215; Murray, 1980a, p. 52; Murray, 1980b, p. 13; London, Washington and Los Angeles, 1985–6, p. 50, no. 5; Warsaw, 1992, p. 68, no. 7; Beresford, 1998, p. 94; Houston and Louisville, 1999–2000, p. 164, no. 53; London 2002, p. 146, no. 33.
VERSIONS AND COPIES: 1. Autograph copy, Edinburgh, University of Edinburgh (on loan to the National Gallery of Scotland), canvas, 38 x 43 cm.

This picture probably dates from the late 1650s; the architectural setting is unmistakably Italianate, while both the humble subject-matter and the earthy, shadowed foreground are typical of the *Bamboccianti*. The extremely bold diagonal – part physical roof-line, part the shadow that the roof casts on the building next to it – that divides the picture also divides sun from shade, and the precisely-judged shift in tone and colour between the two 'halves' of the picture defines the scene's atmosphere and its sense of warmth. A glimpse into a dark window space beyond the central scene shows us the blacksmith's roaring furnace and the smith himself hammering metal. We must assume that the two hobbit-like characters shoeing the ox are the smith's sturdy and capable children. With so much going on, it is a while before the eye comes to rest on the typically Du Jardin-esque animal at the heart of this scene: the ox, poised like a bulky ballerina at the barre, with the worried but dignified expression of a put-upon Dowager.

A Smith shoeing an Ox was once in the collection of George Craufurd (Crawford), a Scottish merchant who had spent much of his life in Rotterdam. Hofstede de Groot confused this painting with another version of the scene by Du Jardin, formerly in the collection of Sir James Erskine of Torrie, subsequently bequeathed to the University of Edinburgh, and now on deposit to the National Gallery of Scotland.[8] An annotation in a copy of the 1806 sale catalogue (The Hague, RKD) notes 'Genl Sir Js Erskine has one of the same subject', proving that Dulwich's version must be the Craufurd picture as the Edinburgh picture was already in Scotland by this date.

8 See HdG336.

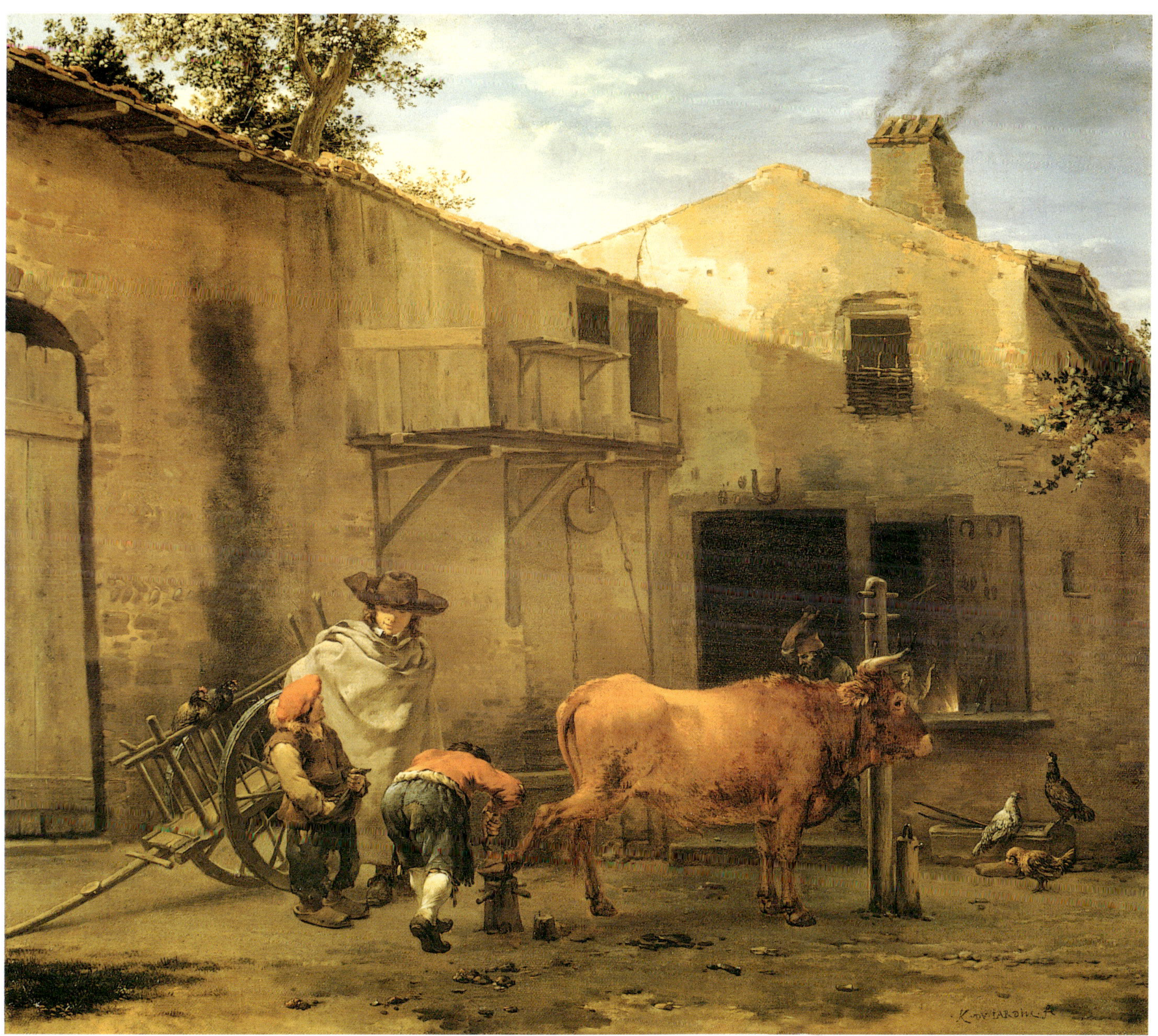

20 Attributed to Carel Cornelisz. DE HOOCH

(Active 1620–died 1638 Utrecht)

A Ruined Temple

DPG No. 23, Bourgeois Bequest, 1811

Conceivably traces of an 'H' in the rocks, bottom left.
Oak panel, 16.2 x 23.7 cm

Prov.: London, Sir Francis Bourgeois, 1811; Bourgeois Bequest, 1811.

Ref.: Richter and Sparkes, 1880, p. 23, no. 16 (as by Breenbergh); 1905 cat., p. 6, no. 23 (as Breenbergh); Cook, 1914, pp. 15–16, no. 23; 1926 cat., no. 23; Roethlisberger, 1969, p. 33 (under no. 62); Murray, 1980a, pp. 30–1; Murray, 1980b, p. 8; Roethlisberger, 1981, p. 103, no. 317 (as 'very possibly' De Hooch); Beresford, 1998, p. 130 (attributed to De Hooch).

This little painting and its pair *Landscape with Roman Ruin* (cat. no. 21), were attributed to De Hooch ('very possibly') only quite recently (by Roethlisberger, 1981). Before that they had always been attributed to Breenbergh, and if not by him, then both paintings are at the least very much in his style. The figures in *A Ruined Temple* are particularly reminiscent of the better-known master. Frustratingly, both paintings have traces of a signature, not sufficiently legible to be much help, although *Landscape with Roman Ruin* also carries a date, 1633, which could suit either artist.

The temple in this piece is a poetic variation on the theme of the famous circular 'Temple of Venus' at Tivoli, sketches of which would have been part of the stock-in-trade of any self-respecting Dutch artist who had spent time in Italy. The ruined building in *Landscape with Roman Ruin* has not so far been identified, although Roethlisberger noted that it derives from a drawing by Breenbergh (formerly of the Sir Robert Witt Collection, London) dated 1626. Both images are typical of the 'first generation' of Dutch Italianate artists, ultimately influenced by the Flemish Paul Bril and the German Adam Elsheimer, but revelling in the discovery of the picturesque qualities of the Roman campagna and its ruins. Typically Dutch, however, is the use of figures to inject an element of everyday life into scenes of decayed Roman grandeur – shepherding in one, laundering in the other.

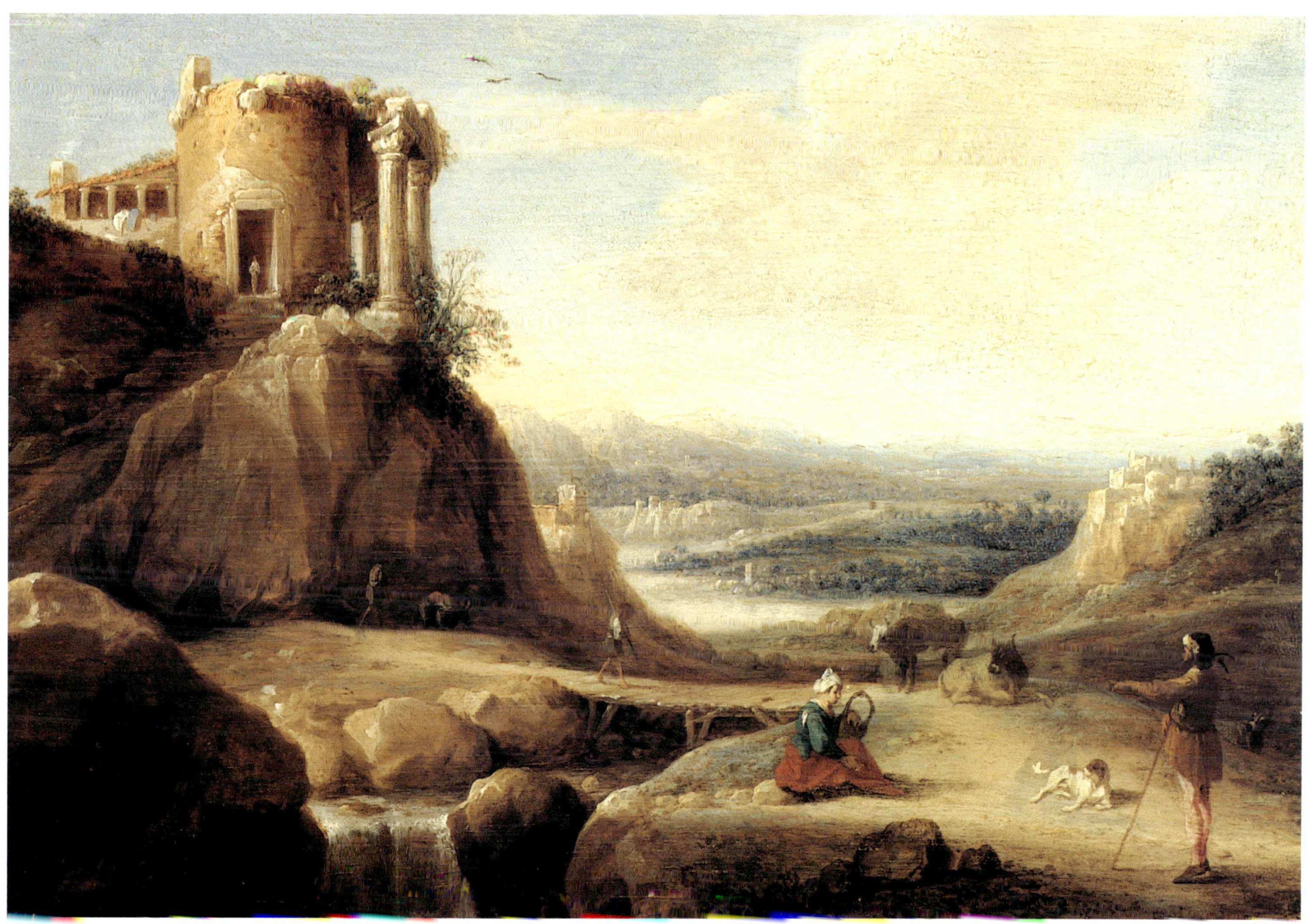

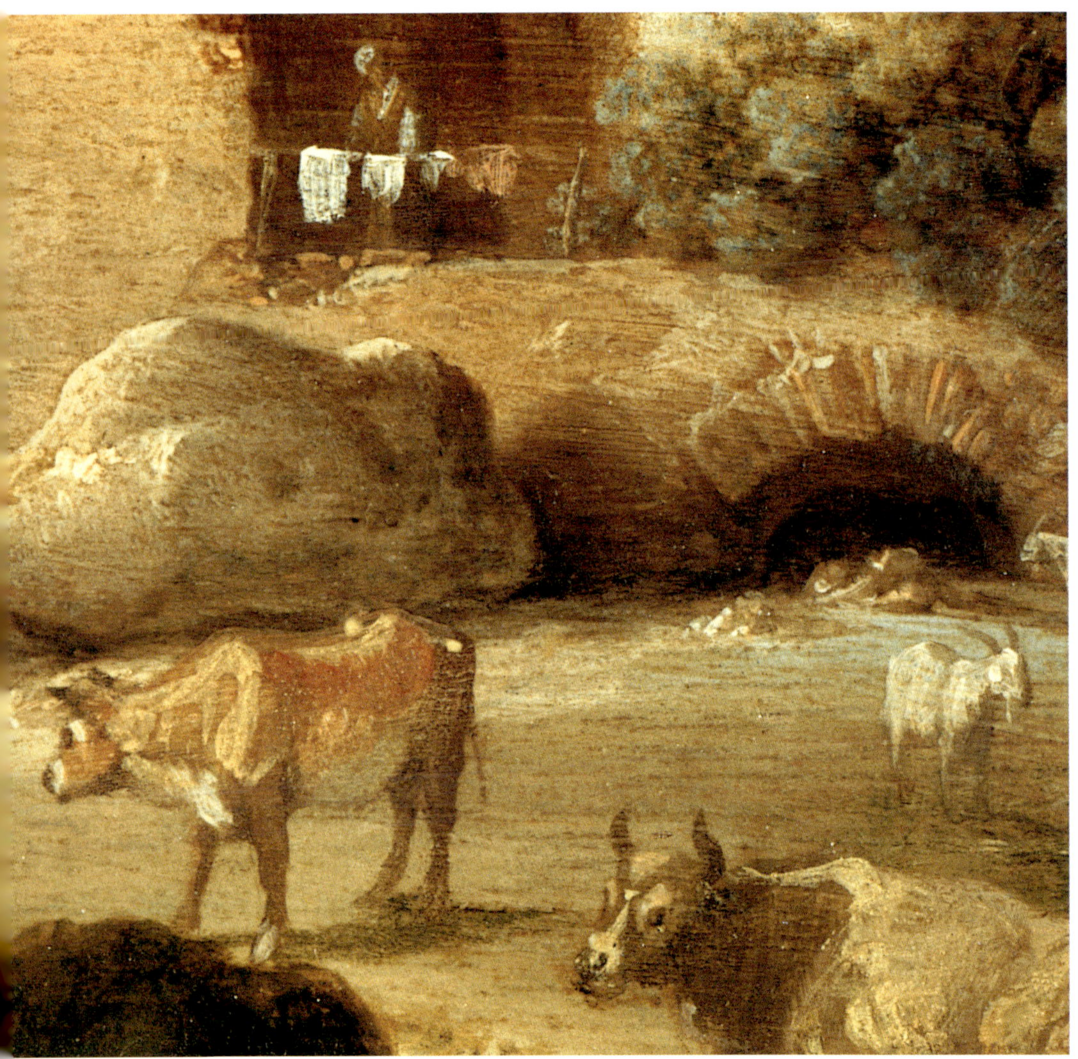

detail

21 Attributed to Carel Cornelisz. DE HOOCH

(Active 1620–died 1638 Utrecht)

Landscape with a Roman Ruin

DPG No. 26, Bourgeois Bequest, 1811

Signed and dated indistinctly on rock, lower right: H[…][t?]/1633
Oak panel, 16.2 x 23.7 cm

Prov.: London, Sir Francis Bourgeois, 1811; Bourgeois Bequest, 1811.

Ref.: Richter and Sparkes, 1880, p. 23, no. 15 (as by Breenbergh); 1905 cat., p. 7, no. 26 (as Breenbergh); Cook, 1914, p. 17, no. 26; 1926 cat., no. 26; Roethlisberger, 1969, p. 33 (under no. 62); Murray, 1980a, pp. 30–1; Murray, 1980b, p. 8; Roethlisberger, 1981, p. 103, no. 318 (as 'very possibly' De Hooch); Beresford, 1998, p. 130 (attributed to De Hooch).

Versions and Copies: 1. Drawing by Breenbergh, Location unknown (formerly Sir Robert Witt coll.), 11.3 x 16.6 cm.

See entry for cat. no. 20.

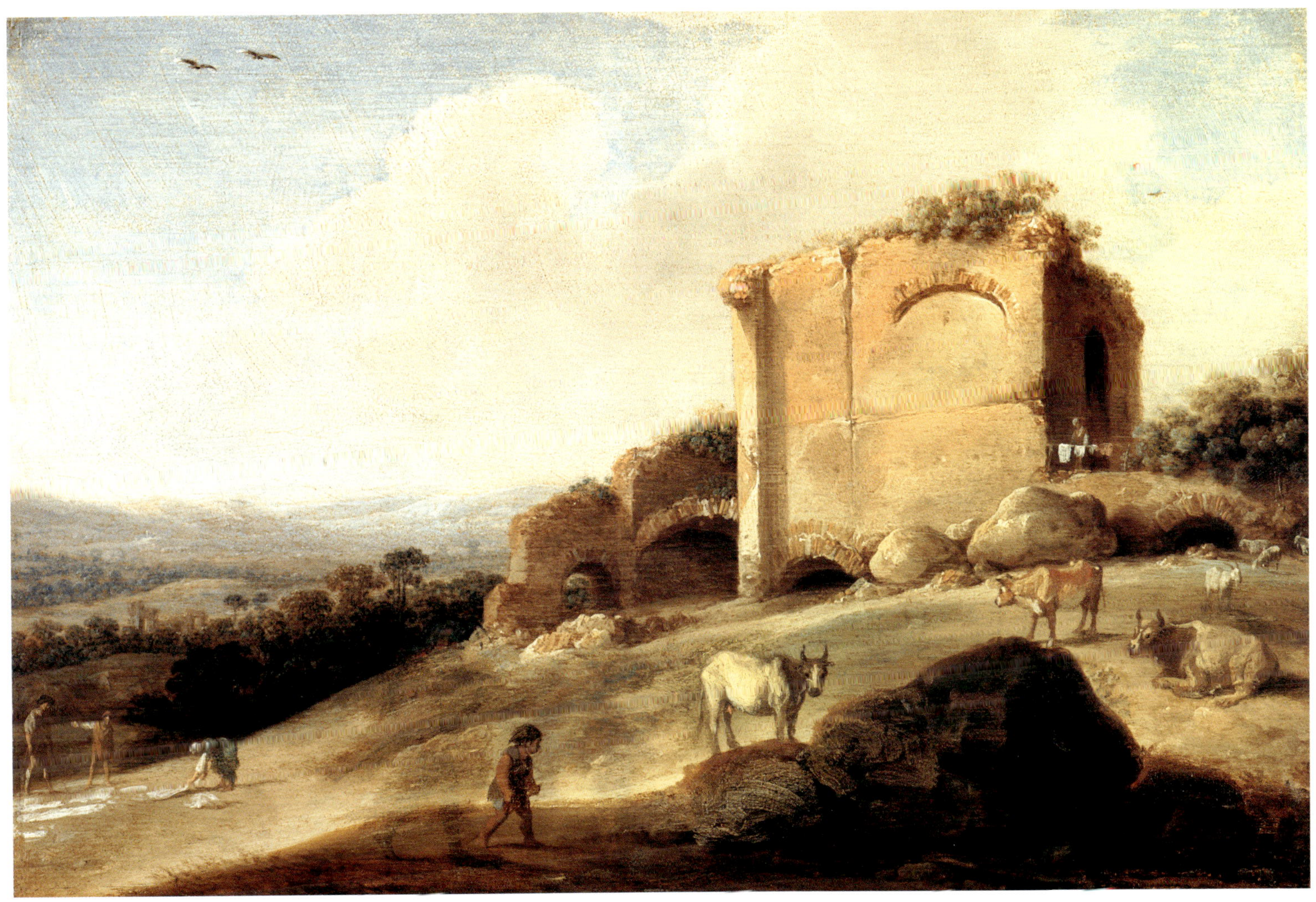

22 Jan van KESSEL

(Amsterdam 1641–1680 Amsterdam)

A Wood near The Hague, with a View of the Huis ten Bosch

DPG No. 210, Bourgeois Bequest, 1811

Oil on canvas, 118.7 x 154.9 cm

Prov.: London, Sir Francis Bourgeois, 1811; Bourgeois Bequest, 1811.

Ref.: 1816 cat., (as Ruisdael); Smith, 1829–42, pp. 278–9, no. 168 (as Wynants, with figures by Adrian Van der Velde); Jameson, 1845, p. 488, no. 278 (as Ruysdael); Richter and Sparkes, 1880, pp. 146–7, no. 278 (as monogrammed by J. van Ruisdael); Michel, 1890, I, p. 86 (as Ruisdael, under Wijnants influence, figures by A. van de Velde); 1905 cat., p. 57, no. 210; HdG, 1911, IV, p. 230, no. 761 (as Ruisdael with figures by Lingelbach); Simon, 1927–30, p. 75 (as Van Kessel); Rosenberg, 1928, p. 118, n. 7 (as Kessel); The Burlington Magazine, 'Editorial', 1953, p. 34 ('Huis ten Bosch in background. Perhaps painted by Wynants in collaboration with Jan Kessel. (H.G.)'); Gerson, 1953, pp. 34, 51, n. 17 (as Wynants and van Kessel); Murray, 1980a, pp. 117, 143 (as Jan Wynants); Murray, 1980b, pp. 26, 31 (as by Jan Wynants); London, Washington and Los Angeles, 1985–6, p. 120, no. 35 (as Wijnants); Norwich, 1988, pp. 130–1, no. 88 (Wijnants); Davies, 1992, pp. 129–31, no. 21; Beresford, 1998, p. 141; Slive, 2001, p. 622, dub23.

Until recently, the authorship of *A Wood near the Hague* has been long disputed. To Francis Bourgeois it was by Jacob van Ruisdael. John Smith, writing in 1835, preferred an attribution to Jan Wijnants and suggested that the figures were by Adrian van de Velde. In 1880 Richter recorded a Ruisdael monogram – JVR – on the painting, but it is no longer visible, and Ruisdael's monogram was all too easily applied to many a lesser picture by unscrupulous art dealers. In 1890 Michel reattributed the picture to Ruisdael but couldn't help observing that the trees and plants looked more like Wijnants. The fact of the matter was that neither artist seemed quite right – this was someone who knew both artists and borrowed elements of both their styles. K.E. Simon in 1927 and Jakob Rosenberg in 1928 reached a solution when they independently suggested the picture was by Jan van Kessel, who fitted the bill in terms of his being influenced by the two greater artists, and who furthermore based his figure style on Van de Velde. However, it was not until Alice I. Davies' 1992 monograph on Van Kessel that the attribution was universally accepted. Perhaps the most conclusive piece of evidence for such an attribution is Davies' realisation that a drawing by Van Kessel (Brussels, Koninklijke Musea voor Schone Kunsten, Collection de Grez inv. 1984) is a preliminary study for the larger oak in the centre of the picture.[9] Davies suggested a date of around 1665.

The location of the scene a short distance to the east of The Hague is given by the inclusion of the Huis ten Bosch on the horizon.[10] This small Palladian villa was designed by Pieter Post for Amalia van Solms, wife of the Stadtholder, Prince Frederik Henrik and built between 1645 and 1652. It is currently the home of the Queen of the Netherlands. After Frederik Henrik's death in 1647, Jacob Jordaens, to a scheme by Constantijn Huygens, decorated the main room of the house (the Oranjezaal) as a memorial to the prince. It is this room whose octagonal drum and cupola can be seen in the background.

9 A.I. Davies, *Jan van Kessel (1641–1680)*, Doornspijk, 1992, p. 245, no. d32.
10 Smith misidentified the scene as taking place in a wood near Haarlem.

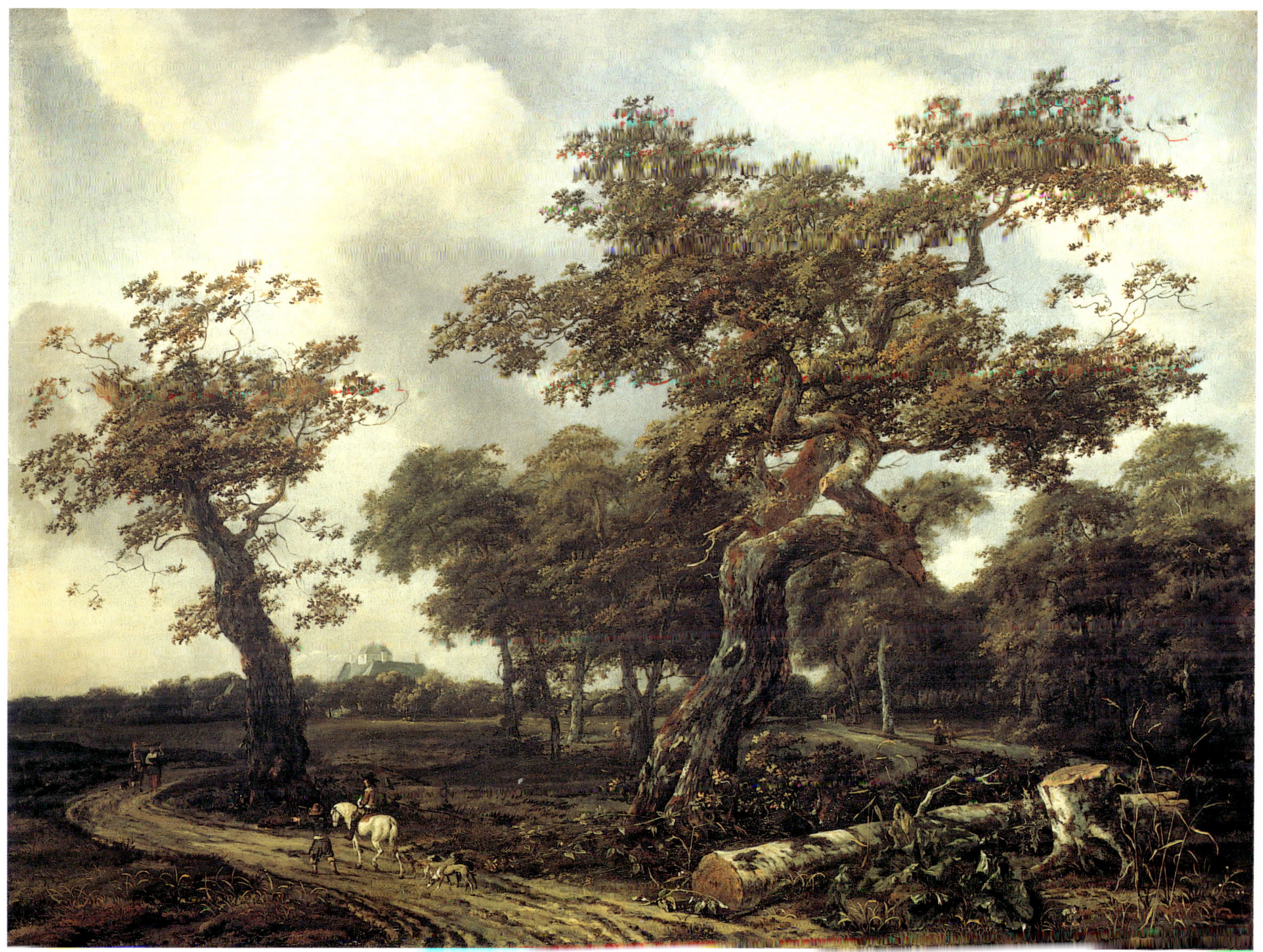

23 Jan LAPP

(The Hague c. 1600?–after 1662 Amsterdam)

Italian Landscape with Figures and Cattle

DPG No. 330, Bourgeois Bequest, 1811

Signed, indistinctly, on plinth, centre left: I… L…ap
Canvas, 56.8 x 64.3 cm

Prov.: London, Noel Desenfans, 1802–1807: London, Skinner and Dyke, Desenfans sale, 18 Mar. 1802, lot 107 (Descriptive Catalogue no. 130, as by Du Jardin) £18.18. Bt in; London, Sir Francis Bourgeois, 1807–1811; Bourgeois Bequest, 1811.

Ref.: Sparkes, 1876, p. 52, no. 216 (as by J. van der Does); Richter and Sparkes, 1880, p. 12, no. 216 (as Van Bergen); 1905 cat., p. 92, no. 330; Thieme-Becker, 1926–50, XXII, p. 377 (as bearing remains of Lapp's signature); Vermeule, 1966, p. 52, fol. 46, no. 8748 (on Villa Torlonia sarcophagus); Bernt, 1970, II, p. 70, fig. 663; Murray, 1980a, p. 28 (as Jan Lapp); Murray, 1980b, pp. 7, 8, 17; Beresford, 1998, p. 145.

Noel Desenfans, who described the picture in great detail in his sale catalogue of 1802, attributed it to Du Jardin. In 1876 John Sparkes noticed the partial signature and suggested J. van der Does. Four years later Richter rejected the attribution and suggested Dirk van Bergen. However, by 1928 Lapp's artistic identity had re-emerged and his authorship of this painting has since been universally accepted. The argument in favour of Lapp having visited Italy is strongly supported by this image, with its strangely exotic mix of emerald poplars and imposing classical statuary. His figures are distinctive also – like a more romantic Pieter van Laer. The whole has a peculiarly dream-like quality, albeit unnaturally enhanced by chemical changes in the pigment over time.

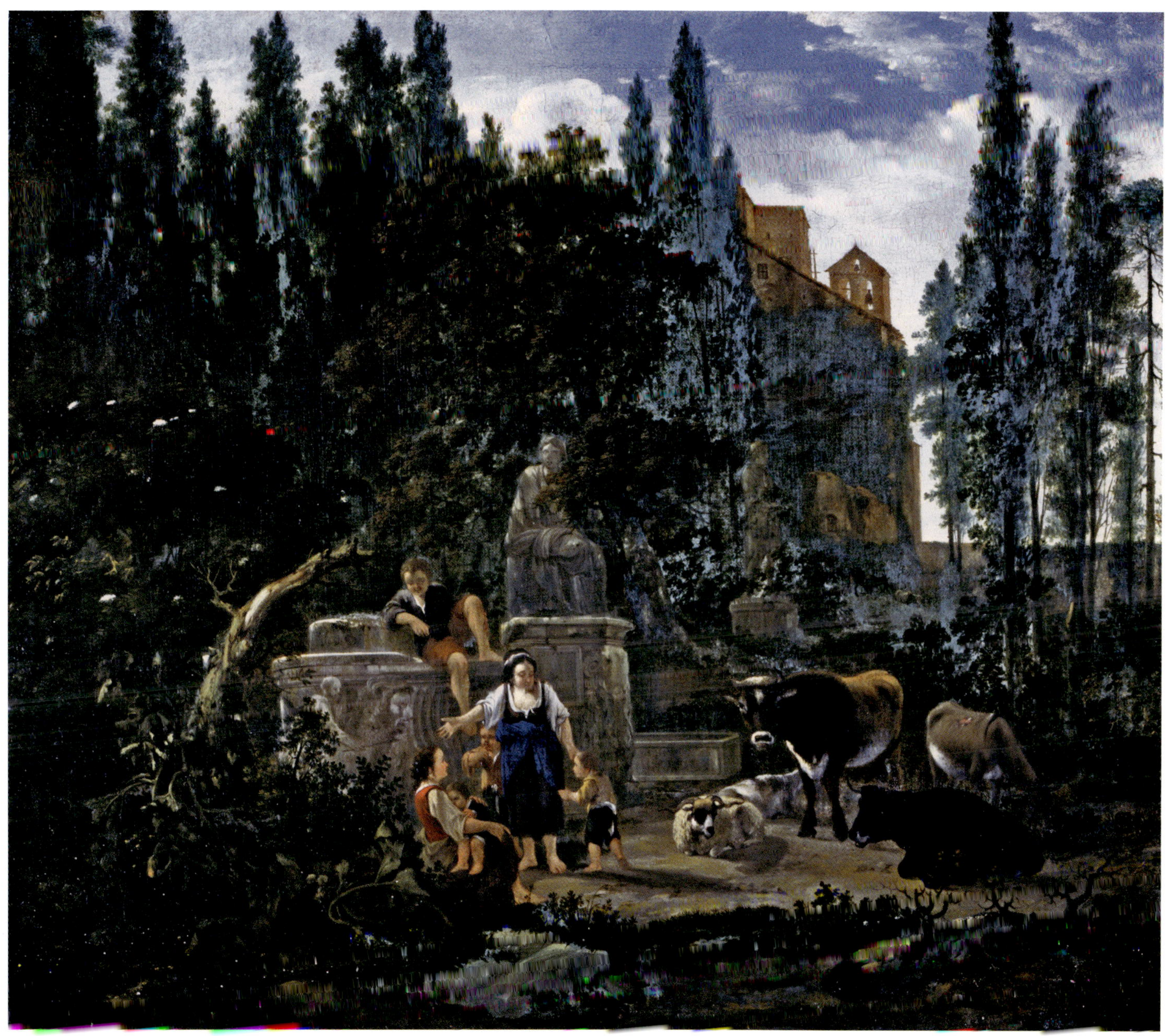

24 Jan LINGELBACH

(Frankfurt am Main 1622–1674 Amsterdam)

Italian Seaport

DPG No. 326, Bourgeois Bequest, 1811

Signed and dated on circular stone, bottom left: I LINGELBACH/ FECIT/ 1670
Canvas, 69.5 x 87.3 cm

Prov.: ?Moses Vanhausen sale, 1783. Bt Desenfans (according to Denning MS, 1859); London, Noel Desenfans, ?1783–1807; London, Sir Francis Bourgeois, 1807–1811; Bourgeois Bequest, 1811.

Ref.: Jameson, 1842, p. 454, no. 77; Richter and Sparkes, 1880, pp. 92–3, no. 77; 1905 cat., p. 91, no. 326; Burger-Wegener, 1976, no. 91; Duparc, 1980, p. 56; Murray, 1980a, pp. 79–80; Murray, 1980b, p. 18; Beresford, 1998, p. 152.

This bustling seaport illustrates the nature of this particular genre very well. The harbour setting is effectively a *capriccio* – an imaginary bringing-together of bits and pieces of classical architecture, statuary and Claudian landscape elements to form a glamorous stage-set for the foreground figures. The whole concept is intensely theatrical, even cinematic, dominated by the man in 'oriental' dress shaded by an umbrella making what can only be described as 'an entrance' to the left, beneath the dominating statue of Neptune, whose posture he seemingly emulates. The other key figure – the mounted man wearing a feathered turban, with his back to us – is presumably part of the other man's retinue. Other, less exotic, figures from central casting sit about observing the scene.

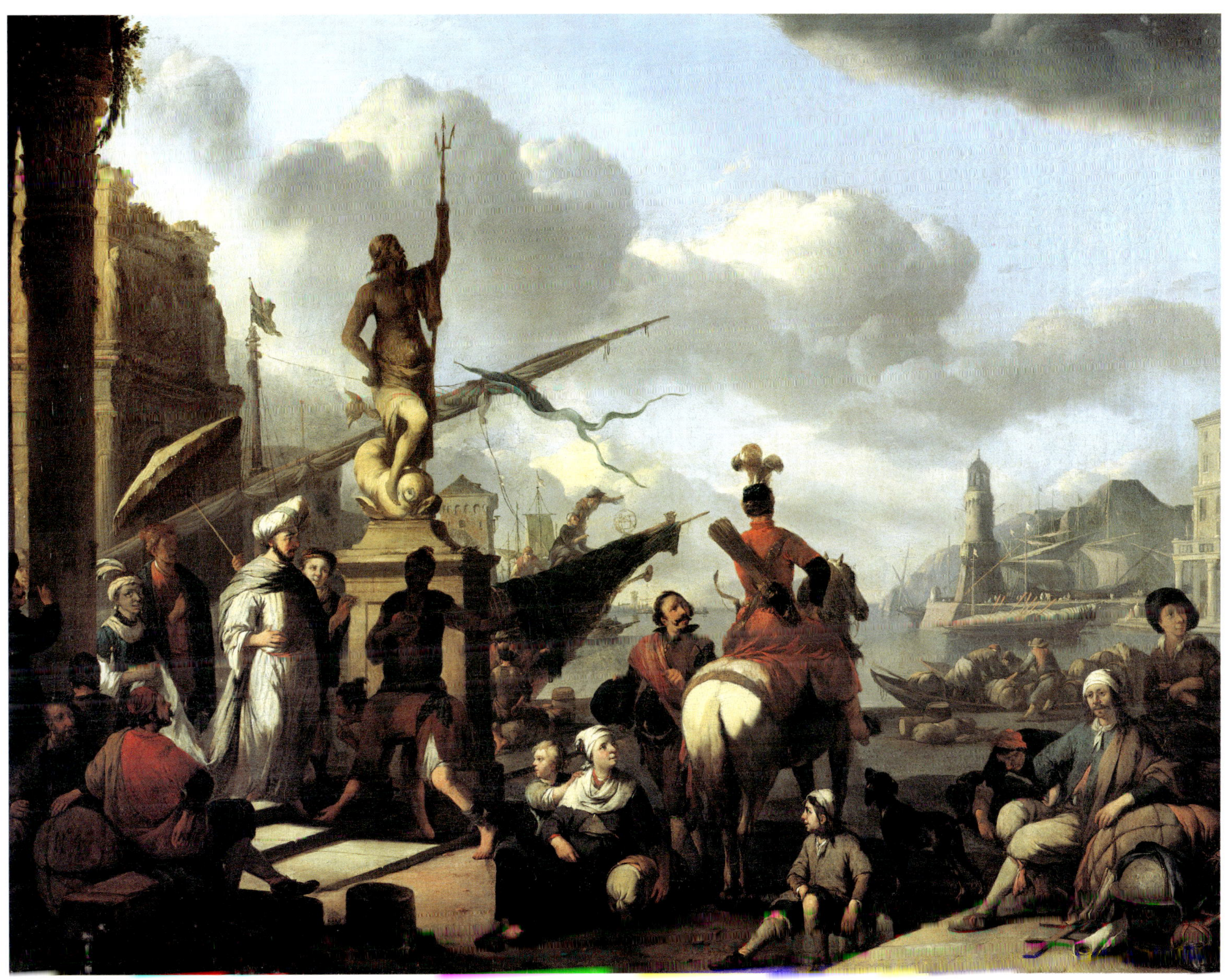

25

Cornelis van POELENBURCH

(Utrecht 1594/5–1667 Utrecht)

Valley with Ruins and Figures

DPG No. 338, Bourgeois Bequest, 1811

Poplar panel, 34.5 x 44.5 cm (oval)

Prov.: Monaco, Jacques François Léonor de Goyon, Duc de Valentinois, Comte de Matignon et de Thorigny, Duc d'Estouteville, 1725 (from an inscription on the verso); London, Sir Francis Bourgeois, 1811; Bourgeois Bequest, 1811.

Ref.: Richter and Sparkes, 1880, p. 23, no. 110 (as Breenbergh); 1905 cat., p. 94, no. 338; Roethlisberger, 1968, p. 391; Chiarini, 1972, p. 30 (first attribution to Poelenburch); Murray, 1980a, p. 32 (as Breenbergh); Murray, 1980b, p. 32; Roethlisberger, 1981, p. 39, no. 58; Sluijter-Seiffert, 1984, p. 116; Beresford, 1998, p. 178; Houston and Louisville, 1990–2000, p. 170, no. 56; London 2002, p. 80, no. 6; London, 2002, p. 80, no. 6.

The panel used for this picture is poplar – a wood associated with Italy. It is likely, therefore, that it may have been produced during Poelenburch's stay in Rome, perhaps around 1627. The tiny, decorative figures have led in the past to a general attribution (first challenged by Chiarini in 1972 in favour of Poelenburch) to Breenbergh; and Nicolette Sluijter-Seiffert (letter, DPG archive, 11 Aug. 1997) proposed that Breenbergh may indeed have painted the figures. However, Laurie Harwood has pointed out that such figures are not entirely without precedent in Poelenburch's work. More difficult is trying to arrive at a reason for the elaborate costumes of the two figures on the left, in a scene which might otherwise be assumed to be a simple genre painting with shepherds. Their presence suggests there might possibly be a specific narrative intended.

If the date is correct, then this is the earliest classical landscape at Dulwich. Its careful arrangement of receding wedges is anchored by the ruin at its centre. Everything leads the eye inwards by balanced and easy stages. But the extreme formality of the composition is belied by the brilliance of light and observation of detail – whether it be sunshine on a rock face, the sudden gleam of reflection on water, or the infinitely tiny washing-line strung under the ruined arch.

The provenance of the painting is first documented by an inscription on the reverse that states it was in the collection of the Duc de Valentinois in 1725. This was Jacques François Léonor de Goyon, Comte de Matignon et de Thorigny, Duc d'Estouteville, who was created Duc de Valentinois on 24 July 1715. He acceded as Prince Sovereign of Monaco on 29 December 1731, and abdicated from that position on 8 November 1733. The picture may have remained in Monaco until January 1793 when the Grimaldi dynasty was temporarily deposed, their collection dispersed, and Monaco annexed by France.

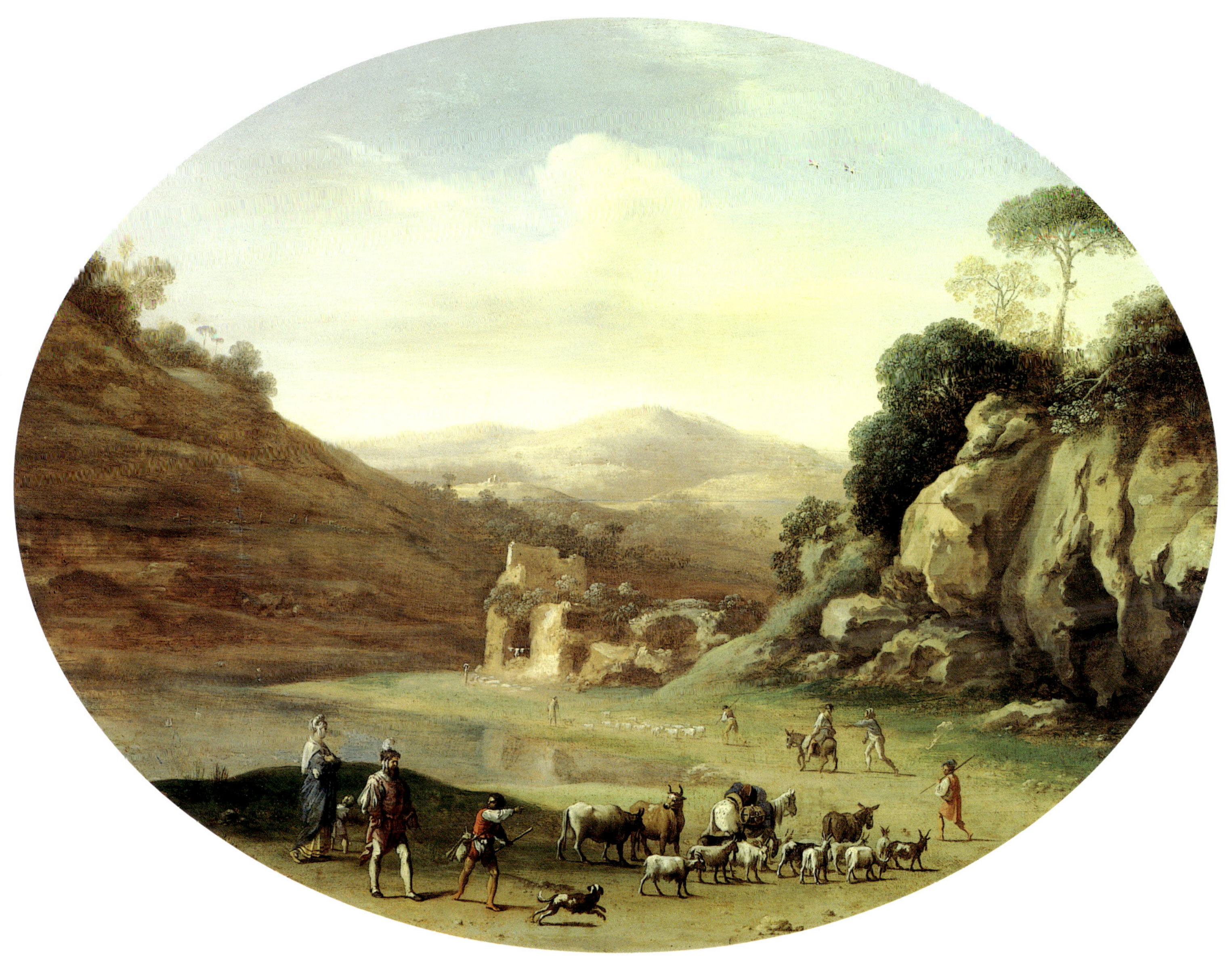

26 Adam PYNACKER

(Schiedam 1620/1–1673 Amsterdam)
Landscape with Sportsmen and Game
DPG No. 86, Bourgeois Bequest, 1811

Signed, bottom centre right: A Pynacker (AP in monogram)
Canvas, 137.8 x 198.7 cm

Prov.: ? Amsterdam, no. 548 Heerengracht, Cornelis Backer (1633–1681) coll., bef. 1681; by descent to C. Backer: his sale, Leiden, 16 Aug. 1775, lot 4. Bt Delfos for 1310 fl; Abraham Delfos (1731–1820); Mr. Diderick, Baron van Leyden, 1804: his sale, Paris, Delaroche, 7 Nov. 1804, lot 75. Bt Paillet for Ff 3500; Alexandre Joseph Paillet (1743–1814), 1804; London, Sir Francis Bourgeois, 1811; Bourgeois Bequest, 1811.

Ref.: Possibly Houbraken, 1718–21, II, p. 97–9; Patmore, 1824a, p. 22, no. 71; Smith, 1829–46, VI, p. 294, no. 28; Jameson, 1842, p. 463, no. 130; Richter and Sparkes, 1880, p. 115, no. 130; 1905 cat., p. 22, no. 86; HdG, 1926, IX, p. 525, no. 9 (and also perhaps p. 539, no. 72 – decoration in the house of C. Backer, Amsterdam); Cook, 1914, pp. 49–50, no. 86; Gerson, 1953, pp. 34, 51; Plietzsch, 1960, XVII, p. 136; London, 1976, p. 68, no. 83; Wright, 1978; Murray, 1980a, pp. 97–8; Murray, 1980b, p. 22; Duparc, 1980, p. 86, under no. 132; Harwood, 1985, p. 487; Boston and Amsterdam, 1987, p. 67; Harwood, 1988, pp. 92–3, no. 77, pp. 31–3; Fleischer, 1989, p. 57; Montreal, 1990, p. 158, under no. 49; Williamstown and Sarasota, 1994, pp. 32–3; Beresford, 1998, p. 189; Houston and Louisville, 1999–2000, p. 186, no. 64; London, 2002, p. 174.

Versions and copies: 1. Partial copy, ?John Crome, Silver Birches, Norwich Castle Museum, inv. no. 112.536, probably 1820.

This very large painting is one of the keystones of Pynacker's oeuvre, and one of the greatest paintings at Dulwich. Laurie Harwood has proposed a date of c. 1665 for the picture, from Pynacker's Amsterdam period. It features many stylistic characteristics of this phase – cool tonality, sharp definition and an astonishing, almost surreal, focus on the foreground group of birches to the left, rendered in illusionistic detail. The most surreal element of the picture, however, is a chemical accident. What was once merely a dazzling display of decorative leaf-painting in the middle foreground is now more notable for the leaves' exceptionally unnatural blue colour – but viewers should remember that blue + yellow = green, and in this case the yellow that Pynacker used was clearly, chemically speaking, fugitive. At any rate, it has gone, leaving Pynacker looking even more modern and striking.

Pynacker borrowed the dogs from a painting by Ludolf de Jongh, *Before the Hunt* (location unknown). The curious elf-like figure with the hunting horn very much gives the impression of having wandered in from another kind of painting altogether; while he may in fact be by Pynacker, it would not be unusual for such a figure to have been painted by some other artist. Mrs Jameson in the 19th century suggested Berchem – surely not, but other candidates might include Abraham Hondius or Lingelbach. A contribution by Hondius would provide a *terminus ante quem*, as he moved to London in 1666.

Hofstede de Groot suggested this painting may have been in the collection of Cornelis Backer (1633–81) which was part of the decorative scheme of his house at no. 548 Heerengracht, Amsterdam, which was completed in 1665.[11] If this is true then *Landscape with Sportsmen and Game* has one of the earliest provenances for a Pynacker painting, along with other of his works thought to have been owned by Backer – the pendants *Landscape with Waterfall* and *Hilly Landscape in Evening* (both Rotterdam, Mus. Boijmans-van Beuningen).

11 See HdG72 and H.F. Wijnman, 'Beschrijving van elk pand aan de Herengracht met zijn eigenaars en bewonders', *Vier eeuwen Herengracht*, Amsterdam, 1076, p. 597.

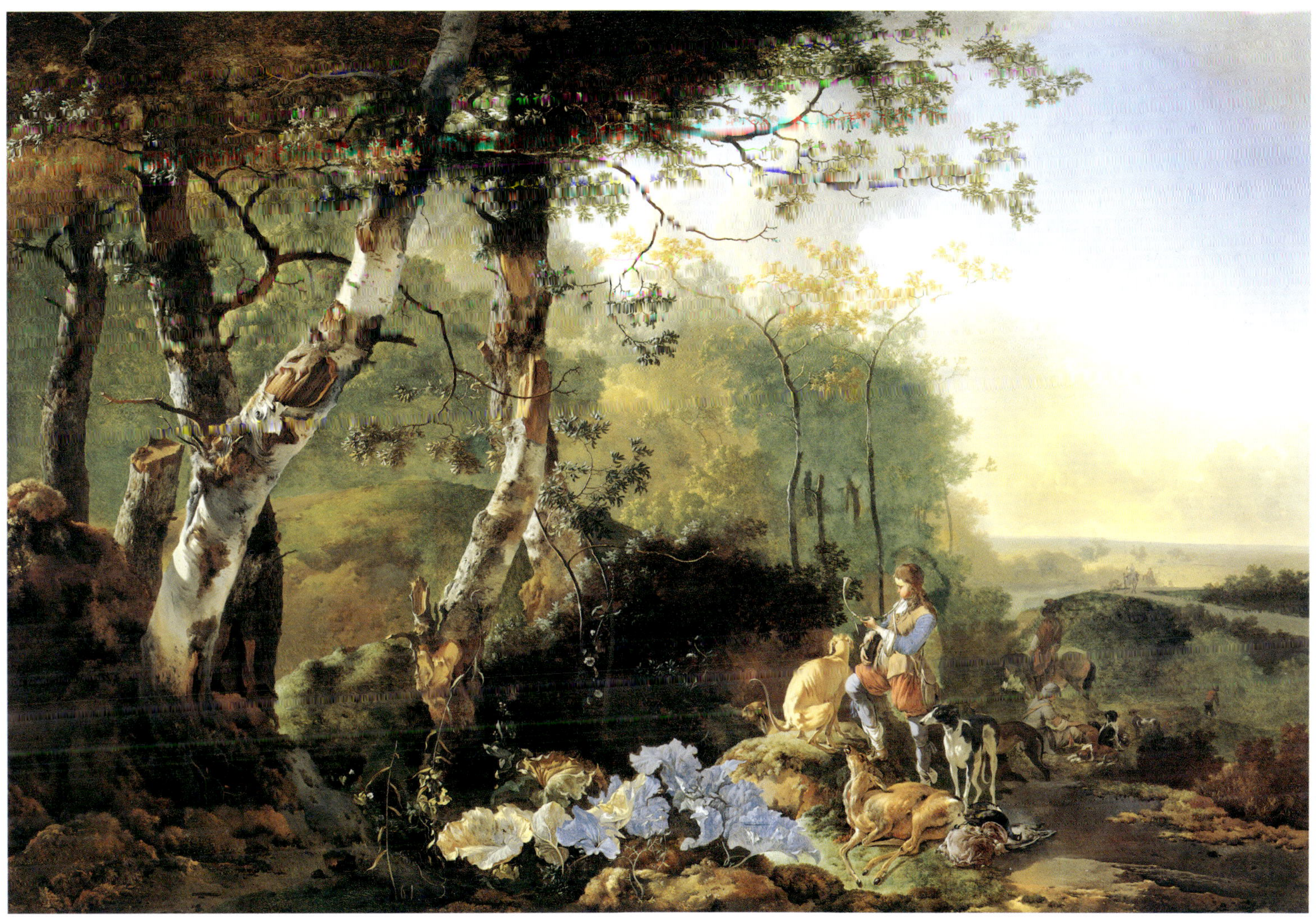

27 Adam PYNACKER

(Schiedam 1620/1–1673 Amsterdam)
Bridge in an Italian Landscape
DPG No. 183, Bourgeois Bequest, 1811

This exquisite painting is generally considered to be one of the most beautiful works at Dulwich. Laurie Harwood emphasized Pynacker's debt to the example of Jan Both, proposing a date of 1653/4, writing: 'Everything from the overall composition to the treatment of light and the representation of trees and foreground foliage can be directly associated with Both's Campagna views.' But it is the remarkable drama of the figures silhouetted against the sky – a sky that opens up again below them in the reflections beneath the delicate bridge – that gives the painting its special quality. Here is one of the most heroically poetic dogs in art, gazing into the sunset.

The picture is first documented in the significant collection of the French politician Charles-Alexandre Calonne (an important, if unpopular, man – Controller-General of Finance to Louis XVI, 1882–7), a friend of Noel Desenfans. In 1789 Calonne had mortgaged his collection to Desenfans in order to fund his support of a counter-revolutionary coup in France. When this failed Desenfans and his business partners foreclosed the debt, placing the paintings up for sale in 1795. By this stage, however, Desenfans had already sold his share of the collection and he or Sir Francis Bourgeois presumably acquired *Bridge in an Italian Landscape* at this juncture.

Signed indistinctly above lily leaves, lower right:
A Pijnaker (AP in monogram?)
Oak panel, 43.8 x 52.7 cm

Prov.: C.A. de Calonne (1734–1802); his sale, London, Skinner and Dyke, 26 Mar. 1795, lot 46 ('Pynacker–A Landscape with a Bridge and Cattle, a fine clear pleasing picture'). Sold, £33.12.0; London, Sir Francis Bourgeois, 1811; Bourgeois Bequest, 1811.

Ref.: Smith, 1829–46, VI, p. 292, no. 17; Buchanan, 1824, I, p. 231; Jameson, 1842, p. 466, no. 150; Richter and Sparkes, 1880, p. 115, no. 150; 1905 cat., p. 48, no. 183; HdG, 1926, IX, pp. 539–40, no. 74; Cook, 1914, p. 117, no. 183; Plietzsch, 1960, XVII, p. 136; Reiss, 1975, p. 176; Murray, 1980a, p. 98; Murray, 1980b, p. 22; Harwood, 1985, p. 486; Harwood, 1988, pp. 61–2, no. 32; Williamstown and Sarasota, 1994–5, p. 48, no. 6; Beresford, 1998, p. 189; Houston and Louisville, 1999–2000, p. 184, no. 63; London, 2002, p. 166, no. 41.

Versions and Copies: 1. Copy. Location unknown (Formerly Dresden, Gemäldegalerie, oil on canvas, 58.2 x 74.3 cm, inv. no. 5 s68 [catalogue 1961, no. 59; Harwood, 1988, no. 32a]). 2. Engraving, R. Cockburn.

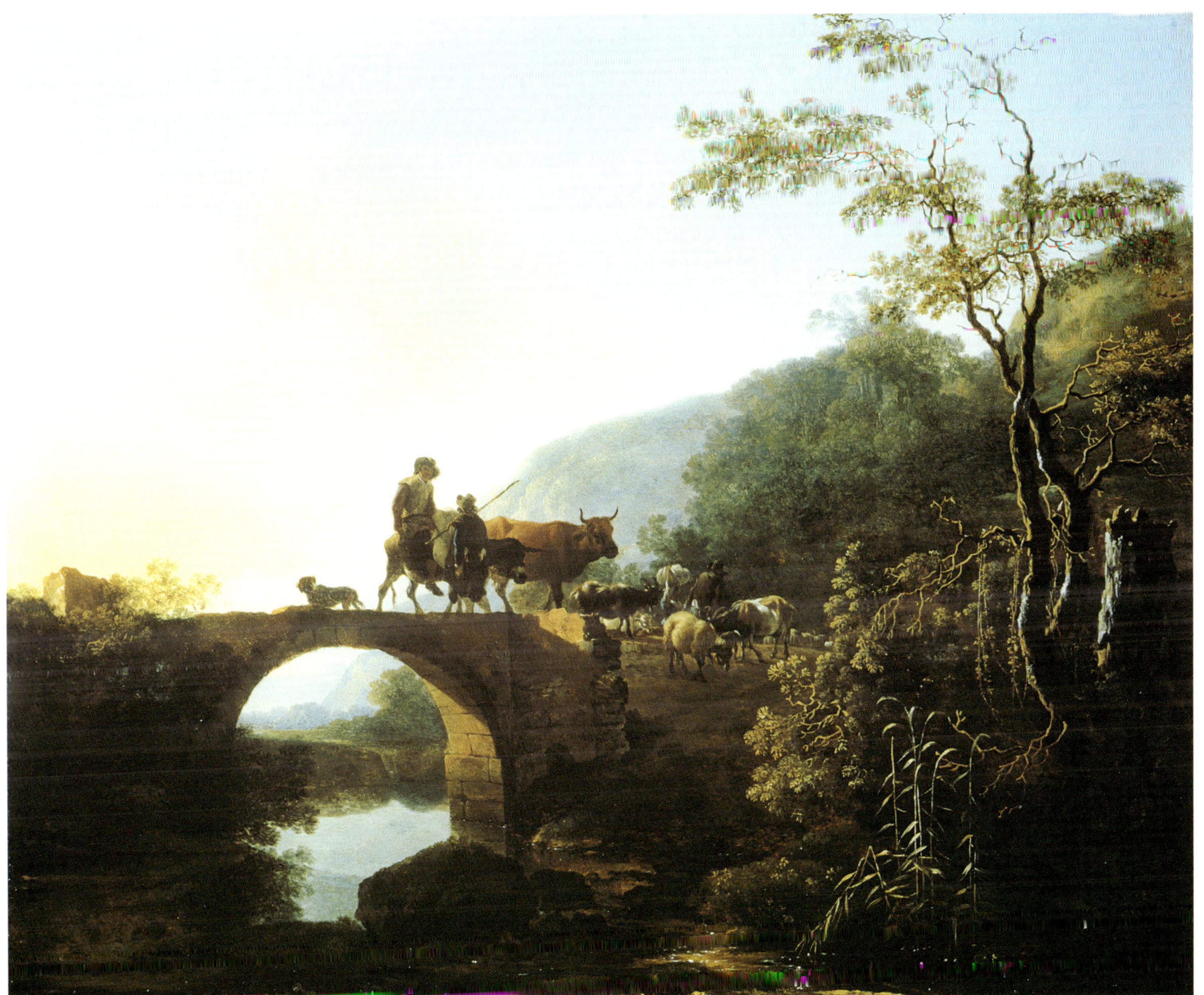

28

William ROMEYN

(Haarlem c. 1624–after 1693 Haarlem?)

Classical Landscape

DPG No. 3, Bourgeois Bequest, 1811

Signed, bottom right: W. ROMEYN (WR in monogram)
Canvas, 35.2 x 41.9 cm

Prov.: ?London, Sir John Gayer (bap. 1584–d.1649), bef. 1649; London, Sir Francis Bourgeois, 1811; Bourgeois Bequest, 1811.

Ref.: Jameson, 1842, p. 444, no. 10; Waagen, 1854, II, p. 344; Wurzbach, 1906–10, p. 468; Richter and Sparkes, 1880, p. 138, no. 8; 1905 cat., p. 1, no. 3; Thieme-Becker, 1907–50, XXVIII, p. 563; Cook, 1914, pp. 3–4, no. 3; 1926 cat. no. 3; 1953 cat. no. 3; Murray, 1980a, p. 299; Beresford, 1998, p. 203.

Pack animals, heavily loaded, and resting cattle and sheep, occupy the foreground of this little painting and its apparent pair, *Landscape* (cat. no. 29). In the case of *Classical Landscape* here the backdrop is of a generic cityscape heavily reminiscent of the Roman forum, with its mix of classical archway, ruins and towering church. The pack animals are accompanied by a mounted muleteer. There is a strong suggestion of evening; the animals give the impression of resting after a long day. Romeyn has handled the poetic light with considerable delicacy.

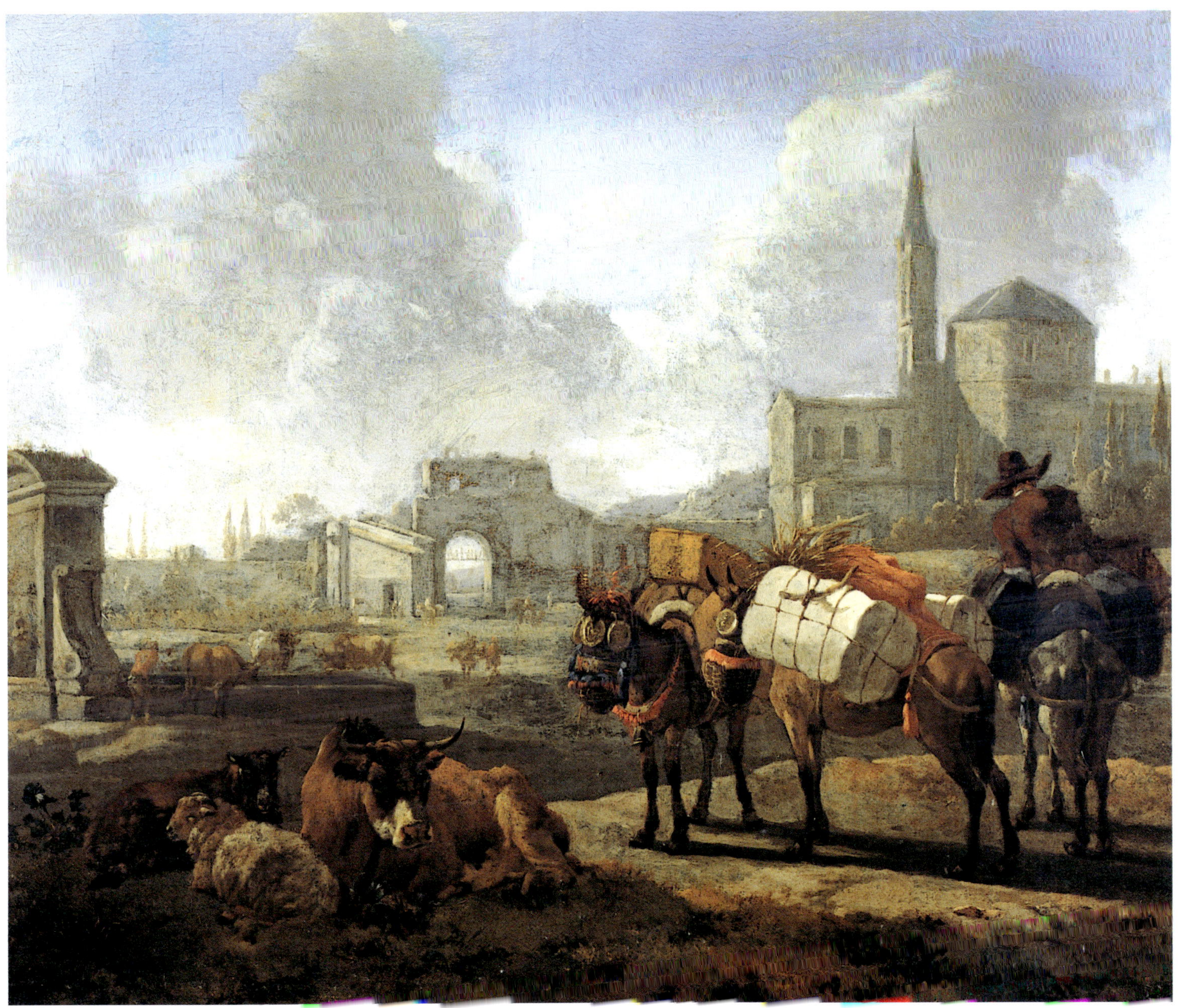

29 **William ROMEYN**

(Haarlem c. 1624–1692/4 Amsterdam)

Landscape

DPG No. 5, Bourgeois bequest, 1811

Signed, bottom right: W. ROMEYN (WR in monogram)
Canvas, 35.7 x 41.9 cm

Prov.: London, Sir John Gayer (bap. 1584–d.1649), bef. 1649; London, Sir Francis Bourgeois, 1811; Bourgeois Bequest, 1811; 1813 inv. no. 180 (Upper Room. West: 'Romayne – A WOMAN MILKING A GOAT, ASS, & SHEEP (comp to 1 [1813, inv. no. 183]) [support and dimensions] 'c' [canvas] '2 2.3').

Ref.: Waagen, 1854, II, p. 344; Richter and Sparkes, 1880, p. 138, no. 10; 1905, cat., p. 2, no. 5; Cook, 1914, p. 7, no. 5; 1926, cat. no. 5; 1953, cat. no. 5; Murray, 1980a, p. 299. Beresford, 1998, p. 203.

This has always been considered to be a partner piece to cat. no. 28 on the previous page. They are the same size, and their subject matter is certainly related, although this time the pack animal is accompanied by sheep and goats, one of which is being milked by the kneeling milkmaid. Each composition is dominated on one side by a tall structural element – the towering campanile to the right of the *Classical Landscape* is answered here by the blasted oak to the left of this composition. The backdrop, however, is rural, with a very Du Jardin-esque mountain and sky.

The recent identification of an intriguing wax seal[12] ('Ermine a fleur de lys on a chief a mullet') on the reverse of the stretcher as that of the merchant and mayor of London (1646) Sir John Gayer (bap. 1584–d. 1649), implies that this picture at least was painted before Romeyn's arrival in Italy in 1650[13], and indeed that it made its way to England before 1649, when Gayer died. This would make it one of his earliest known works, its obvious Italianate elements derived presumably from Berchem.

12 By Mr Melvyn Jeremiah, file at Dulwich.
13 For this see *Papworth's Ordinary of British armorials*, Bath, 1977.

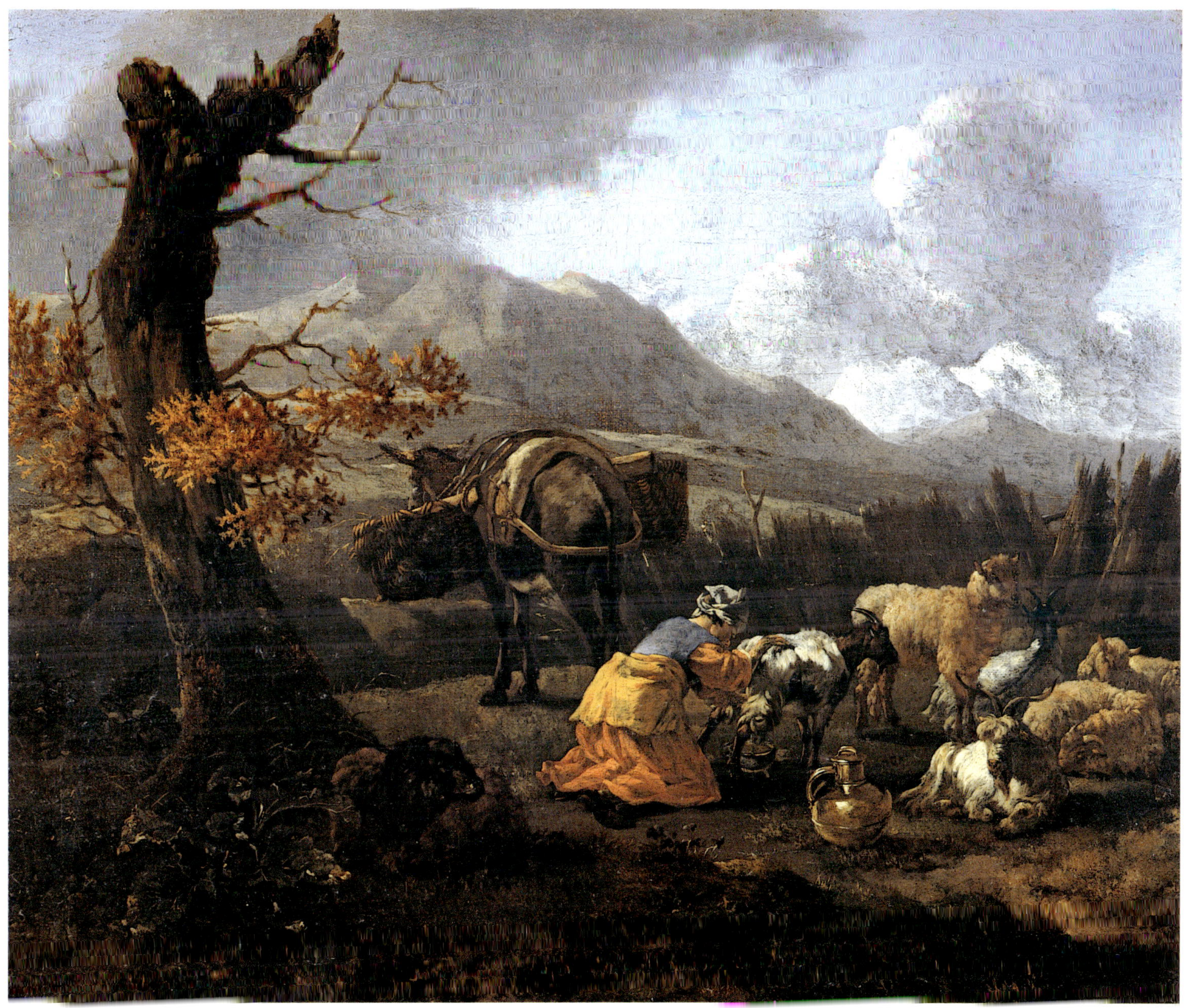

30 Jan WEENIX

(Amsterdam 1642–1719 Amsterdam)
Landscape with Shepherd Boy
DPG No. 47, Bourgeois Bequest, 1811

Signed and dated, bottom left: J. Weenix/ 1664
Canvas, 81.6 x 99.6 cm

Prov.: London, Noel Desenfans, 1804–1807: 1804 Insurance List, no. 79 ('Weeninx – A Landscape with Sheep'). £100; London, Sir Francis Bourgeois, 1807–1811; Bourgeois Bequest, 1811.

Ref.: Richter and Sparkes, p. 184, no. 147; Jameson, 1842, p. 466, no. 147; 1905 cat., p. 11, no. 47; Cook, 1914, p. 27, no. 47; Stechow, 1948, pp. 195–6; Bernt, 1970, III, pl. 1376; London, 1976, p. 95, no. 122; Murray, 1980a, p. 137; Murray, 1980b, p. 29; Schloss, 1983, pp. 72–3, fig. 2; London, Washington and Los Angeles, 1985–6, p. 118, no. 34; Beresford, 1998, p. 257; Houston and Louisville, 1999–2000, p. 202, no. 73; London, 2002, p. 201, no. 57.

The painting comes from early in Weenix's career – it is dated 1664, the year in which he is first recorded as a member of the Utrecht painter's guild – and closely imitates the style of his father, Jan Baptist Weenix, who had died four years earlier. It is not known whether Weenix travelled to Italy, but the column, which seems to derive from the Temple of Vespasian, appears in numerous paintings by Jan Baptist Weenix, and could easily have been copied from drawings made by his father in Rome. A superficially charming genre scene such as this was nevertheless more than likely to have borne a freight of secondary meaning in its time. The boy's care for his dogs and sheep was probably intended as an allegory of industry – a message reinforced by the smaller figures in the background, apparently travelling a bustling trade route.

The technique is fluid and watercolour-like. It always drew attention – in 1842 Mrs Jameson called the picture 'cleverly painted', while in 1948 Stechow described it as 'calligraphic'.

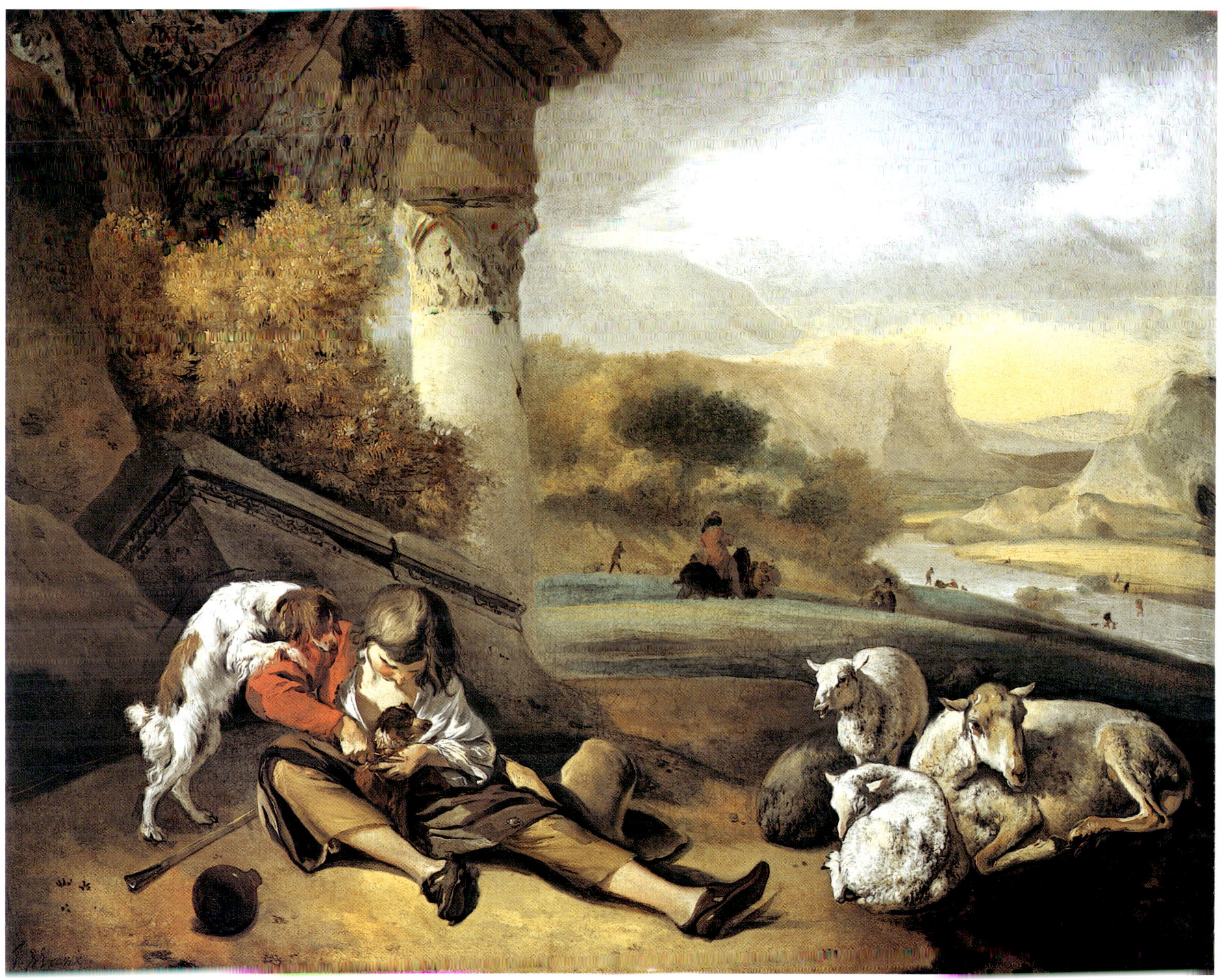

31 Thomas WIJCK

(Beverwijck c. 1616–1677 Haarlem)
Italian Courtyard
DPG No. 247, Bourgeois Bequest, 1811

Canvas on panel, 38.3 x 31.1 cm

Prov.: London, John Philip Kemble (1757–1823), his gift to Bourgeois; London, Sir Francis Bourgeois, 1811; Bourgeois Bequest, 1811.

Ref.: Jameson, 1842, p. 458, no. 103 (as Jan Miel); Richter and Sparkes, 1880, p. 96, no. 103 (as Jan Miel); 1905 cat., p. 67, no. 247; Kren, 1978, pp. 197–8, no. D24 (first attribution to Wijck); Murray, 1980a, p. 300 (as Jan Miel); Beresford, 1998, p. 259 (as Wijck).

This little picture is a characteristic exercise in the style of the *Bamboccianti*, followers of Pieter van Laer (*Il Bamboccio*). A ramshackle courtyard, notable for its antiquity, but not for its antiquities, shelters a small group of women and children doing nothing in particular. These figures are reminiscent of Andries Both, and even of the young Lingelbach. Recent cleaning revealed that the seated woman in particular and her older son wearing the big hat are painted with considerable delicacy and finesse – what light and colour there is in the picture flickers round this little group. These dark courtyards no doubt reflected life as it was lived; but they also strongly evoke a sense of history – of baroque built on medieval built on ancient Roman – that gives these scenes a timeless character (something still true in parts of Rome to this day). Originally catalogued as by Jan Miel, in 1978 Thomas Kren correctly attributed *Italian Courtyard* to Thomas Wijck.

The picture arrived in Bourgeois's collection by interesting means. An inscription records that it was given to Bourgeois by his friend, the great Shakespearian actor, John Philip Kemble. Most likely this was before 1804, in which year Bourgeois parted ways with Kemble in high dudgeon at Kemble's replacing Bourgeois' painting of 'Kemble in Coriolanus' with another by Thomas Lawrence.[14]

14 Farington recorded that: 'Taylor mentioned that Bourgeois has broke off from Kemble in consequence of Kemble having given Bourgeois picture of 'Kemble in Coriolanus' to [James] Boaden [of the Oracle], and placed in His drawing room over the fire place Lawrence's portrait of Him.–Kemble having heard of Bourgeois indignation called on him to explain, but according to Bourgeois acct. on Hearing Kemble ask for Him He called that Kemble might hear him, that "He was not at home."–This had been preceded by Kemble having, when Bourgeois was present, expressed that a Club shd. be formed to consist of men most eminent in every Class of liberal study, & in enumerating mentioned Lawrence in the Painting department, on which Bourgeois asked if Kemble thought Him the proper representative ? who replied in the affirmative, which Bourgeois sd. He cd. not agree to.' Farington, entry for 13 Sep. 1804. The portrait of Kemble is now at the Soane Museum, London.

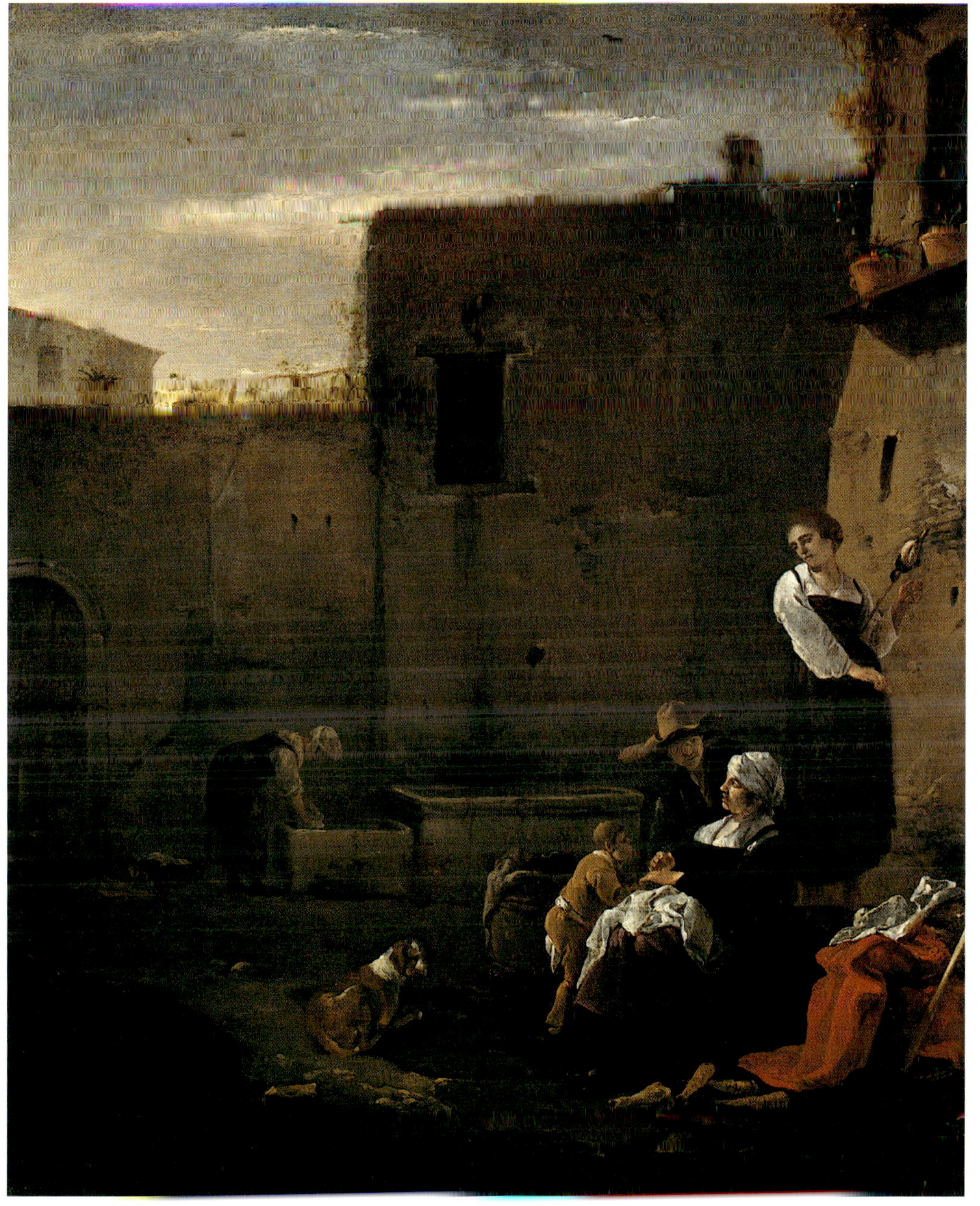

32 Jan WIJNANTS

(Haarlem? 1631/2–1684 Amsterdam)
Landscape with Cow drinking
DPG No. 114, Bourgeois Bequest, 1811

Signed, bottom right: J wijna[n]t[s]
Oak panel, 15.6 x 18.7 cm

Prov.: London, Michael Bryan, 1801; his sale, London, Christie's, 6 Mar. 1801, lot 51 ('Wynants – A Pair of small brilliant Landscapes'). Bt Bourgeois for £26.5; London, Noel Desenfans and/or Sir Francis Bourgeois, 1801–1807: 1804 Insurance List, no. 23 or 24 ('Wynants–A Landscape' or 'Wynants–Ditto' [A Landscape]). £50; London, Sir Francis Bourgeois, 1807–1811; Bourgeois Bequest, 1811.

Ref.: Patmore, 1824, p. 182; Smith, 1829–42, VI, p. 278, no. 165; Jameson, 1842, p. 445, no. 11; Richter and Sparkes, p. 186, no. 12; 1905 cat., p. 29, no. 114; HdG, 1923, VIII, p. 544, no. 312 (as signed in full); Cook, 1914, pp. 67–8, no. 114; Murray, 1980a, p. 143; Murray, 1980b, p. 31; Beresford, 1998, p. 260; Houston and Louisville, 1999–2000, p. 200, no. 71; Eisele, 2000, pp. 152–3, no. 151; L. Harwood in London, 2002, p. 191, no. 52.

Versions and Copies: 1. Engraving, R. Cockburn.

The *Landscape with Cow Drinking* and its pair, *Landscape* (cat. no. 33) are dune landscapes of the late 1650s, with not a hint of the Italianate about them. The two pictures are effectively variations on the same theme, each dominated by rising ground on the right, with a stand of trees in the centre middle ground and a distant landscape opening up to the left, reached by a winding path. However, the landscapes are articulated differently through their contrasting skies, and through two differing exercises in the use of Ruisdael-like tree focal points. In cat. no. 33 it is a blasted oak used as a dominant *repoussoir* on the left; here a brightly-lit dead tree stands out like a shaft of lightning against the dark trees. Tiny figures and cattle (in *Landscape* only) emerge on close study to attract the eye and further define the landscape; the presence of people helps us recognise the paths, while the cow brings the eye to the expanse of water at the bottom left of this work. Light falls differently in each: *Landscape with Cow Drinking* has the more dramatic effects as a huge raincloud fills the sky, while a bright patch of sunlight catches the top of the hill. These two brilliant tiny paintings are masterclasses of their genre.

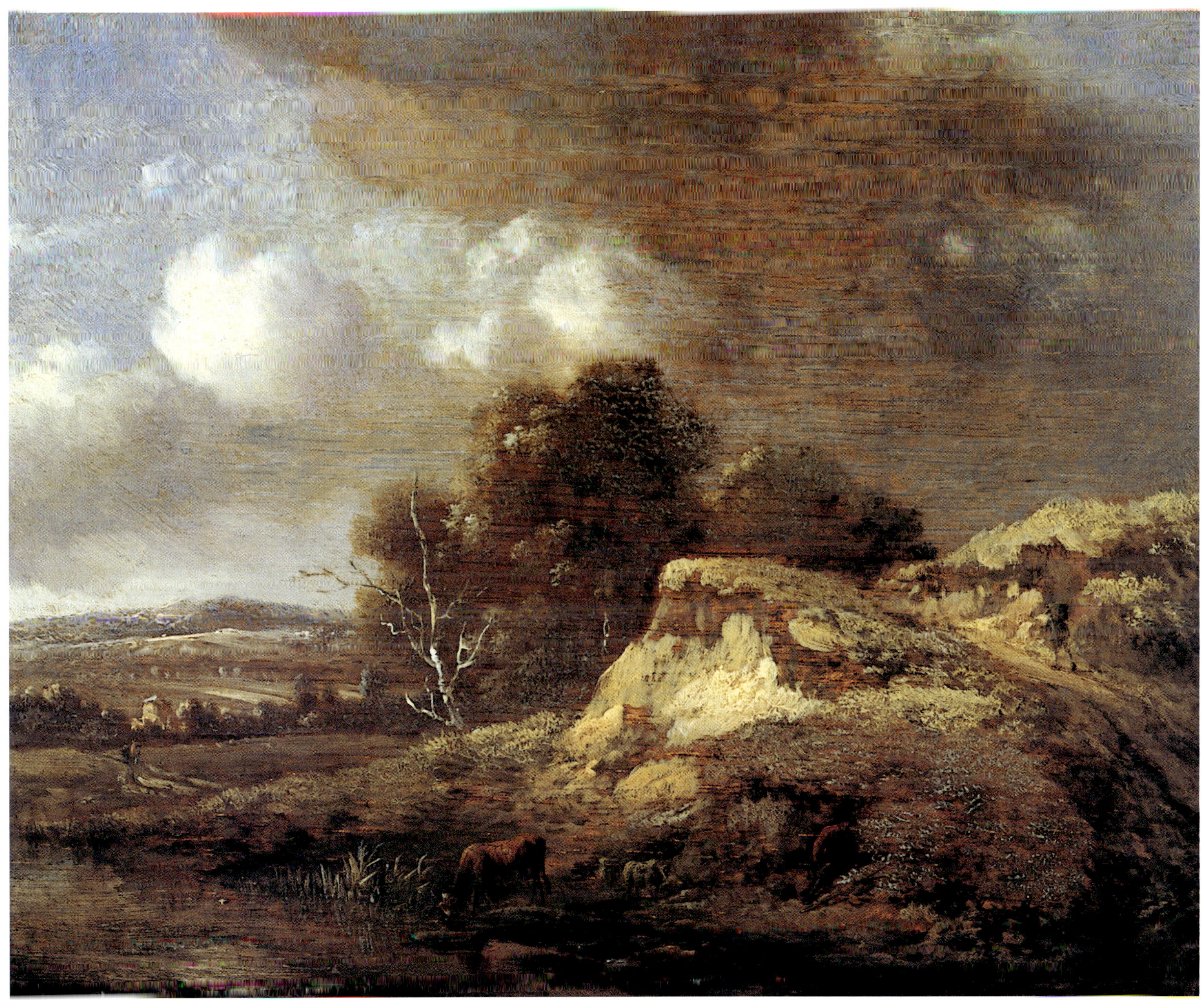

33 Jan WIJNANTS

(Haarlem 1631/2–1684 Amsterdam)

Landscape

DPG No. 117, Bourgeois Bequest, 1811

Oak panel, 15.8 x 18.8 cm

Prov.: London, Michael Bryan, 1801; his sale, London, Christie's, 6 Mar. 1801, lot 51 ('Wynants – A Pair of small brilliant Landscapes'). Bt Bourgeois for £26.5; London, Noel Desenfans and/or Sir Francis Bourgeois, 1801–1807: 1804 Insurance List, no. 23 or 24 ('Wynants–A Landscape' or 'Wynants–Ditto' [A Landscape]). £50; London, Sir Francis Bourgeois, 1807–1811; Bourgeois Bequest, 1811.

Ref.: Patmore, 1824, p. 182; Smith, 1829–42, VI, p. 278, no. 165; Jameson, 1842, p. 445, no. 11; Richter and Sparkes, p. 186, no. 12; 1905 cat., p. 29, no. 114; HdG, 1923, VIII, p. 544, no. 312 (as signed in full); Cook, 1914, pp. 67–8, no. 114; Murray, 1980a, p. 143; Murray, 1980b, p. 31; Beresford, 1998, p. 260; Houston and Louisville, 1999–2000, p. 200, no. 71; Eisele, 2000, pp. 152–3, no. 151; L. Harwood in London, 2002, p. 191, no. 52.

Versions and Copies: 1. Engraving, R. Cockburn.

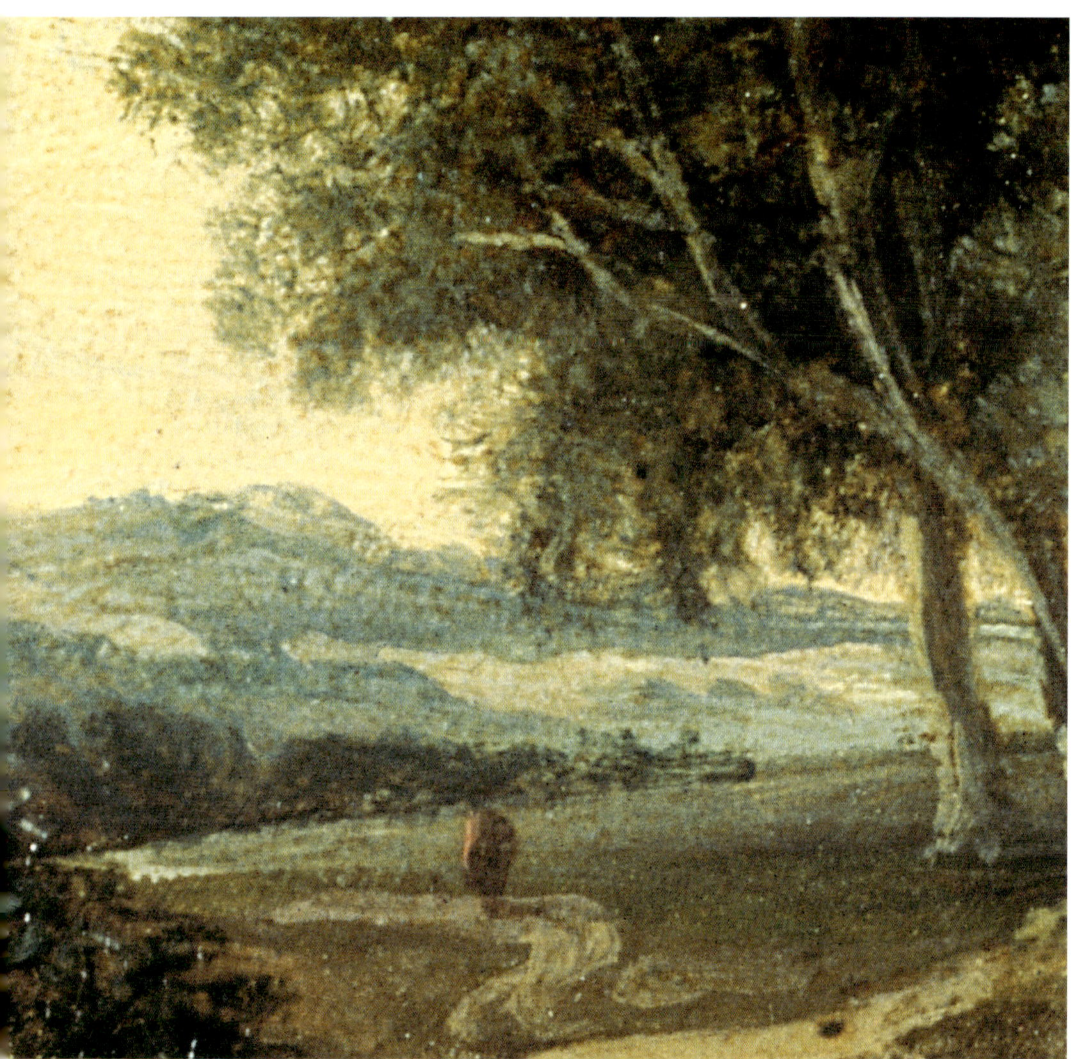

detail

See entry for cat. no. 32.

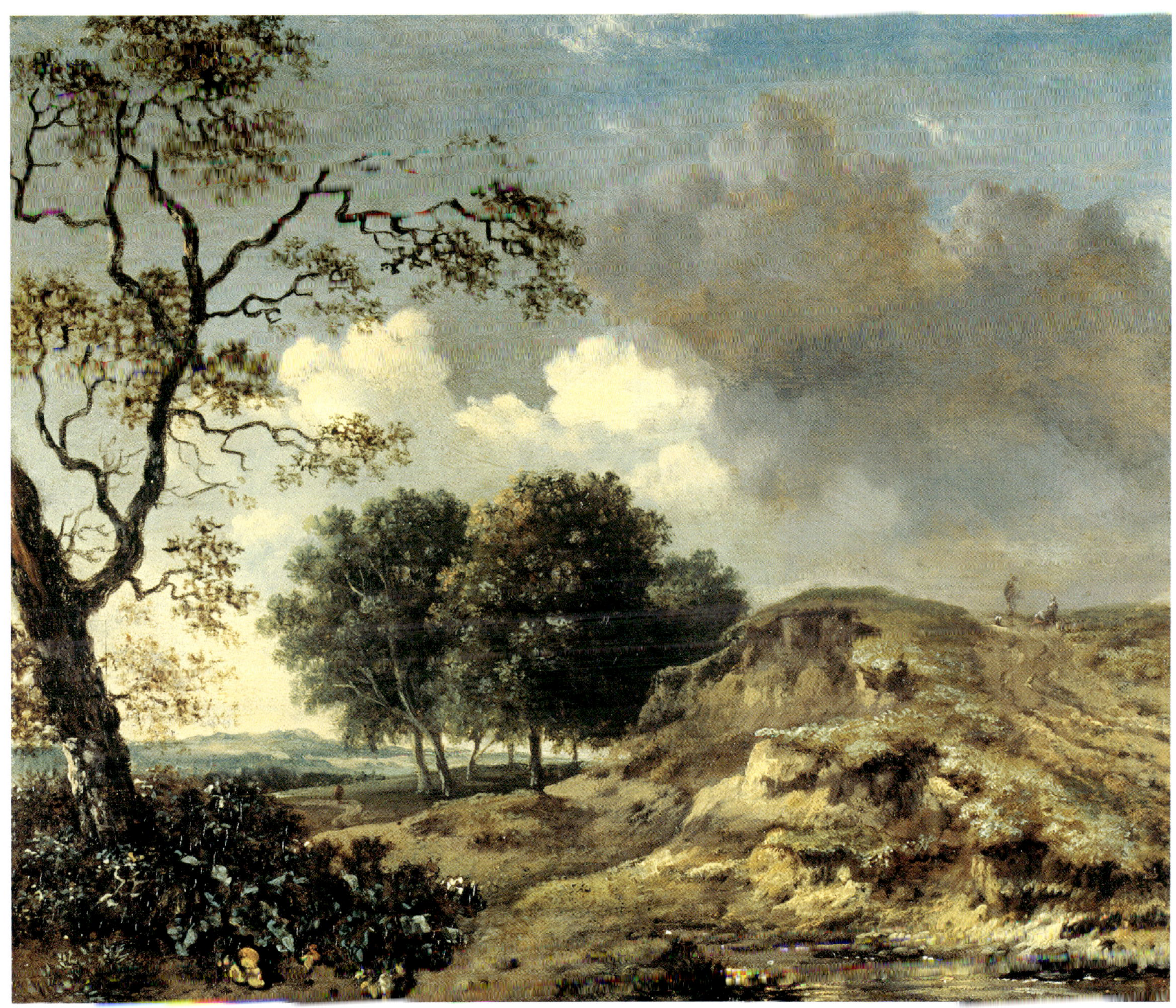

34 Philips WOUWERMANS

(Haarlem 1619–1668 Haarlem)
Halt of Cavaliers at an Inn
DPG No. 77, Bourgeois Bequest, 1811

Although dating can be problematic in this artist's considerable oeuvre, there is one useful distinction in his early work: before 1646 he used a different monogram – 'PH W'. Post-1646, he changed his signature to PHILS .W (PHILS in monogram). This painting is therefore certainly pre-1646, and F. Duparc (DPG archive, letter on file, 1997) suggested it dates from 1642/3. Here the influence of Pieter van Laer is at its clearest, in terms of its strongly diagonal composition, its earthy colours, and the focus on the beautifully-observed interaction of resting 'cavaliers' in the foreground. Even the horses reflect the more down-to-earth aesthetic of Van Laer, and the furthest right of the three is first cousin to the horse in Van Laer's *Landscape with Hunters*, now in the Mauritshuis, dated to just after Van Laer's return to Haarlem in 1639.

Signed, bottom right: PH W (PH in monogram)
Oak panel, 43.8 x 61 cm

Prov.: M. de Brunoy, 1749–1776; his sale, Paris, Joullain fils, 2 Dec. 1776, lot 34. Bt Dubois, 5405 livres; London, Skinner and Dyke, Desenfans sale, 27 Feb. 1795, lot 63); London, Sir Francis Bourgeois, 1807–1811; Bourgeois Bequest, 1811.

Ref.: Smith, 1829–42, I, p. 286, no. 309; Jameson, 1842, p. 462, no. 125; Waagen, 1854, II, p. 343; Richter and Sparkes, 1880, p. 190, no. 125; 1905 cat., pp. 19–20, no. 77; HdG, 1908, II, p. 373, no. 425 (as pendant to DPG79); Cook, 1914, pp. 43–4, no. 77; Murray, 1980a, p. 140; Murray, 1980b, p. 30; Beresford, 1998, p. 265.

Versions and Copies: 1. According to HdG (819) the main group is exactly repeated in a picture then in a private collection. 2. J.P. Foster (DPG archive, letter on file, dated 27 June 1988) refers to a copy or version formerly in a private collection in Poland.

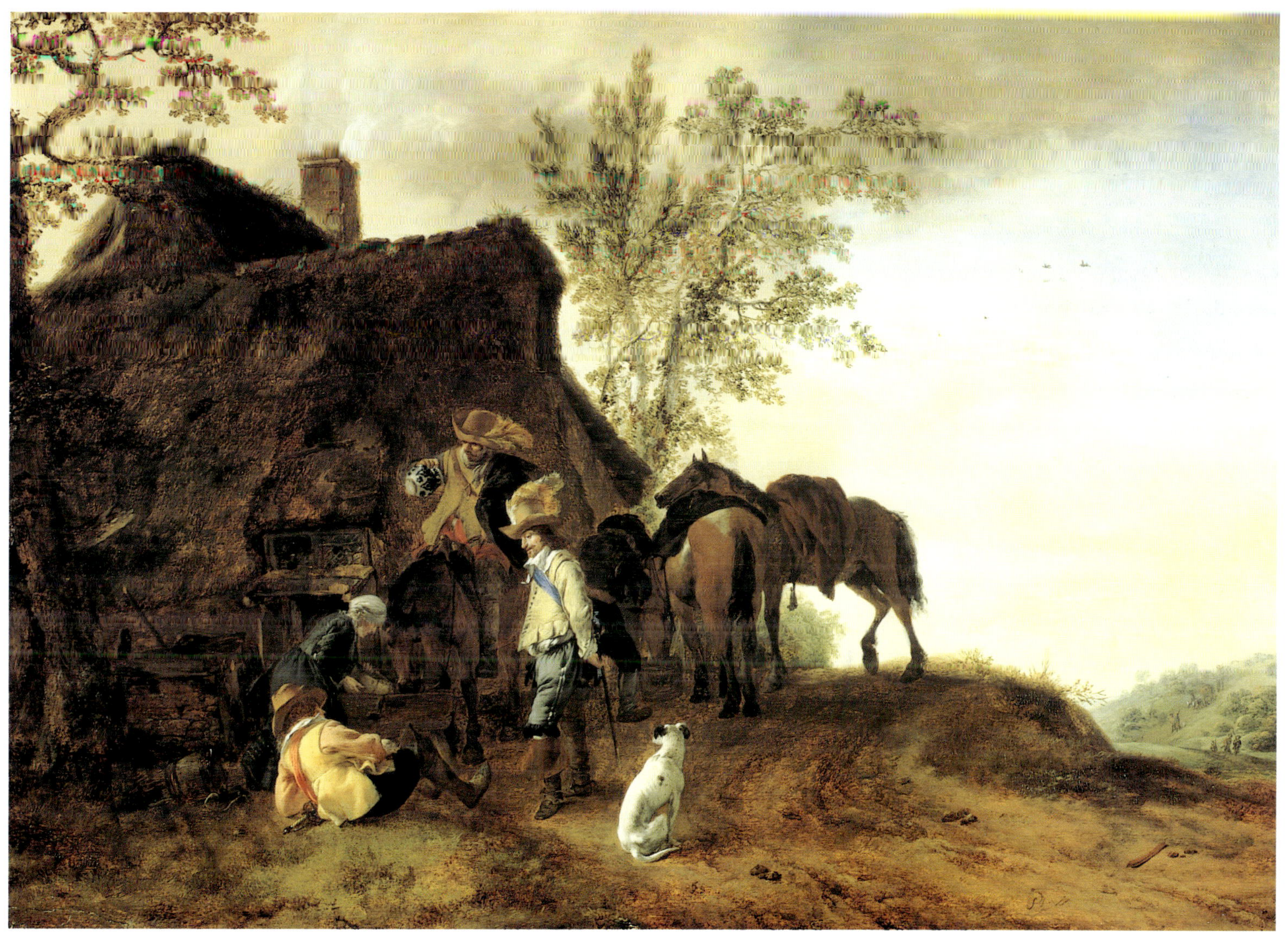

35 **Philips WOUWERMANS**

(Haarlem 1619–1668 Haarlem)

Halt of a Hunting Party

DPG No. 78, Bourgeois Bequest, 1811

Frederick Duparc has suggested a date for this painting in the early 1660s (DPG archive, letter, 1997). This is the grandest of Wouwermans' landscapes at Dulwich, and a comparison with the previous painting (cat. no. 34) sums up very neatly the journey that the artist's style has taken. This is an altogether more polite affair: aristocratic couples out hunting with hawks, dogs and a retinue of servants in an airy panoramic landscape. Wouwermans uses colour to focus our eyes on the resting couple on the left – white horse, red cloak, green dress, yellow jacket, orange dog. Gesture plays its part too, and Wouwermans has orchestrated a genteel ballet of movement and counter-movement across the frieze of figures. The scene is bracketed by a repeated gesture – the doffing of a hat. In one case, it signifies mere manners, part of the exaggerated fluff of courtship; in the other grim reality – an old beggar asks for alms. The beggar, with the defecating dog directly below him, forms a typically Dutch punctuation mark to undercut what could only be described as an access of too much French-ness.

Halt of a Hunting Party was once in the celebrated collection of the Duc d'Orleans before passing, as Mme Anne Leclair has pointed out (DPG archive, letter on file, 31 Mar. 2004), into that of the Marquis de Voyer d'Argenson, where it was inventoried c. 1750. Fredericksen has noted that this painting certainly appears in London at the 1806 sale of the collection of George Craufurd (Crawford), a Scottish merchant whose family had long been resident in Rotterdam and whose brother James was British consul-general in that city. The picture was purchased, along with Du Jardin's *A Smith Shoeing an Ox* (cat. no. 19), by 'North' and next appears in the 1813 inventory of Bourgeois' collection. Bourgeois was friends with the Crawford family (London, British Library, correspondence), and a frequent visitor to their home, so must have known both pictures; it seems likely that North was acting as his agent.

Signed, bottom right: PHILS . W (PHILS in monogram)
Canvas, 55.6 x 82.9 cm

Prov.: Paris, Orléans collection, by 1739); Asnières castle, Marquis Voyer d'Argenson (1722–1782), his inventory [Poitiers, Bibliothèque Universitaire], c. 1750, no. 78 ('"Dépar pour la chasse à l'oiseau" du Cabinet du M. le Chevalier d'Orlèans'); Jan Danser Nijman, 1797; his sale, Amsterdam, (v.d. Schley... Roos), 16 Aug. 1797, lot 303. Bt Van Zanten (or Van Santen, most likely Van Santvoort), 1800 fl 162l; Rotterdam and London, George Craufurd, 1806; his sale, London, Christie's, 'Crawford' sale, 26 Apr. 1806, lot 27. Bt North for £362.5; London, Sir Francis Bourgeois, 1811; Bourgeois Bequest, 1811.

Ref.: Patmore, 1824a, p. 42, no. 119; Smith, 1829–42, I, p. 262, no. 215; Waagen, II, p. 343; Richter and Sparkes, 1880, p. 191, no. 173; 1905 cat., p. 20, no. 78; HdG, 1908, II, p. 456, no. 659; Cook, 1914, p. 44, no. 78; Wilenski, 1955, p. 178; Rosenberg, Slive and Ter Kuile, 1966, p. 281, pl. 141A; Murray, 1980a, p. 140; Murray, 1980b, p. 30; London, Washington and Los Angeles, 1985–6, p. 124, no. 37; Warsaw, 1992, no. 29; Slive, 1995, pp. 210–11, fig. 288; Beresford, 1998, p. 266; Houston and Louisville, 1999–2000, p. 198, no. 70; Amsterdam, 2000, p. 266, no. 178; London, 2002, p. 187, no. 50.

Versions and Copies: 1. Engraving, J. Moyreau, Oeuvres de P.W…, Paris, 1737–62, no. 38. 2. Engraving, R. Cockburn.

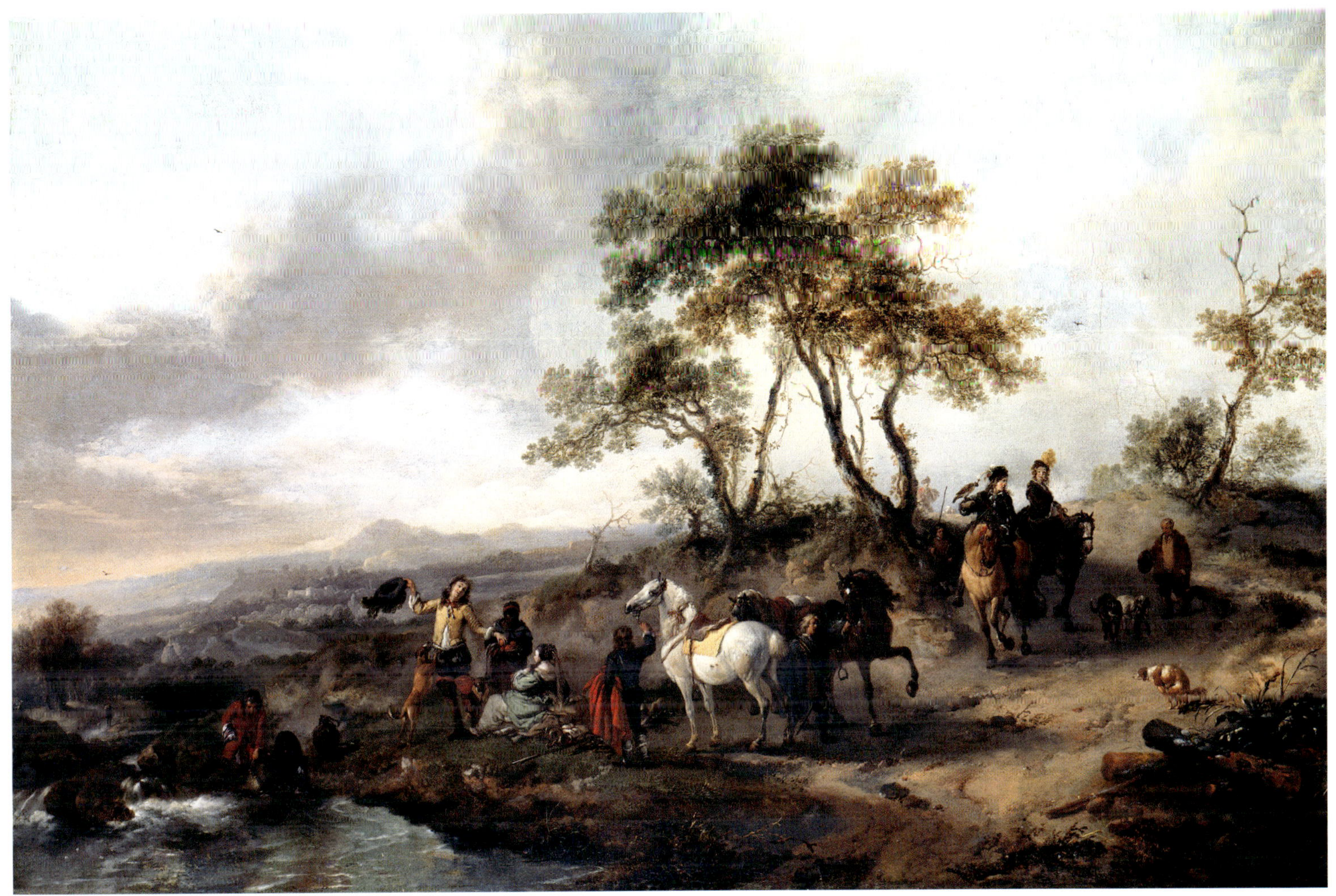

36 Philips WOUWERMANS

(Haarlem 1619–1668 Haarlem)
Two Horsemen near a Fountain
DPG No. 79, Bourgeois Bequest, 1811

This picture has often been considered a companion piece to *Halt of Cavaliers at an Inn* (cat. no. 34). Apart from their similar size, and their superficially identical subject matter (woman gives water to resting riders; dog in attendance) it is hard to imagine why such a conclusion would have been reached. They are certainly not of the same date: the use of the PHILS . W (PHILS in monogram) signature indicates that the picture was produced after 1646 and F. Duparc (DPG archive, letter on file, 1997) has suggested convincingly a dating of 1650/2. Stylistically, the piece can easily be seen as a transitional work on the road to the sophistication and mastery of the *Halt of a Hunting Party* (cat. no. 35). It has the same frieze-like arrangement of characters, the same slightly skewed horizontal panorama, even the careful balance of gesture. However, the woman on the left's gesture looks stiff and studied in comparison to the theatrical posturing of the man with the hat in later painting, and the horses have yet to achieve that Arabian perfection of form and movement.

Signed, bottom right: PHILS . W (PHILS in monogram)
Oak panel, 44.1 x 61.3 cm

Prov.: M. de Brunoy, 1749–1776; his sale, Paris, Joullain fils, 2 Dec. 1776, lot 34. Bt Dubois, 5405 livres; London, Noel Desenfans, 1795–1807: London, Skinner and Dyke, Desenfans sale, 27 Feb. 1795, lot 39; London, Sir Francis Bourgeois, 1807–1811; Bourgeois Bequest, 1811.

Ref.: Patmore, 1824a, p. 42, no. 119; Smith, 1829–42, I, p. 205, no. 308; Waagen, 1854, II, p. 343; Jameson, 1842, p. 462, no. 126; Richter and Sparkes, 1880, p. 190, no. 126; 1905 cat., p. 20, no. 79; HdG, 1908, II, p. 336, no. 293; Cook, 1914, p. 44, no. 79; London, 1952–3, p. 112, no. 205; Murray, 1980a, pp. 140–1; Murray, 1980b, p. 30; Beresford, 1998, p. 266.

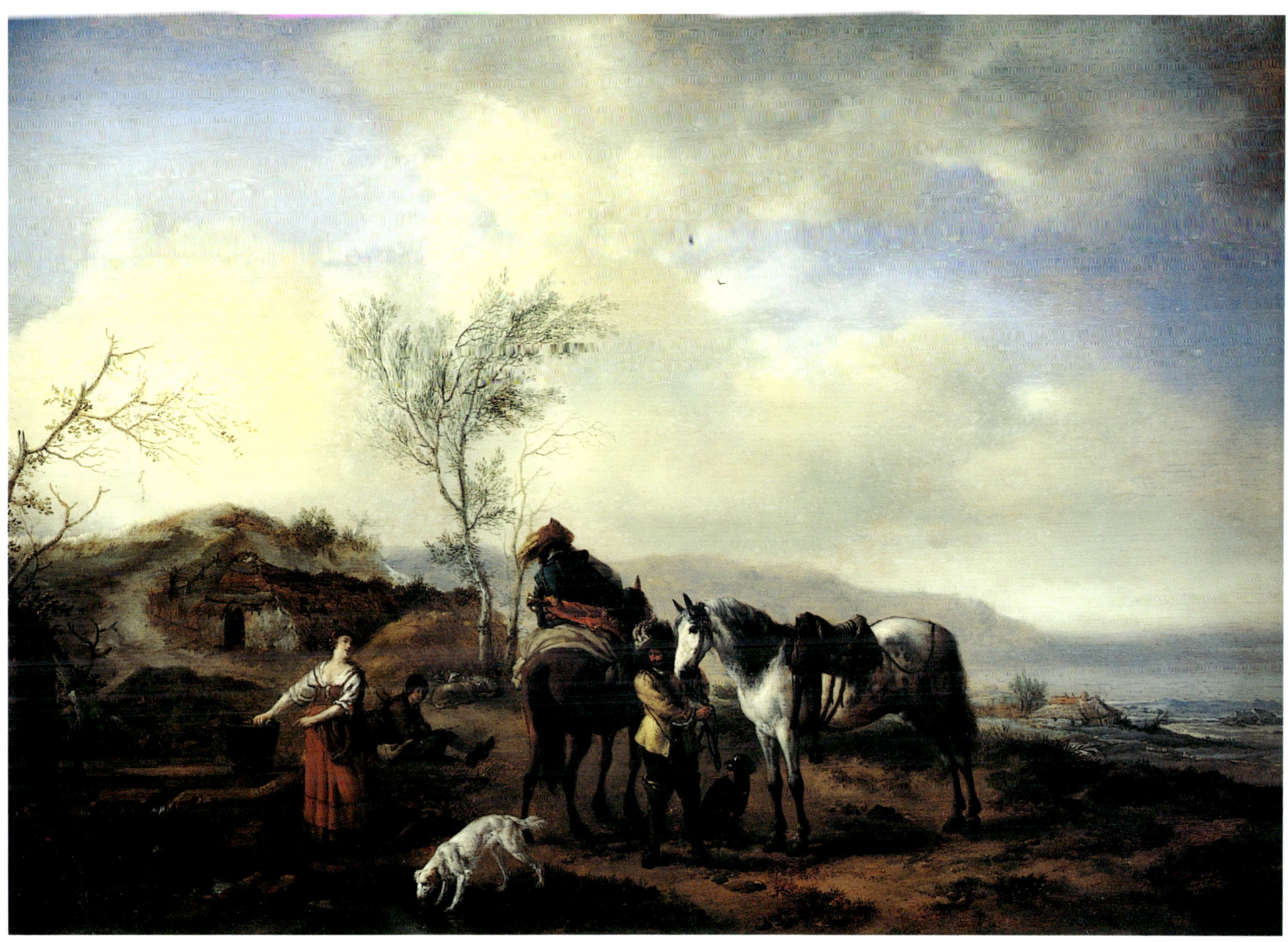

37 **Philips WOUWERMANS**

(Haarlem 1619–1668 Haarlem)

The Return from Hawking

DPG No. 91, Bourgeois Bequest, 1811

Signed, bottom left: PHILSW (PHILS in monogram)
Oak panel, 47.3 x 64.8 cm

Prov.: London, Noel Desenfans, 1804–1807: 1804 Insurance List, no. 84. £400; London, Sir Francis Bourgeois, 1811; Bourgeois Bequest, 1811.

Ref.: Richter and Sparkes, 1880, p. 191, no. 136; 1905 cat., p. 23, no. 91; HdG, 1908, II, p. 471, no. 705; Cook, 1914, p. 54, no. 91; Murray, 1980a, p. 141; Murray, 1980b, pp. 30–1; Beresford, 1998, p. 267.

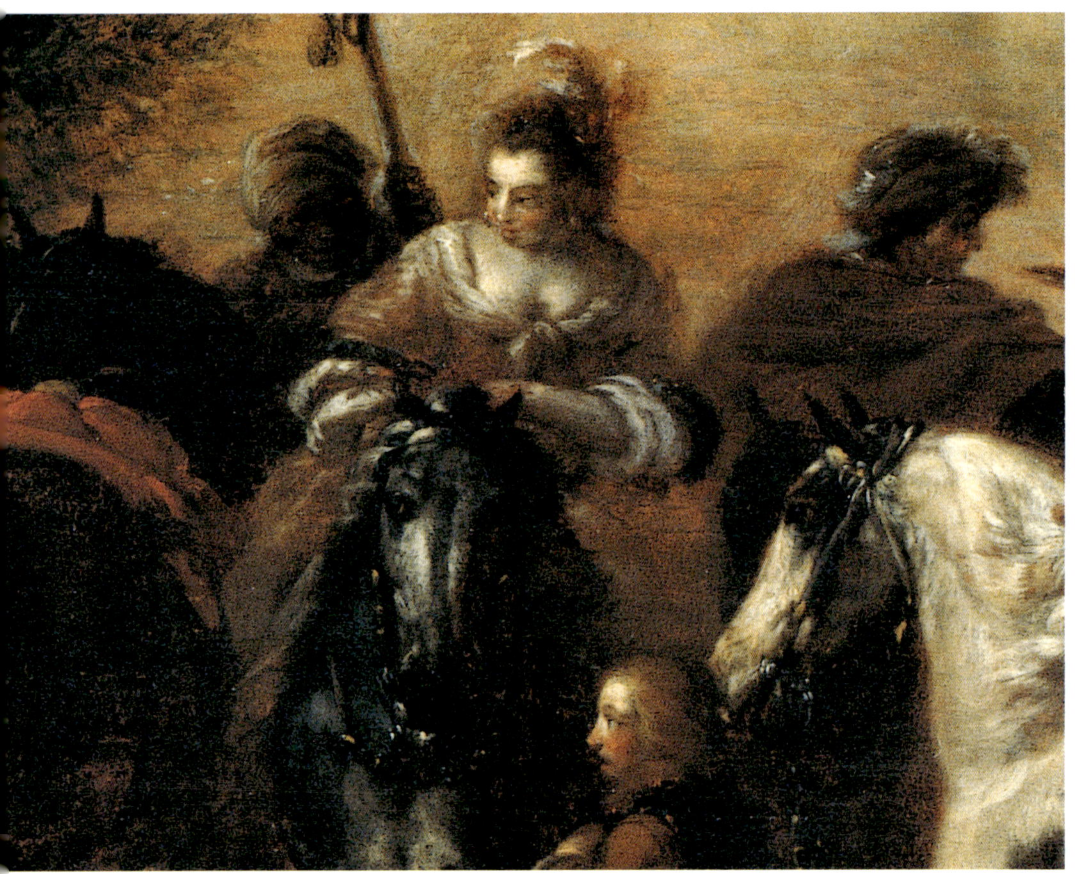

detail

The scene depicts the moment when a group of riders have returned from the hunt. In the centre can be seen a group of horses whose riders have dismounted. Between them is a lady on horseback, a black slave holding a parasol above her. To the left, servants are preparing a picnic under an arbour, beneath the walls of a country villa. F. Duparc (DPG archive, letter on file, 18 Aug. 1997) has dated the picture to the first half of the 1660s.

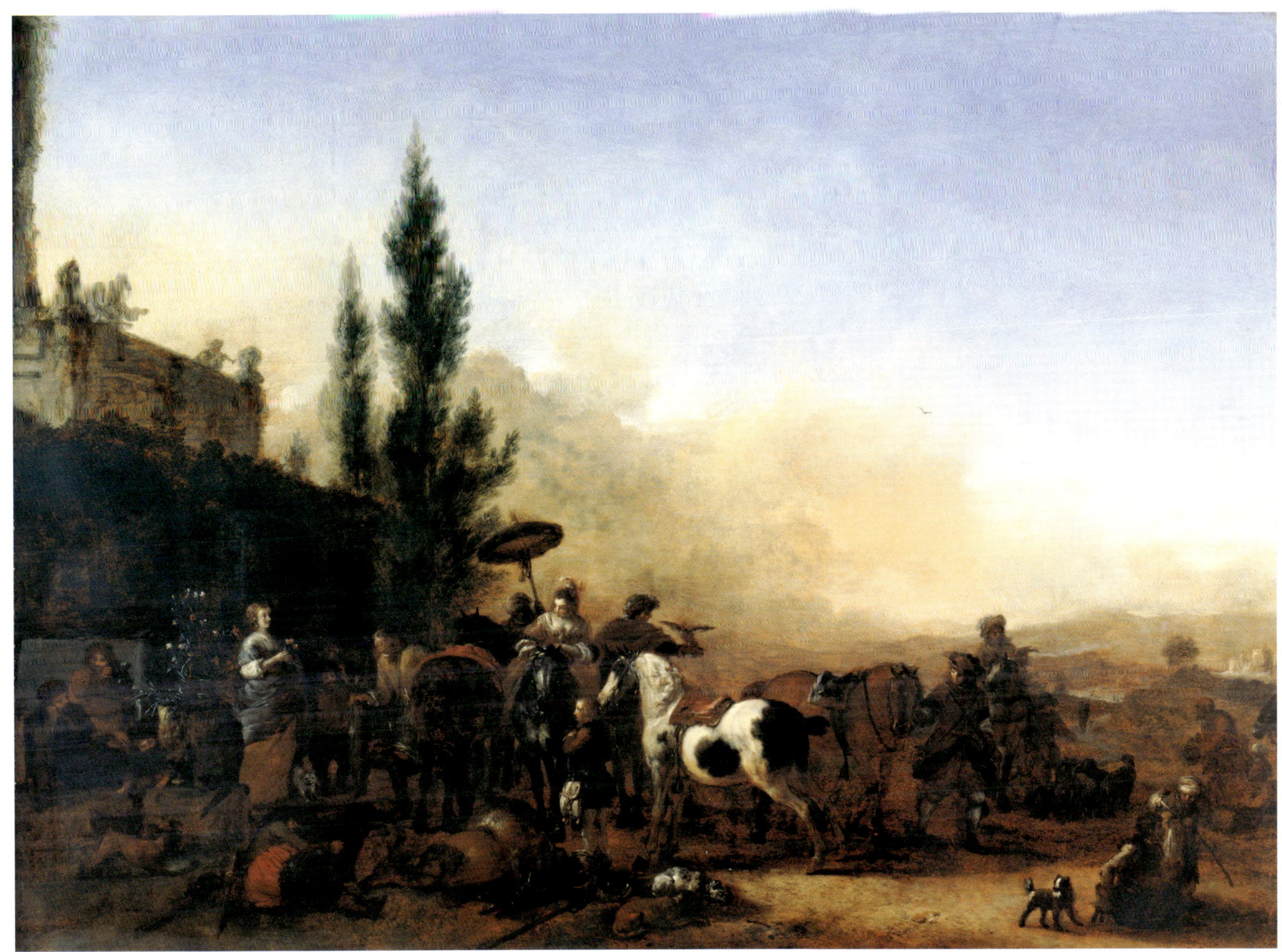

38 Philips WOUWERMANS

(Haarlem 1619–1668 Haarlem)

Halt of Travellers

DPG No. 97, Bourgeois Bequest, 1811

Signed, bottom left: PHILS W (PHILS in monogram)
Oak panel, 45.1 x 41.6 cm

Prov.: London, Noel Desenfans, 1802–1807: London, Skinner and Dyke, Desenfans sale, 17 Mar. 1802, lot 124 (Descriptive Catalogue no. 114. £220.10); London, Sir Francis Bourgeois, 1807–1811; Bourgeois Bequest, 1811.

Ref.: Smith, 1829–42, Vol. I, pp. 266–7, no. 232; Jameson, 1842, p. 466, no. 144; Richter and Sparkes, 1880, p. 190, no. 144; 1905 cat., p. 25, no. 97; HdG, 1908, II, pp. 342–3, no. 317 (both, probably wrongly, as exhibited at the British Gallery in 1815); Cook, 1914, p. 57, no. 97; Murray, 1980a, p. 141; Murray, 1980b, p. 31; Beresford, 1998, p. 268.

Halt of Travellers is an early work, though using the post 1646 signature style of PHILS . W (PHILS in monogram). Duparc has suggested a date of c. 1647/9 (DPG archive, letter on file, 1997). The use of a diagonal skyline and the coarse figures is typical of Wouwermans' output during a period when he was heavily under the influence of Pieter van Laer. On the other hand, Hofstede de Groot pointed to the influence of Isaac van Ostade on the work in the depth of its colouring.

First recorded in Desenfans' 1802 sale, according to the Descriptive Catalogue this painting was acquired from a collector at Amsterdam, which seems likely as it does not seem to appear in Dutch sale catalogues from 1790 to 1802. It is therefore likely that the earlier provenance of the picture will continue to be obscure.

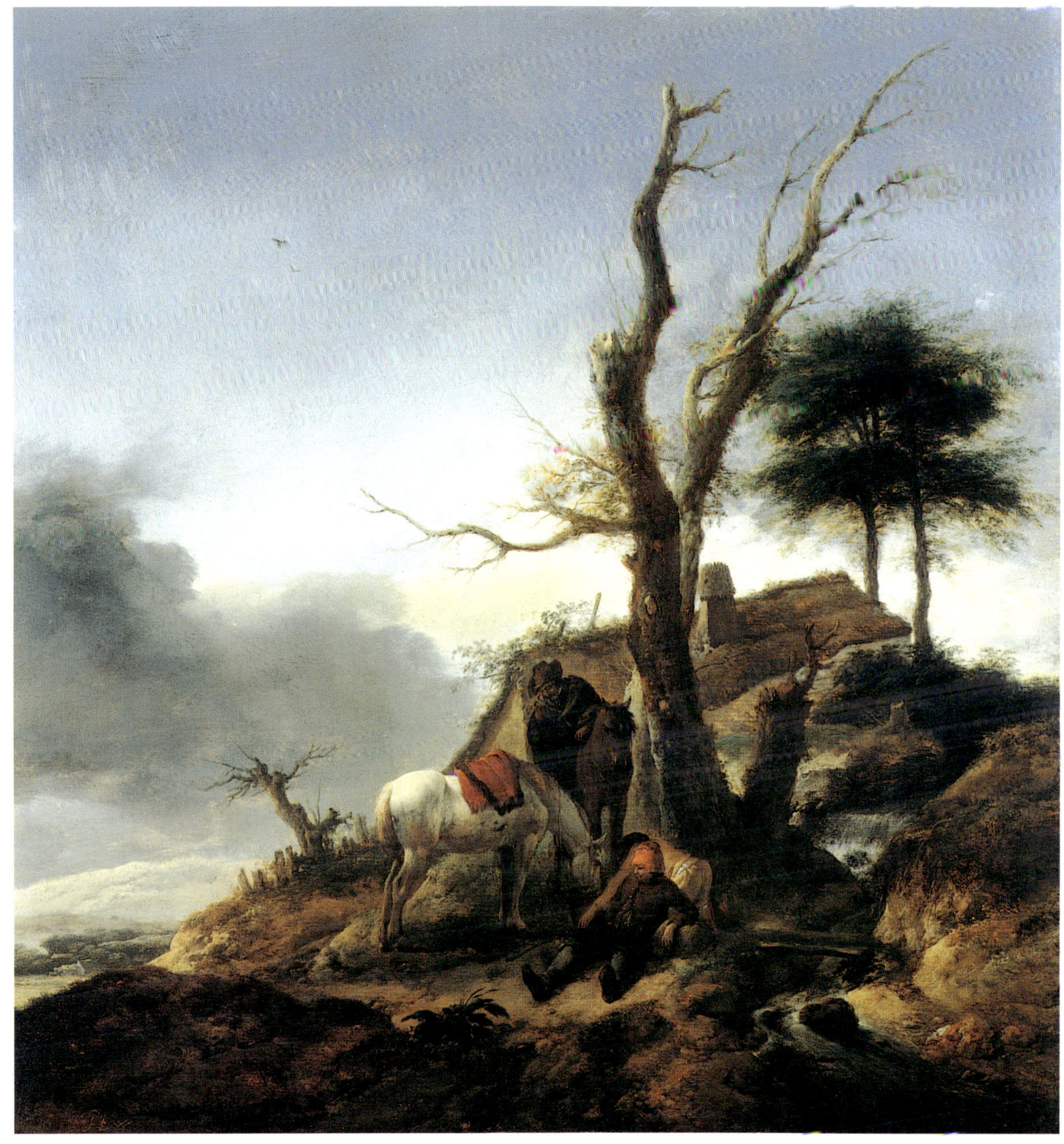

39 Philips WOUWERMANS

(Haarlem 1619–1668 Haarlem)
Peasants in the Fields: Hay Harvest
DPG No. 182, Bourgeois Bequest, 1811

Signed, bottom left: PHILS W (PHILS in monogram)
Oak panel, 41.3 x 35.9 cm

Prov.: Soeterwoude, J. van Bergan van der Grijp and others sale, 25 Jun. 1784, lot 134. Bt Fouquet, 1,225 florins [Acc. to HdG]; London, Noel Desenfans, 1804–1807: 1804 Insurance List, no. 83. £600; London, Sir Francis Bourgeois, 1807–1811; Bourgeois Bequest, 1811.

Ref.: Patmore, 1824b, p. 181; Smith, 1829–42, Vol. I, p. 286, no. 311; Jameson, 1842, p. 480, no. 228; Waagen, 1854, II, p. 343; Richter and Sparkes, 1880, pp. 190–1, no. 228; 1905 cat., p. 48, no. 182; HdG, 1908, II, pp. 559–60, no. 941; Cook, 1914, pp. 116–17, no. 182; Murray, 1980a, p. 141; Murray, 1980b, p. 31; Duparc, 1993; Beresford, 1998, p. 269.

Versions and Copies: 1. Engraving, R. Cockburn, no. 50, 1816.

Frederik Duparc has proposed (DPG archive, letter on file, 1997) a date in the second half of the 1650s because of its silvery tonality. Here, Wouwermans' trademark white horse is of a stockier variety than the elegant mount of his 1660s *Halt of a Hunting Party* (cat. no. 35). The composition and its atmosphere are more reminiscent of the gentle observational humour of Karel du Jardin than the 'low-life' scenes of Pieter van Laer. The point is well made by a comparison between this picture and the earlier *Halt of Travellers* (cat. no. 38), with which it has much in common in terms of composition. In atmosphere, in the balance of light and dark, and in the sense of enveloping air and space, however, the later picture represents a considerable progression.

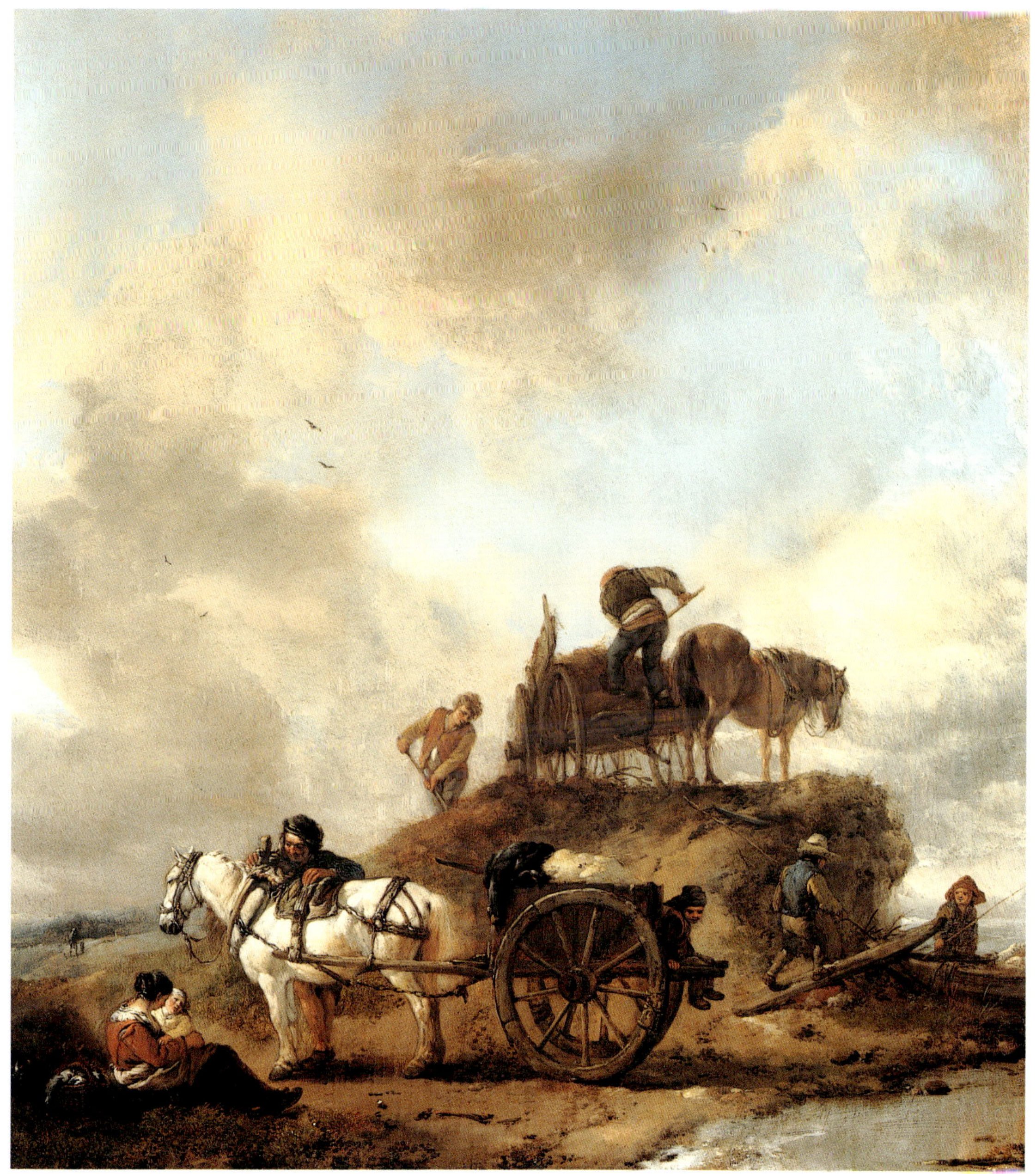

Artists' Biographies

Nicolaes BERCHEM

(Haarlem 1620–1683 Amsterdam)

Nicolaes Berchem is one of the towering figures of the Dutch Italianate style. Son of the great still-life master Pieter Claesz, he began his education with his father. He may have also studied with several other artists, including Van Goyen, Moeyaert, Pieter de Grebber and Jan Wils. He seems to have enjoyed the environment of the studio, for he was a notable teacher as well as serial pupil: not only to Romeyn and Du Jardin, but also, according to Houbraken, Pieter de Hooch and Jacob Ochtervelt, amongst others. It is perhaps this ability to mix and share ideas with other artists that is the secret of his prolonged influence. Notably, he was a good friend of Jacob van Ruisdael – travelling with him to Westphalia, if the pictorial evidence is to be believed. Up to three trips to Italy have been proposed for him, although none are documented; it is pretty certain, however, that he must have gone in the early 1650s. The influence of Berchem is strongly in evidence well into the 18th and 19th centuries, particularly in France. Anyone thinking that the stylised decorativeness and brilliant brushwork of Francois Boucher came out of nowhere need only look at Berchem's decorative figure work, which can look astonishingly rococo. His Dutch Italianate landscapes are amongst the most vibrant and distinctive of all; but he was remarkably inventive and varied in his output, producing fancy history pieces, battle scenes and allegories. His figure style was an elegant development of Van Laer's, and just as influential. He was extremely well paid, and earnt it, producing a very large body of work.

Jan BOTH

(Utrecht? c. 1615–1652 Utrecht)

Jan Both was one of the most influential and important of the Dutch Italianate painters, the presiding genius of the so-called 'second generation'. Unlike Aelbert Cuyp, Both had not only travelled to Italy, but had collaborated with Claude himself (and Herman van Swaneveldt) on a seminal commission in the development of landscape painting as a genre – two major landscape series for the Buen Retiro palace in Madrid, commissioned by Don Manuel de Moura, Marqués de Castel Rodrigo and ambassador of Philip IV. Both had an artistic family background; his father Dirck Boot [sic] was a glass painter, and his elder brother Andries another Dutch Italianate artist whose career was cut short when he drowned in a Venetian canal in 1642. Sandrart, who knew both brothers, claimed that they studied with Abraham Bloemart, and that Jan also worked with Honthorst. His style owes little or nothing to either.

Abraham van CALRAET

(Dordrecht 1642–1722 Dordrecht)

Dulwich owns five pictures by this artist. Thanks to similarities of style and to the simple fact of signing with his initials (A.C.) the true authorship of his work, and this was certainly the case with these five paintings, was regularly lost under attribution to Aelbert Cuyp (in this case until 1953, although Bredius had suggested the genuine attribution as early as 1919). Calraet's relationship with Cuyp is not entirely clear: an apprenticeship with Dordrecht's leading artist would seem to have been probable, and according to Houbraken, Calraet's brother Barent certainly trained with Cuyp. He owned works by, and copies after, both Cuyp and Wouwermans, and the latter artist provides the other key influence on his style.

Govaert CAMPHUYSEN

(Gorinchem? 1623/4–1672 Amsterdam?)

Camphuysen's animal paintings and his preference for dramatic lighting effects link him visually with both Paulus Potter and Adriaen van de Velde, artists who share a similarly atmospheric and poetic intensity. Starting out as a portrait painter in Amsterdam in the early 1640s, but moving on to animals and landscape by c. 1650, in general his early career seems to have been unsuccessful in that one of the dated documents associated with him is a 1652 inventory of his house and possessions, drawn up before a sale to pay off his debts. He left this low point behind and set out for Stockholm and life as a court painter; he is recorded there in 1655 working for the Dowager Queen Hedvig Eleonora. His will, drawn up in 1667, confirms that he had by then returned to Amsterdam. His works are not particularly well-known, and many – like Dulwich's – were misattributed to the more famous Potter.

Aelbert CUYP

(Dordrecht 1620–1691 Dordrecht)

Cuyp was one of the greatest Dutch landscape painters. He travelled widely in Holland and in the Rhineland, but never apparently went to Italy. However, enough of the visual language of the Dutch Italianates was available and familiar in Holland from the work of, for instance, Jan Both in Utrecht, for his work to have an undeniable Italianate feel to it, particularly in the treatment of light. By any standards, Cuyp's mastery of romantic half-light, particularly in his middle distances, is magically poetic. His delicate trees remind us more of Claude than of Ruisdael. He rather defies labelling, yet aspects of his output regularly tempt us to try – the 18th-century English market that discovered and idolised him thought of him as the 'Dutch Claude'. During his lifetime and immediately afterwards, he was not well-known at all outside Dordrecht, and his marriage in 1658 to an extremely wealthy widow helped eclipse his reputation – he was well-known, but for owning land rather than painting it. Indeed he seems to have stopped painting altogether, and his last thirty years were spent as a pillar of society.

Cuyp's remarkable popularity in Britain began in the last quarter of the 18th century. By the time the market for his works peaked, around 1870, about 75%

of all known Cuyps were in British collections, and his influence on British artists from Gainsborough to Constable was profound. Noel Desenfans, co-founder of Dulwich Picture Gallery, played an important role in the 'discovery' of Cuyp by the English. The Gallery owns six magnificent Cuyps, five other pictures no longer attributed to him, and five works which Desenfans thought were by Cuyp but which are in fact by Abraham Calraet – a common error until relatively recently.

Karel DU JARDIN

(Probably Amsterdam 1621/2–1678 Venice)

Du Jardin trained with Berchem (it is supposed, although no documentary evidence exists to prove it) and probably made a trip to Italy in the 1640s (again supposition, but generally accepted). He was chiefly a painter of Dutch Italianate landscapes, but also produced some ambitious history paintings, and even some portraits. He made probably his second trip to Italy in 1675, and rejoiced in the *Schildersbent* nick-name of 'Goat-beard'. His keen observation of animals, seen with affection and humour, often marks him out from the routine Van Laer-isms of other Italianate painters; this has led to suggestions that he may have worked with Paulus Potter at some stage.

Carel Cornelisz.DE HOOCH

(Active 1620–died 1638 Utrecht)

About Carel de Hooch very little is known, and his style is so close to that of Bartholomeus Breenbergh and Cornelis van Poelenburch it seems remarkable his name has come down to us at all. He died in Utrecht, and was made a member of the Guild there in 1633; but he was recorded as a painter in Haarlem in 1628. He must have worked in the orbit, at least, of Breenbergh, who was based close by, in Amsterdam.

Jan van KESSEL

(Amsterdam 1641–1680 Amsterdam)

Van Kessel has been doomed to a double obscurity. Firstly, he shares a name with a family of Flemish artists working in very different styles, leading to considerable confusion. Then, he swims in that enormous pool of minor artists whose work can be described as 'school of Ruisdael'. It seems almost impossible that he should not in fact have been a pupil of the great landscapist. He was certainly satisfied to work in his style, and to repeat Ruisdael's range of subject matter, although he was clearly aware of Hobbema and Wijnants also. He works the same territory – the dune and forest landscape surrounding Haarlem – as other fellow alumni of the 'school of Ruisdael' like Jan Vermeer of Haarlem and Anthonie van Borssum.

Jan LAPP

(The Hague c. 1600?–after 1662 Amsterdam)

Works by Jan Lapp are rare; there are some dated examples from 1636. Even his identity as an artist was obscure until the early 20th century. Nothing very much is known about him, apart from the fact that he was documented as a member of the painters' guild in The Hague in 1625. His works (as in this case) often lurked beneath an attribution to Karel du Jardin, with whose style – and Paulus Potter's – he has something in common. His work is undeniably Italianate, though whether as a result of a personal trip to Italy is unknown.

Jan LINGELBACH

(Frankfurt am Main 1622–1674 Amsterdam)

Although born in Germany, Lingelbach's family was in Amsterdam by the time he was twelve, and it is almost certain therefore that he trained in that city – although there is no documentation to tell us with whom. He died there also, and is documented there from 1653. However, it is less certain, through lack of evidence, how he spent his time in the 1640s. According to Houbraken he went to France in 1642, and is recorded in Rome in 1647–9, but he may well have arrived earlier. Either way, he spent several years in Italy, developing another strand of Pieter van Laer's seminal 'low-life' genre scenes into heavily populated, romantically colourful depictions of Carnival and bustling seaports reflecting a glamorous evocation of a multicultural mercantile society which no doubt appealed to the Dutch world view. Jan Baptist Weenix and Lingelbach made harbour scenes into a popular Italianate genre in its own right.

Cornelis van POELENBURCH

(Utrecht 1594/5–1667 Utrecht)

Poelenburch trained with Abraham Bloemart in his native Utrecht, then travelled to Rome by 1617, remaining in Italy for at least six (probably more like eight) years. He is one of the most important of the so-called 'first generation' Dutch Italianate artists, part of that initial group who, along with Claude Lorrain, developed the new genre of classical landscape. Highly visible influences on his work were the German (but based in Rome) painter Adam Elsheimer and the Flemish/Roman landscapist Paul Bril. Elsheimer died in 1610, but the impact of his small-scale, stunningly-detailed and highly imaginative works was still prominent in Rome. From him Poelenburch ultimately derived his preference for working on a small scale on panel or copper, as well has his high finish and interest in mythological themes. Bril was also a specialist in tiny, jewel-like, highly-coloured landscapes. Poelenburch's own work has a cooler tonality, and his landscapes are firmly grounded in close observation of the Roman campagna. During his stay in Rome he became one of the founder members of the *Schildersbent*, boasting a *bentvueghel* nickname of 'Satyr'. From 1627 until his death he worked in Utrecht – with the exception of a brief period as court artist to Charles I of England, from 1637 to 1641. He was one of the most popular artists of his day, particularly admired for his figures. Later generations tended to confuse attributions with Bartholomeus Breenbergh, a confusion that has only been sorted out comparatively recently.

Adam PYNACKER

(Schiedam 1620/1–1673 Amsterdam)

According to Houbraken, Pynacker spent three years in Italy in the 1640s; but it is quite possible that he was there in his capacity as wine merchant, employed by his merchant father. By 1649 he was in Delft, but he died in Amsterdam, where he had moved in 1661. Although there are echoes of various artists in his work – Potter and Both must have influenced him, and Berchem certainly did – and he counts as a Dutch Italianate, Pynacker's style was intensely individual always. He died in poverty; but his unique genius seems to be more immediately accessible to modern audiences than, say, that of Berchem.

William ROMEYN

(Haarlem c. 1624–after 1693 Haarlem?)

William Romeyn was born in Haarlem; he is recorded there in 1642 as a pupil of Nicolaes Berchem, who clearly influenced his style. He can also be strongly reminiscent of Karel du Jardin. He visited Rome in 1650–1 and developed a very typical Dutch Italianate style, with considerable skill. He was well enough thought of to serve as *hoofdman* in his native Haarlem's Guild of St Luke, and his early work is good enough to have been regularly mistaken for Du Jardin or Berchem.

Jan WEENIX

(Amsterdam 1642–1719 Amsterdam)

Weenix was trained by his father, Jan Baptist Weenix, an artist so thoroughly imbued with the spirit of Italy as to take to signing his works Gio[vanni] Batt[ist]a. Weenix Senior specialised in Italianate landscapes with classical ruins, and developed a particularly distinctive line in colourful harbour scenes. Weenix the younger became best known for large still lifes of dead game, but he started out in the manner of his father.

Thomas WIJCK

(Beverwijck c. 1616–1677 Haarlem)

Thomas Wijck spent most of his career in Haarlem, but travelled to Italy c. 1640 (he was back home in 1642). In the 1660s, after the Restoration of Charles II, he visited London, where he apparently witnessed and painted the Great Fire. The galvanising influence on Wijck was that of the *Bamboccianti* in Rome; although he doesn't date his works, those that are most Italianate in their details are certainly closer to the beginning of his career. Many drawings survive, and he made good use of those he had done in Rome – they lend a real sense of authenticity to works produced miles, and years, away from the Eternal City.

Jan WIJNANTS

(Haarlem? 1631/2–1684 Amsterdam)

The date of Wijnants' birth is unknown; it could be as late as 1635 – and many past scholars have assumed it was much earlier. His father was an art dealer based in Haarlem, and it makes perfect sense for that town to have been Wijnants' birthplace and home, given how much of his landscape output seems to have focused on the very particular dune landscape that surrounds it. After an interlude in Rotterdam in the 1650s, the last twenty-four years of his life were spent in Amsterdam. He ran an inn there as a supplement to his income, but was continuously in debt nevertheless. Wijnants, like many other landscapists, regularly used other artists to add the figures to his works, and collaborated in this way with Adriaen van de Velde (whom he is supposed to have taught) and Lingelbach. The overwhelming influence on his work was clearly Jacob van Ruisdael, from whom he borrowed subject matter and motifs – he may possibly have studied with him. However, he was open to other influences; he certainly came in contact with the Italianate artists (Pynacker, for instance, was in Rotterdam at the same time as Wijnants), and in his Amsterdam period his landscapes bask in Italian light. While he could never really be described as Dutch Italianate, at least some of his landscapes can. Wijnants has been slightly short-changed by art history; his name is certainly not as well known now as it was in the 18th century, when the young Gainsborough was clearly familiar with, and influenced by, his work.

Philips WOUWERMANS

(Haarlem 1619–1668 Haarlem)

Wouwermans was the son of one artist (Pauwels), and brother to two more (Pieter and Johannes, both of whom seem to have been subsumed into their more talented brother's studio). The return of Pieter van Laer (*Il Bamboccio*) from Italy to Haarlem in 1638 seems to have caught the young Wouwermans at a seminal moment (he joined the Haarlem Guild in 1640). The story, told by Houbraken, that Wouwermans acquired sketches and notebooks of Van Laer's after the latter's death, whether true or not, certainly reflects the impact of Van Laer's famous figure style and subject matter on the younger artist. As Wouwermans developed, a more courtly and decorative style emerged, and he was always famous for his horses. His landscapes are not strictly Italianate (there is no evidence that he ever visited Italy), but have a certain silvery picturesque quality that appealed to an aristocratic market, particularly in France, where he was heavily collected. Hunting and military scenes were his specialties. He was amazingly prolific, even discounting the fact that some work by his brothers probably still lurks within his accepted oeuvre, and very successful – he died a rich man. His reputation remained exceptionally high throughout the 18th century and into the 19th, when it finally struck the rock that seems to have temporarily sunk most of the Italianate artists. However, when Dulwich's founders were putting together their collection, he was at a peak of collectability. Desenfans and Bourgeois acquired a dozen paintings then attributed to him (seven are still).

Select Bibliography

1905 cat.: *Catalogue of the Pictures in the Gallery of Alleyn's College of God's Gift at Dulwich, with Biographical Notices of the Painters*, London, 1905

1926 cat.: E. Cook, *Catalogue of the Pictures in the Gallery of Alleyn's College of God's gift at Dulwich, revised and further revised and completed by the Governors*, London, 1926

1953 cat.: *A Brief Catalogue of the Pictures in Dulwich College Picture Gallery*, 1953

Amsterdam 2000: Amsterdam, Rijksmuseum, *The Glory of the Golden Age*, exh. cat. (Judikje Kiers and Fieke Tissink), 2000

Amsterdam, Boston and Philadelphia, 1987: Amsterdam, Rijksmuseum; Boston, MA, Museum of Fine Arts; Philadelphia, PA, Museum of Art, *Masters of 17th-century Dutch Landscape Paintings*, exh. cat., ed. P. Sutton, 1987–8

Anon., *Beauties of the Dulwich Picture Gallery*, London, 1824

Beresford, 1998: R. Beresford, *Dulwich Picture Gallery: Complete Illustrated Catalogue*, London ,1998

Bernt, 1970: W. Bernt, *The Netherlandish Painters of the Seventeenth Century*, Revised ed., 3 vols, London, 1970

Bredius, 1919: A. Bredius, 'Further light upon the painter Calraet', *Burlington Magazine* 35, (September) 1919

Bredius and Moes, 1903: A. Bredius and E.W. Moes, 'De Schilders Camphuysen', *Oud Holland* 21, 1903

Brochhagen, 1957: E. Brochhagen, 'Karel Dujardins spate Landschaften', *Bulletin, Musées Royaux des Beaux-Arts* VI, Brussels, 1957, p. 236ff

Brochhagen, 1958: E. Brochhagen, '*Karel Dujardin: Ein Beitrag zum Italianismus in Holland im 17. Jahrhundert*', Ph.D diss., U. Cologne, 1958

Buchanan, 1824: W. Buchanan, *Memories of Painting*, 2 vols, London, 1824

Burger Wegener, 1976: C. Burger Wegener, *Johannes Lingelbach, 1622–1674*, Schwerin, 1976

Burke, 1976: J.D. Burke, *Jan Both. Paintings, Drawings and Prints*, New York, 1976

Burnett, 1969: D.G. Burnett, 'The Landscapes of Aelbert Cuyp', *Apollo* 89, 1969, pp. 372–80

Chiarini, 1972: M. Chiarini, 'Filippo Napoletano, Van poelenburgh, Breenbergh e la Nascita del paesaggio realistico in Italia', *Paragone* XXIII, 1972

Chong, 1992: A. Chong, '*Aelbert Cuyp and the Meaning of Landscape*', Ph.D diss., New York University, 1992

Cook, 1914: E. Cook, *Catalogue of the Pictures in the Gallery of Alleyn's College of God's gift at Dulwich*, London, 1914

Davies, 1992: A. I. Davies, *Jan van Kessel (1641–1680)*, Doornspijk, 1992

Desenfans, N., *A Descriptive Catalogue (with remarks and anecdotes never before published in English) of some Pictures of the Different Schools purchased for His Majesty the Late King of Poland*, 2 vols, London, 1802

Duparc, 1980: F. J. Duparc et al., *Mauritshuis, Hollandse schilderkunst: Landschappen 17de eeuw*, The Hague, 1980

Duparc, 1993: F. J. Duparc, 'Philips Wouwerman, 1619–1668', *Oud Holland* 107, 1993, pp. 257–86

Eisele, 2000: K. Eisele, *Jan Wijnants (1631/32–84): Ein Niederlandischer Maler der Ideallandschaft im Goldenen Jahrhundert*, Stuttgart, 2000

Fleischer, 1989: R. G. Fleischer, *Ludolf de Jongh*, Doornspijk, 1989

Gerson, 1953. National Gallery, London, *Netherlandish Art – Part 2*, exh. cat. (H. Gerson), 1953

Harwood, 1985: Laurie B. Harwood, 'Revelling in Contemplation: Adam Pynacker (c. 1620–73) and British Collectors', *Country Life*, August 22, 1985, pp. 486–8

Harwood, 1988: Laurie B. Harwood, *Adam Pynacker (c. 1620–1673)*, Doornspijk, 1988

Hazlitt, 1843: *Criticisms on Art, and Sketches of the Picture Galleries of England*, 1843

HdG: C. Hofstede de Groot, *A Catalogue raisonné of the works of the most eminent Dutch painters of the seventeenth century, based on the works of John Smith, 1907–28*

Houbraken, 1718–21: A. Houbraken, *De Groote Schouburgh*, 1718–21

Houston and Louisville, 1999–2000: The Museum of Fine Arts, Houston, Texas; The Speed Art Museum, Louisville, Kentucky, *Rembrandt to Gainsborough: Masterpieces from Dulwich Picture Gallery*, exh. cat. (Ian Dejardin, Desmond Shawe-Taylor and Giles Waterfield), 2000

Jameson, 1842: A.B. Jameson, *Hand-book to the Public Galleries of Art in and near London*, London, 1842

Kilian, Jennifer M. *The Paintings of Karel du Jardin (1626–1678), Catalogue Raisonné*, Studies in the Arts of the Low Countries 8, 2005

Kren, 1978: T. Kren, *Jan Miel (1598–1664), a Flemish Painter in Rome*, II, diss., Yale University, 1978

London, 1995: *Conserving Old Masters*, exh. cat., Dulwich Picture Gallery, London, 1995

London, 1903: *Exhibition of Works by the Old Masters and Deceased Masters of the British School, Including a Collection of Paintings by Aelbert Cuyp...*, Royal Academy, London, 1903

London and Leeds, 1947: *Some Pictures from the Dulwich Gallery*, The National Gallery, London, 1947

London, 2002: Dulwich Picture Gallery, London, *Inspired by Italy: Dutch Landscape Painting 1600–1700*, exh. cat., ed. L. Harwood, 2002

London RA, Dutch, 1952/3: *Dutch Pictures 1450–1750*, Royal Academy, London, 1952/3

London, 1973: *Aelbert Cuyp in British Collections*, The National Gallery, London (cat. by Stephen Reiss), 1973

London, Washington and Los Angeles, 1985–6: National Gallery of Art, Washington D.C.; Los Angeles County Museum of Art, *Collection for a King: Old Master Paintings from the Dulwich Picture Gallery*, exh. cat., 1985–86

Michel, 1890: E. Michel, *Jacob van Ruysdael et les paysagistes de l'ecole de Harlem*, Paris, 1890

Montreal, 1990: The Montreal Museum of Fine Arts, *Italian Recollections: Dutch Painters of the Golden Age*, exh. cat. (Frederik J. Duparc and Linda Graif), 1990

Murray, 1980a: P. Murray, *The Dulwich Picture Gallery: A Catalogue*, London, 1980

Murray, 1980b: P. Murray, *The Dulwich Picture Gallery: A Handlist*, London, 1980

Norwich, 1988: Norwich Castle Museum, *Dutch and Flemish Painting in Norfolk*, exh. cat. (Andrew W. Moore), 1988

Patmore, 1824: P.G. Patmore, *British Galleries of Art*, London, 1824

Plietzch, 1960: E. Plietzch, *Hollandische und flamische Maler des XVII. Jahrhunderts*, Leipzig, 1960

Reiss, 1953: S. Reiss, 'Aelbert Cuyp', *Burlington Magazine* 95 (Feburary 1953), pp. 42–7

Reiss, 1975: S. Reiss, *Aelbert Cuyp*, London, 1975

Richter and Sparkes, 1880: J. P. Richter and J.C.L. Sparkes, *Catalogue of the Pictures in the Dulwich College Gallery with Biographical Notices of the Painters*, London, 1880

Rijksmuseum, Amsterdam, *Karel du Jardin 1626–1678*, exh. cat. (Jennifer M. Kilian), 2007

Roethlisberger, 1969: M. Roethlisberger, *Bartholomeus Breenbergh, Handzichnungen*, Berlin, 1969

Roethlisberger, 1981: M. Roethlisberger, *Bartholomeus Breenbergh, The Paintings*, Berlin and New York, 1981

Rosenberg, 1928: J. Rosenberg, *Jacob van Ruisdael*, Berlin, 1928

Rosenberg, Slive and Ter Kuile, 1966: J. Rosenberg, S. Slive and E.H. Ter Kuile, *Dutch Art and Architecture, 1600 to 1800*, Harmondsworth, 1966

Ruskin, 1843: J. Ruskin, *Modern Painters*, vols I–V, London 1843

Schaar, 1958: E. Schaar, *'Studien zu Nicolaes Berchem'*, Ph.D dissertation, U. Cologne, 1958

Schloss, 1983: C. Schloss, 'The Early Italianate Genre Paintings by Jan Weenix (c. 1642–1719)', *Oud Holland* XCVII, 1983

Simon, 1927–30: K. E. Simon, *Jacob van Ruisdael, Eine Darstellung seiner Entwicklung*, Berlin 1927 (reprinted with errata and addenda, 1930)

Slive, 1995: S. Slive, *Dutch painting 1600–1800*, New Haven and London, 1995

Slive, 2001: S. Slive, *Jacob van Ruisdael: a complete catalogue of his paintings, drawings, and etchings*, New Haven and London, 2001

Sluijter-Seiffert, 1984: N.C. Sluijter-Seifert: *Cornelis van Poelenburch*, c. 1593–1667, Leiden, 1984

Smith, 1829–42: J. Smith, *A Catalogue Raisonné of the works of the Most Eminent Dutch, Flemish, and French Painters*, 9 vols. London, 1829–1842

Sparkes, 1876: J.C.L. Sparkes, *A Descriptive Catalogue of the Pictures in the Dulwich College Gallery with Biographical Notices of the Painters*, London, 1876

Stechow, 1948: W. Stechow, 'Jan Baptist Weenix', *Art Quarterly*, XI, pp. 180–99, 1948

Thieme-Becker, 1907–1950: Thieme and Becker, *Allgemeines Lexicon der bildenden Kunstler*, 37 vols, Leipzig, 1907–50

Trnek 1992: R. Trnek, *Die hollandischen Gemalde des 17. Jahrhunderts in der Gemaldegalerie der Akademie der Bildenden Kunste*, Vienna/ Cologne/ Weimar, 1992

Vermeule, 1966: Cornelius C. Vermeule, *The Dal Pozzo – Albani Drawings of Classical Antiquities in the Royal Library at Windsor Castle*, Philadelphia, 1966

Waagen, 1854: G.F. Waagen, *Treasures of Art in Great Britain: Being an Account of the Chief Collections of Paintings, Drawings, Sculptures, Illuminated Mss., &c., &c.* 3 vols + index, London (J. Murray), 1854

Warsaw, 1992: Kolekcja dla Króla, *exh. cat., Royal Castle*, Warsaw, 1992

Washington, London and Amsterdam, 2001–2: National Gallery of Art, Washington; National Gallery, London; Rijksmuseum, Amsterdam, *Aelbert Cuyp*, exh. cat., ed. A.K. Wheelock, Jnr, 2001–2

Waterfield, 1988: G. Waterfield, *Dulwich Picture Gallery: Rich Summer of Art: A Regency Picture Collection Seen through Victorian Eyes*, London, 1988

Waterfield, G., 'That White-faced Man: Sir Francis Bourgeois', *Turner Studies*, 1989, 9, pp. 45–6

Williamstown and Sarasota, 1994: Sterling and Francine Clark Art Institute, Williamstown, and John and Mable Ringling Museum of Art, Sarasota, *A Golden Harvest, Paintings by Adam Pynacker*, exh. cat. (Laurie B. Harwood), 1994

Whitley, 1928: W.T. Whitley, *Artists and Their Friends in England, 1700–1799*, 2 vols, London and Boston, 1928

Wilenski, 1955 : R. H. Wilenski, *Dutch Painting*, London, 1955

Wright, 1978: C. Wright, *The Dutch Painters: 100 seventeenth century masters*, London, 1978

Wurzbach 1906–10: Alfred von Wurzbach, *Niederlandisches Kunstler-Lexicon*, 3 vols, Vienna and Leipzig